Peter Jackson Rova

Devotion and Artifice

Religion and Reason

Founded by
Jacques Waardenburg (†)

Edited by
Gustavo Benavides, Michael Stausberg, and Ann Taves

Volume 57

Peter Jackson Rova

Devotion and Artifice

Themes of Suspension in the History of Religions

DE GRUYTER

ISBN 978-3-11-221360-5
e-ISBN (PDF) 978-3-11-046060-5
e-ISBN (EPUB) 978-3-11-045998-2
ISSN: 0080-0848

Library of Congress Control Number: 2023934443

Bibliographic information published by the Deutsche Nationalbibliothek
The Deutsche Nationalbibliothek lists this publication in the Deutsche Nationalbibliografie; detailed bibliographic data are available on the Internet at http://dnb.dnb.de.

This volume is text- and page-identical with the hardback published in 2023.
Printing and binding: CPI books GmbH, Leck

www.degruyter.com

Hé quoi ! vous ne ferez nulle distinction
Entre l'hypocrisie et la dévotion ?
Vous les voulez traiter d'un semblable langage,
Et rendre même honneur au masque qu'au visage,
Égaler l'artifice à la sincérité,
Confondre l'apparence avec la vérité,
Estimer le fantôme autant que la personne,
Et la fausse monnaie à l'égal de la bonne ?

"But what! Will you make no distinction between hypocrisy and devotion? Will you treat them as a common language, and give the same honor to a mask as to a face, equate artifice with sincerity, confuse appearance with the truth, value the phantom as much as the person, and counterfeit money as good as the real?"

Molière, Le Tartuffe ou l'imposteur (act 1, scene 6, verse 334)

Contents

A Note on Transliteration and Abbreviations — IX

Acknowledgements — XI

1 Theoretical Preliminaries — 1

I Pre-Ancient Themes (Reservoir)

2 Hyperboles of Identity and Difference — 17

3 Fame and Social Eating — 33

4 Itinerancy and Afterlife — 51

II Ancient Themes (Confluence)

Resumé and Preamble — 77

5 The Stargazer's Sacrifice — 78

6 Apparitions and Apparatuses — 93

7 Antinomies of the Cross — 109

III Nascent Modernity (Reflux)

Preamble — 139

8 The Return of the Pagans — 140

9 Postscript: Survivals of Religion in the Western Imaginary — 166

A Note on Transliteration and Abbreviations

I have consistently followed standard principles of diacritical transliteration. As for ancient Indian and Iranian languages, contemporary transliteration standards are meant to be fully reversible with regard to the scripts used in the manuscripts, and there exists no satisfying standard of simplification. Ancient Greek is transliterated according to the norms of Brill's New Pauly (BNP). Here, long vowels with separate Greek characters (η, ω) are marked with macron (*ē, ō*) unless they have a circumflex accent (ˆ). Improper diphthongs with a so-called iota subscript (ᾳ, ῃ, ῳ) are transliterated as *ai, ēi, ōi.*

Block quotes from the Greek are not transliterated, but are always followed by an English translation. The translations are my own unless otherwise indicated. Whenever applicable, classical texts and authors are abbreviated according to the conventions of Liddell-Scott-Jones' *Greek-English Lexicon* (LSJ) and Lewis and Short's *Oxford Latin Dictionary* (OLD).

Transliterations of classical Arabic follow the conventions of Brill's *Encyclopedia of Islam* (EI) and the *International Journal of Middle Eastern Studies* (IJMES).

https://doi.org/10.1515/9783110460605-001

Acknowledgements

It took me a long time to complete this book, not just because I underestimated the intellectual challenges that lay ahead, but also because of some drastic yet profoundly enriching changes to my private life. I dedicate this book to my wife Felice and my two daughters Alma and Pax – none of which I knew, and one of which did not even exist when this book was first outlined – in recognition of their loving companionship.

A generous grant from the research project LAMP: Languages and Myths of Prehistory (funded by Riksbankens Jubileumsfond) enabled me to put all other obligations aside and prepare a first final draft of the manuscript in the spring of 2022. I wish to extend a heartfelt thanks to the project manager Jenny Larsson and other members of the project team for supporting me and providing all sorts of valuable intellectual input, not least concerning Indo-European matters.

At an early stage in the editing process, a group of distinguished peers kindly accepted to read individual chapters with an opportunity to add comments and react to inaccuracies with regard to their respective areas of expertise: Francesco d'Errico, Norbert Oettinger, Almut Hintze, Stephanie Jamison, Guy Stroumsa, Hans Ruin, Jan Bremmer, Philip Halldén, and Egil Asprem. I wish to express my sincere gratitude for their forthcomingness and encouragement, leaving all blame on myself for remaining flaws.

I owe a debt of gratitude to my esteemed first teacher, friend, and eventual colleague Erik af Edholm as well as to my longtime friend Gabor Bora for critically ingesting the whole manuscript, offering numerous perceptive comments and remarks to which I have only partially been able to respond in the final version of this text.

Equally engaging has been the feedback I received from the series editors, Gustavo Benavides and Michael Stausberg, at various stages of the writing process. I would like to thank them for initially showing interest in my book proposal as well as for their encouragement and patience along the way.

My warm thanks go to Ann Broughton for proofreading the manuscript before final submission, to the Royal Gustavus Adolphus Academy in Uppsala for financially supporting the proofreading as well as to Joachim Katzmarek, Katrin Mittmann, Aaron Sanborn-Overby, and other members of the De Gruyter staff for their assistance and professionalism in the publishing process.

As for the large group of unnamed others with whom I have been fortunate to share ideas over the years, I must deign to thank them all collectively to spare myself the embarrassment of having left someone out.

https://doi.org/10.1515/9783110460605-002

1 Theoretical Preliminaries

1.1

This study tries out a simple assumption on a richly variegated data set, in a long-term perspective, and in a tradition of comparison considered by many to be hopelessly outdated. As the story goes, contemporary scholars of religion are dissuaded from the daunting task of free-solo cross-cultural comparison by the bad examples of their predecessors. In order to improve, some engage exclusively in scrutinizing the modern discourse on religion, others interrogate discrete texts and traditions in a style of increasing specialization, and others yet test competing hypotheses and make empirical predictions on a global scale in the grand tradition of scientific collaboration.[1] This is not pointed out as an insinuation of dissent, for I consider all such lines of inquiry potentially relevant and compatible. What worries me is rather the occasional complacency with which scholars group each other into mutually exclusive camps. Such tendencies induce cowardice and narrow-mindedness by (at worst) disabling the kind of controlled conversation with our own kind and its past, in a speculative style resistant to testable prediction, that uniquely characterizes the humanities.[2]

As a contribution to this ongoing conversation, I have selected a series of historical cases, some of which have surfaced in previous publications, to tease out from them a sense of cohesion and continuity. By bringing them together under one umbrella, I now hope to make more explicit the assumptions that first led me into such seemingly disconnected areas of inquiry. I prefer to think of these examples as interconnected points in a continuous trajectory. While the cases have not been selected on the grounds of circumspect principles, I remain confident that they will yield some forensic gain both within and without the thematic trajectory to which I have assigned them. If the project proves tenable, what ultimately lies at stake is the scholarly concept of religion. How are we to understand this cross-cultural propensity? Why have we come to think of it the way we do?

1 Consider, for instance, the bulk of Russell McCutcheon's publications as characteristic of the first approach, whereas the last approach is typically defined by Harvey Whitehouse's involvement in the *Seshat: Global History Databank* at the University of Oxford.

2 The "unpleasant dilemma" facing the humane (as opposed to the natural) sciences from Galileo onwards consists in, to quote Carlo Ginzburg's perceptive characterization (Ginzburg 1990, 124): "either to assume a lax scientific system in order to attain noteworthy results, or assume a meticulous, scientific one to achieve results of scant significance."

https://doi.org/10.1515/9783110460605-003

And in what terms may our future explorations be furthered by such retrospect considerations?

Without relapsing into traditional apologetics, I wish to proceed from the great mass of evidence that shows religious subjects to be active participants in the work of culture rather than victims or perpetrators of its deceptive machinations. Against the popular tendencies to identify an original impulse of religion either in primitive responses to the riddles of nature and existence, or in a shrewd desire to control the will of others, we need to account for the many historical circumstances in which religion has been equally involved in the devaluation of intellectual curiosity as in programs designed to overcome the temptations of civic deception. This is a particularly urgent task in a time when the conceived issue of religion – both from the outside and from within, by its critics as well as by its caretakers – is being reduced to the stereotypes and overexposures with which a majority of religious participants, past as well as present, would never comply apart from what transiently appears and disappears.

1.2

Throughout this study, I will be using *suspension* as a generic term for a pattern of behavior induced by the ability in humans to prevent certain persistent impressions about themselves and their world from being in force. The English term (from Latin *suspendo, suspensio*) literally denotes the action of "hanging up" (*sub* + *pendo*), but it figuratively comes to denote a momentary deprivation of conditions or positions.[3] Since my primary focus of interest lies on the historical impact of suspended mental actions, referred to in the following as actions of judgement and disbelief, I shall begin by clarifying some of the conceptual ambiguities with which these actions have become associated.

Samuel Taylor Coleridge's phrase for the voluntary withholding of scepticism (*willing suspension of disbelief*) and the associated phrase to describe a disciplined concession to doubt and uncertainty (*suspension of judgement*), have a long and fascinating prehistory. The two formulas can be traced back to concepts in ancient Greek and Roman epistemology, jurisprudence, rhetoric, and theology (*dispensatio, dispositio, epiméleia, epokhḗ, oikonomía, hyperbolḗ*, etc.), all of which revolve around the voluntary disposition towards excess and deficit. Furthermore, such various actions of suspension have a common ground in the momentary affirma-

3 The figurative sense *to be doubtful* or *make uncertain* is already attested in classical authors such as Livy (39.29) and Ovid (*Met.* 7.308).

tion of obliqueness as opposed to an everyday (premature and habitual) mode of orientation in the world. Today, a rash distinction between religious and scientific dispositions of mind might imply the former to be irrational and concerned with unfounded beliefs, whereas the latter appears rational and concerned with disbelief. I suggest that we create a more flexible analytical framework by having such antinomies dissolve into attitudes that both require momentary deferral, into acts of suspended judgement and disbelief. None of these attitudes are entirely commonsensical, nor need they exhaust one another.

For the sake of clarification, I shall begin by briefly outlining the proper context of Coleridge's formula. It occurs in chapter 14 of the *Biographia Literaria* (Coleridge [1817] 1983), an epochal work of literary criticism in which its author, spurred by the advent of German idealism, expresses his aesthetic predilections. Dictated to his friend John Morgan throughout the summer of 1815, the work was initially intended by Coleridge as a counterpoise to William Wordsworth's *Preface* to the second edition of *Lyrical Ballads* (1800), but it soon grew into a far more comprehensive statement on the application of philosophically deduced rules to poetry and criticism (I: 5[4]).

Lyrical Ballads had first been published anonymously in 1798 as the result of a conjoint experiment. Apart from Wordsworth's major contribution to the collection, four of the poems were written by Coleridge (including his famous *The Rime of the Ancyent Mariner*). It appears from the latter's retrospect account that the original plan of the experiment was defined by an agreed division of labor. Wordsworth was "to propose to himself as his object, to give the charm of novelty to things of every day," (II: 7) whereas Coleridge's endeavors:

> it was agreed (...) should be directed to persons and characters supernatural, or at least romantic; yet so as to transfer from our inward nature a human interest and a semblance of truth sufficient to procure for these shadows of imagination that *willing suspension of disbelief for the moment* [my italics], which constitutes poetic faith. (II: 6)

When we turn to Wordsworth's 1800 *Preface*, it is striking to note the stubbornness with which he derives the sole aesthetic principle of the collection from his own side of the original bargain. He complains about the craving for extraordinary incident produced in urban populations deadened by the uniformity of labor (117[5]). A poem's worthy purpose to strengthen and purify human affections should rather be attained through the ordinary language of repeated experience (115–116), not

4 The pagination, with a Roman numeral indicating the original first or second volume, refers to the 1983 edition of *Biographia Literaria* (Coleridge [1817] 1983).
5 The pagination refers to W. J. B. Owen's edition of the 1800 Preface (Owen 1957).

through the personification of abstract principles and mechanical devices of style (118). Although Coleridge would continue to hold Wordsworth's poetry in high esteem, he considered the latter's preface to be misdirected in its rejection of all those phrases and forms of style that did not conform to a purported language of real life (II: 8). Coleridge was anxious to distinguish the creative act of imitation from the deceptive sense of sameness that ensues from mere copying (II:72). Unlike the copy, the imitation acknowledges its own artificiality and dissimilarity. Wordsworth's mistake, according to Coleridge, thus lay in depreciating the mediatory power of imagination. In restricting the merits of representation to that which is truly real and natural, he had failed to distinguish the image from what is essentially only a copy.

Coleridge expounds on his formula in a letter to the Scottish journalist Daniel Stuart from 1816 (Griggs 1959, 641–643). Less concerned with poetics in the strict sense, he is now taken up with developing a new theory of stage illusion. Furthermore, it appears that he is not merely employing religious terminology (*religiously disbelieve, the suspended power to disbelieve, the voluntary Lending of the Will to suspension*) in order to elucidate artistic experience, but that his theorizing in fact involves a personal stance on religious doctrine. While being influenced by Unitarian ideas during his late student years, Coleridge eventually returned to what he considered to be orthodox Christianity. In his refutation of the presumption of an "absolute *De*lusion" – promulgated by French seventeenth-century theoreticians such as Nicolas Boileau and Pierre Corneille – as being equally illogical as Samuel Johnson's notion of commonsensical drama spectatorship, he explicitly does so by linking Johnson and the French critics to Christian rationalistic tenets from which he sought to dissociate himself: Irenicism in the case of Johnson and Unitarianism in the case of the French critics (Griggs 1959, 642).[6]

Coleridge contends that both the denial and approval of solid belief yield inaccurate solutions to the problem of stage illusion. If we consider the spectator to be either deceived by the illusion or to approach it broad awake, it is because we falsely posit scrutiny as the only viable alternative to misinterpreted perception. The dichotomy entails a fallacy of exhaustive hypotheses. In his attempt to conceptually overcome this double bind by evoking the *willing suspension of disbelief,* Coleridge seems to be contemplating media virtuality in a fashion quite ahead of his time. At the same time, however, he intervenes in an age-old theological controversy regarding the epistemology of faith – also referred to as fideism or the so-called doctrine of belief against reason – the early history of which I discuss in chapter 7.

---

6 For further comments on the context of the letter to Stuart, see Tomko 2015, 44–51.

We need to specify in what sense Coleridge's formula differs from what is commonly understood as *suspension of judgement*. Is not disbelief just another form of judgement *held in suspense* while we willingly subject ourselves to an illusion? The confusion ensues from the fact that the original Greek concept of *epokhḗ* could broadly denote a sudden pause or retention (from a verb *epékhō* "hold back, keep in check"), whereas its understanding in Pyrrhonian scepticism concerned a much more restricted practice of the will. What was to be kept in check by the Pyrrhonian sceptic was not the critical ability as such, but rather the established systems of dogma through which philosophical judgements were habitually made. The extended Stoic concept of *epokhḗ* was intended to include practical judgements of everyday life (HWPh, II: 595). The judgement held in suspense, both in the Stoic and modern sense of the formula, should thus not be confused with a well-founded judgement, but rather with the preconceived opinions from which we derive rash conclusions. The indeterminate source of such rash conclusions can only be uncovered through an intentional act of retention. Familiar examples of means to suspend judgement are the principle of reproducibility in experimental sciences, and the withholding of ad hominem reasoning in forensic procedure. A similar suspension of immediate judgement is seen in social practices designed to turn an indeterminate output into an exterior objective of choice, such as a lot drawn "at random" (*propetḗs*) [Pi. *N.* 6.63]). There is consequently a negative correlation between the sense in which a judgement can be considered "precipitate" (*propetḗs*) and the sense in which it may be suspended in obeisance to an indeterminate source exterior to the obedient subject. This is a point to be further elaborated on in chapter 6.

1.3

Since acts of volitional suspension are understood to be acts of the mind, they are also subordinated to a meta-cognitive conceptual framework associated with the scientific study of the mind. I should emphasize, however, that this study is not premised on any particular trend in psychology or the cognitive sciences. Instead, I shall try to remain as neutral as possible with regard to hypothesizing what the mind *is* or *does* on the basis of accumulated scientific knowledge. I am concerned with cognitive abilities (whether innate or socially acquired) that, unlike telepathy and telekinesis, conform to an intuitive understanding of the human mind. In accepting the likewise uncontroversial assumption that these abilities have cross-cultural pertinence, we can assume that they developed very long ago, and hence need not even be unique to anatomically modern humans.

What the volitional suspension of judgement and disbelief shares with other cognitive abilities, such as remembering and prospection, is the ability to mentally situate oneself where one is not presently situated. When we project ourselves into a simulation of a time, place, or perspective beyond the present moment, we are no longer merely stimulus-dependent (Spreng et al., 2009).[7] This is the simplest possible qualification of what it means to remember a place, prospect future events, and imagine fictitious circumstances. Recent studies of the cognitive capacity to traverse subjective time – so-called mental time travel (Szpunar 2011, Suddendorf and Corballis 2007) – emphasize this capacity as being predetermined by what Endel Tulving has called autonoetic consciousness (Tulving 1985). Regardless of whether we consider this capacity to be uniquely human or not, it necessarily involves awareness of one's self existing in subjective time (Szpunar 2011, 410). Now that self-projection allows us to apprehend things differently, furthermore, it will not just imply a digression from present circumstances. It would be more accurate to propose that a different apprehension of present circumstances implies a self-projection into these circumstances.

In a meta-analytic study pursued by R. Nathan Spreng et al. (2009), quantitative evidence is presented in support of the proposition that the same core network underlies a number of cognitive processes previously studied as distinct. The processes in question, all of which seem to elicit similar patterns of brain activity, come under the heading of remembering, prospection, navigation (= topographical orientation), theory of mind, and default mode (including stimulus-independent thought and mind-wandering). While such coordinated approaches to the basis of self-projection may support inferences about the early emergence of complex social processes – such as deception, perspective taking, and alliance building (Spreng et al. 2009, 505) – the current study serves a different purpose. My point of departure is rather a set of traits that may already be considered behaviorally modern, but where controversy is involved in specifying what they are, how they might be identified, and how to understand the consequences of their historical impact. I thus put aside assumptions about the social selection pressures by which human brain evolution was ultimately driven; partly because they lie outside the scope of this study, and partly because there is no scholarly consensus that a fully developed human mind is a sufficient factor in explaining the emergence of behavioral modernity (see, for instance, d'Errico 2003).

Despite my ambition to maintain disinterest in explaining the causal role of consciousness, I need to make a reservation on purely methodological grounds.

7 The distinction between "sensation" (*aísthēsis*) as always being present, and "imagination" (*phantasía*) as not being present, can be traced back to Aristotle's treatise *On the Soul* (*de An.* 428a).

Since I will be focusing on a pattern of behavior linked to the faculty of conscious volition, I refrain from all implicit assumptions about the unconscious mind. This precautionary measure also means that another category is put aside, namely that of self-deception (see, for instance, Trivers 2000). No matter what they are worth in terms of evolutionary theory, notions of unconscious manipulation and unconscious modules of deception provide means of sidestepping a notion that would otherwise prove philosophically untenable: that we are in fact disposed to deceive ourselves. Voluntary acts of withholding judgement and disbelief cannot, for obvious reasons, be considered to involve deception or self-deception. On the contrary, they disclose a pattern of behavior often falsely (or hyperbolically) held to ensue from involuntary inhibition due to a fallacy of exhaustive hypotheses.

The post-war discussion of "play" (*Spiel*) in its complex relation to "deception" (*Schein*) found a way into phenomenological research through the works of Eugen Fink. Here, the problem of volitional suspension is tackled in a style very different from that of contemporary cognitive science on account of phenomenology's familiar stance against psychologizing tendencies in philosophy around the turn of the 19th century. In a preparatory study preceding the monograph *Spiel als Weltsymbol* (1960), Fink insists on excluding the human involvement in games of pretence from the deceptive imagination associated with the German word *Schein* (Fink 2010 [1957], 26). The word *Schein* is ambiguous in the sense that it suggests both the visible appearance of something, and the false appearance behind which something hides what it actually is. Participants in a "world of play" (*Spielwelt*) are not deceived by what they falsely hold to be real (*Schein* 1), but rather experience the reality of a subjective appearance (*Schein* 2) – like the reflection of a tree in a pond – that they are fully capable of distinguishing from its objective cause of appearance. Instead of being fully detached from the real world, players respond to the world *as* play. However, there is a point at which I consider Fink to get ahead of himself, for he seems to claim that the true meaning of play lies in deciphering the world by means of a less playful cultic participation essentially dissimilar from the ludic phenomenon initially placed under scrutiny (Fink 2010 [1957], 25). By thus emphasizing the contrast between playful suspension and serious religious participation, Fink can be said to join in the game announced as his object of study: his theory becomes an exemplar of what it tries to explain. This is precisely what I shall try to avoid in the following, namely to identify an exotic substrate beneath the hyperbolic representations of reality by which we may recognize religion tout court. Apart from the psychologizing preconceptions that phenomenology justifiably avoids, I shall also try to avoid representing religion hyperbolically, that is, by overstating features no longer assumed to accord with its perceived historical and contemporary characteristics.

1.4

It should go without saying that the area of religion affords a particularly promising historical testing ground for exploring themes of suspension. Nevertheless, and for reasons that may themselves be historically significant, they are elusive objects of historical study. One apparent reason for this is that cognitive acts of suspension, despite their long trajectory of execution and consideration in human history, are intrinsic to the very practice of inquiry. The phenomenological method of suppressing preconceived notions (*epokhḗ* [see above]) has typically been prescribed to students of religion as a means of eidetically grasping religious motivations, not as an intrinsic modality of such motivations deserving attention in its own right.[8] The treatment of bracketing as a perennial trait of religious participation, including the understatement of this circumstance in the age-old critical discourse on religion, may thus yield a host of analytical rewards. According to the twofold philosophical critique, religious motivations are typically understood to ensue from premature misconceptions (= a proto-philosophical theory of the world), or from deceptive devices for manipulation designed to foster such misconceptions (= a form of proto-politics).[9] Closer attention to the cognitive process of suspension is thus, by contrast to this somewhat slanted view, expected to create a more cohesive notion of religious belief and participation.

Despite the occasional insistence on unconditional faith, religious participation is widely attested as the result of a voluntary and momentary disposition of mind. We may affirm beliefs by acting *as if* believing what is conceived not to be true, or we may place something under scrutiny by acting *as if not* knowing what is conceived to be true according to rash judgement (Benavides 2010, 245–247).[10] A juxtaposition of these frames of mind should make clear how they differ, but also how they are conjoined by a reluctance to indisposed preconceptions. Whereas the first attitude implies a disposition towards artificiality (or so-called apparatuses), the second implies a disposition towards indeterminacy.

8 The former approach to religion, proceeding from the methodological precept that reality has to be held back in order to be understood, finds its most characteristic formulation in Gerardus van der Leeuw's classical introduction to the phenomenology of religion (Van der Leeuw 1961, 9).

9 The conception of ancient religion as proto-philosophy (or proto-theory) is still manifest in the contemporary understanding of philosophical beginnings, as exemplified by Hans-Georg Gadamer's *Der Anfang der Philosophie* (1996, 130).

10 Gustavo Benavides' discussion of as-if-ness echoes the neo-Kantian philosopher Hans Vaihinger's systematic approach to the foundations of idealistic positivism in *Die Philosophie des Als Ob* (Vaihinger 1922). It should be emphasized, however, that Vaihinger's understanding (unlike Benavides') of the *Als-Ob* comprises virtually all aspects of life and the human approach to the world, including scientific thought and research.

These attitudes may come into conflict, but they may also interact within the same ritual framework. The first attitude implies means of accepting circumstances that are not intuitively apparent, such as the dissimulation of animal consent and divine participation in Graeco-Roman sacrifice, whereas the second implies means of suspending judgement, such as leaving certain choices to arational (rather than irrational) processes in divinatory decision-making, for example the inspection of sacrificial *exta* in order to receive an indeterminate reply.

Another act of suspension hampering the academic study of human affairs is related to the problem of identity and difference, especially the suspension of certain viable assumptions about one's in-group as a foil for defamiliarizing others. Although scholars may claim immunity to such tendencies, an occasional lack of critical self-awareness in this regard is likely to be unavoidable. The timeliness of this circumstance is made obvious by recent scholarly approaches to the emergence of modernity that, on both sides of a broad timescale, are informed by the same implicit notion of profound human otherness.

In a seminal paper deserving attention beyond its historical specificities, film historian Tom Gunning offers a critical evaluation of this persistent conception. His point of departure is the purported panic caused by one of the first public film screenings at the Salon Indien of the Grand Café in Paris. The fifty-second movie, directed and produced by the brothers Lumière in 1895, shows a continuous real time shot of a train arriving at La Ciotat station in southern France. According to numerous accounts in standard works of film history, many of which cite an uncorroborated passage in Georges Sadoul's *Histoire générale du cinéma* from 1948, the audience consisted of credulous spectators who reared back, screamed, or even fled their seats in terror, because they were afraid that the train would run them down. Unable to find any contemporary documents supporting the panic at the Grand Café, Gunning provides sufficient evidence to restore the incredulity of the late-nineteenth century pleasure seekers. By thus reaffirming the spectators' awareness of, and delight in, the illusionistic capacities of a new technology, he also brings attention to the fact that similar technologies have invited audiences to suspend their disbeliefs long before the advent of modern cinema.

Despite its historically situated subject matter, Gunning's essay provides a suggestive illustration of a prevalent human propensity for defamiliarization, typically associating a radical lack of sophistication and agency with a position beyond, or before, the present location of the in-group. Such tropes are not meant to elicit critical examination, but rather to foster affirmative participation as a means to enhance in-group characteristics. They are typically seen to create a hyperbolic sense of generality and distance out of a first-order experience that, initially, rather evokes a sense of confusing particularity and proximity (Smith 2004, 246). To put it bluntly, imagining someone to exist outside of the willing suspension of disbelief may in itself result from a willing suspension of disbelief. In so far as this propensity can be considered characteristically human, it should also be considered modern in a general anthropological sense, namely as a defining criterion of behavioral modernity. We need to consider the possibility that this differentiating urge, alongside the acknowledgement of its artificiality, is not just a secondary trait of human culture, not just a by-product of some regulatory worldview, but a primary function of culture. If the assumption holds true, we may conjecture that this urge sets in whenever the origin of culture is addressed. In trying to imagine such beginnings we are not so much facing an epistemological conundrum, but rather participate in a discourse that illustrates the veritable work of culture. This issue will be further tackled in the next chapter.

1.5

From the viewpoint of western intellectual history and the history of religions, themes of suspension reach a point of particular acuteness and reflexivity in classical, Hellenistic, and late antiquity contexts. In order to appreciate this development, it is helpful to consider previous scholarly work addressing the genesis of philosophy and new modalities of religiosity in antiquity. An appropriate point of departure is the Greek notion of "self-care" (*epiméleia heautoû*). This notion has gained widespread scholarly recognition due to the impact of Michel Foucault, who examined it at length in an attempt to trace the historical constitution of so-called *technologies of the self* in ancient philosophy (Foucault [posthumously] 2001). While extending back at least to the Pythagoreans of the 6th century BCE, and culminating with the rise of Christian monasticism, these techniques receive their first and most tangible formulation in Plato's *Apology* and the (possibly spurious) dialogue *First Alcibades.*

When Socrates stood accused of having corrupted the youth, and of "impiety" (*asébeia*) for dishonoring the gods of Athens by introducing new deities into the city, his philosophical activities were deemed to invert the most prominent token of allegiance to the community. These putatively noble gestures of "piety" (*eusébeia*) are used in the *Apology* as a premise of the groundbreaking notion of self-care:

> Most excellent man, are you who are a citizen of Athens, the greatest of cities and the most famous for wisdom and power, not ashamed to *care* for the acquisition of wealth (*epimeloúmenos*), and for *reputation and honor* (*dóxēs kaì timês*), when you *neither care* (*ouk epimelê*) nor take thought for wisdom and truth and the perfection of your soul? (29d–e, trans. Fowler [s.v. Plato *Ap.*], my italics)

In order to appreciate the semantic subtleties of the Socratic precept – an elaboration of the famous Delphic maxim "know thyself" (*gnôthi seautón*) – we must take into account that the term *epiméleia* was already intrinsically associated with the obligations of public worship. It could evoke a sense of care, if not even zealousness, bestowed upon sacred things; a sense likewise testified by the early usage of the Latin terms *religio* and *religiosus*. We also need to recall that the cultic apparatus of the Greek polis was largely a matter of wealth and reputation. This means that Socrates is placing the civic sacrificial economy under scrutiny, and, more importantly, that he is propagating its replacement by a new economy of the self. A moderate version of such precepts need not exclude a notion of civic care, for Socrates is apparently urging the Athenian citizens to start occupying themselves with their souls, not with the tokens of wealth and reputation, in order to learn how to occupy themselves with the city.

In their more radical renderings, however, similar precepts could also induce breachs of etiquette on a quest for spiritual refinement and transformation, such as the renunciation of home and family, the abandonment of the old gods (the old customs, the old bonds of loyalty), and a call for political violence. When a traditional economy of sacrifice is internalized, inner life is economized through asceticism and self-care. The expected gain is no longer the increasing quantities of wealth and honor, but rather spiritual qualities that may otherwise appear redundant, possibly even corrosive, to a loyal member of the preexisting in-group.

A crucial point to be made with regard to these concerns is that they all reflect a tension between two frames of mind, namely the two kinds of suspended mental actions touched upon above. In the life of a stable community, the suspension of disbelief is enticed by the symbolic and theatrical aspects of public worship, whereas the suspension of judgement becomes instrumental in dealing with changes and crises within that same community through specialized techniques (divination, engineering, forensics, military tactics, and so on). By extension, the latter mindset also emerges as a characteristic feature of antinomian communities – usually enjoying the support of a privileged intellectual laity – seen to challenge the commonsensical ideals and expectations of civic society by emphasizing asceticism, salvation, disinterested exploration, and prophetic knowledge (Kippenberg 1991). While the reality of Greek religion was certainly more complex than such a dyadic model might suggest, the notion of a fundamental opposition between civic and unlicensed forms of religion can still be effectively employed in order to uncover the model's various shades of grey (Kindt 2012, 98).

Max Weber once came close to formulating a sociological law in order to capture this tension: "A religiosity of salvation is elaborated in its most durable form by privileged classes of a people when they are demilitarized and excluded from the interest of political activity" (Weber quoted in Kippenberg 1991, 88). In addition to this important observation, it should be emphasized that the contrasting forces at work in such sociopolitical circumstances are not merely matters of belief and disbelief, but also of the distinct means of suspending belief and disbelief. While a recognition of these frames of mind will no doubt yield analytical rewards on a cross-cultural scale, it is likewise important to acknowledge the historical contingencies that enable such attitudes to gain momentum. Although examples from antiquity may prove particularly elucidating in this regard, such exemplary cases can only acquire sufficient depth and contour if we take pains to explore their prefigurations and repercussions on a much broader timescale.

1.6

As intimated above, the fact that my examples are distributed over such a broad timescale – ranging from the Upper Paleolithic to late modernity – should of course not be taken to imply that I intend to cover this period in a comprehensive survey. Rather, I propose to undertake a limited set of case studies as a basis for reflecting in more general terms upon the following issues: (1) how (and possibly why) have humans sought to prevent viable assumptions about themselves and their world from being in force, (2) how does this propensity manifest itself historically and archaeologically, and (3) in what terms has it been theorized and criticized throughout the ages?

1.6.1

Considering the wealth of topics, traditions, and genres discussed in this book, a few final paragraphs are in order to issue a guideline for the unprepared (and potentially perplexed) reader through the sections and chapters to follow. I should begin by adding a note on my choice of title.

As suggested by the epigraph from Molière's *Tartuffe* (act 1, scene 6, verse 334), it might seem feasible to raise concern about the lack of distinction between two moral registers, between two classes of interpersonal behavior marked by pretense and hypocrisy on the one hand, and sincere devotion to a just and lasting cause on the other. The statement is attributed to the play's so-called *raissoneur*, Cléante, who reproaches the play's foolish protagonist, his brother-in-law Orgon, for being blinded by admiration for the hypocritical religious devotee Tartuffe. Cléante seeks to vouch for a more reasonable form of Christian piety by insisting on making momentous distinctions. This book is also about making distinctions, but without equating the dedication to masks, appearances, and phantoms with deceptive acts of hypocrisy by which fools such as Orgon have been misled throughout the ages. Rather, the sincere devotion to a (practical or theoretical, scientific or spiritual) cause and the temporary affirmation of artifice are not mutually exclusive comportments. They (i. e., devotion and artifice) can be taken to label the complementary means by which humans voluntarily step out of habitual patterns of judgement and disbelief in order to perceive and appreciate the world differently.

The three main sections of this book (reservoir – confluence – reflux) are chronologically arranged so as to roughly suggest three phases in which two complementary modes of behavior (the affirmation of artifice [= suspension of disbelief] and devotion [= suspension of judgement]) can be perceived to coexist and conflate by various degrees of complexity.

By applying a conceptual framework of irrigation, I begin to discuss (in section I) how constitutive elements of these modes of behavior can be traced back to a pre-ancient reservoir. I do so first (in chapter 2) by paying general attention to archeological signatures of suspension – as evidenced, especially, in prehistoric burial practices and the use of personal ornaments – and certain symptomatic traits of "othering" in the contemporary scholarly debate about behavioral modernity, and secondly (in chapters 3 and 4) by comparing pre-ancient systems of hospitality and patronage. These latter systems can be understood to respectively elicit two distinct modes of behavior in the sense that the first (hospitality = suspension of disbelief) evokes lax communal participation and pretense, and the second (patronage = suspension of judgement) evokes attention and theoretical inventiveness.

In section II (confluence) I discuss the gradual collapse and conflation of these once distinct behavioral modes in the ancient Mediterranean world. First (in chapter 5) by paying attention to the philosophical critique of the civic spectacle in terms of theorization and interiorization, then (in chapter 6) by scrutinizing the participatory affirmation of artifice, and finally (in chapter 7) by showing how an emergent Christian (and predominantly Pauline) discourse on faith (Gr. *pístis*, Lat. *fides*) can be taken to eventually short-circuit such modes of behavior through imperial manifestations of Christianity as a universal "religion of truth" (*vera religio*).

In section III (reflux) an attempt is made to account for how a new duality of comportments linked to the suspension of judgement and disbelief begin to reconstitute themselves within the secular domain by the beginning of the early modern period. I do so first (in chapter 8) by sketching out the return of pagan philosophy to the West, and lastly (in chapter 9) by briefly addressing the reconstitution of religious residuals under the secular guise of popular entertainment and scientific reason.

Without entertaining the slightest doubt that this storyline will appear grossly oversimplified to some, I shall not attempt to conceal the fact that it has been conceived in a venturesome spirit of intellectual curiosity. Hence, the kind of critique I could appreciate the most would be characterized by the same daring spirit. My gambit in regard to this kind of scholarly conversation has been to downplay the distinction between credulity and deception, between foolishness and imposture. These are not, as I shall argue in the following, necessarily the most revealing characteristics of religious participation.

I Pre-Ancient Themes (Reservoir)

2 Hyperboles of Identity and Difference

2.1

When visual representations of Neanderthals first began to appear in publications during the 1880s, they conformed to the image of a monstrosity effaced by scientific reason: the apeman or troglodyte inhabiting a borderland between the animal kingdom and our own world in the absence of an interventionist God.[11] The German anthropologist Hermann Schaaffhausen (1816–1893), who first examined the skeletal remains from the Neander Valley in 1857, had soon come to accept Charles Darwin's assumption that the natural evolution of plants and animals also involved the eventual genesis of modern humans. After carefully comparing the bones and cranial cap to those of apes and modern humans, he was nevertheless convinced that they could not represent the so-called missing link between man and animal. A gap still remained, he concluded, that would only be filled in the future (Schaaffhausen 1888, 49).

And yet, when Schaaffhausen instructed the painter Philippart in Bonn to make a reliable rendition of what the wild man must have looked like in real life, the result was a creature with a far more non-human complexion than the cranial features themselves had revealed (fig. 1). Both face, neck, and upper shoulders are covered in hair, leaving only the chin, the nose, and the upper part of the cheek hairless. One has to imagine a body almost completely covered in fur.

It is significant that Schaaffhausen even had to correct Philippart's original draft, because he considered the countenance to appear "a good deal too mild" (*ein viel zu milder*) (Schaaffhausen 1888, 34). My point here is not to downplay the heuristic benefits of phenotypical comparison, but rather to indicate a tenacious rhetoric of excess – of "as if-ness" if you will – at work beneath even the most rigid scientific expositions. Schaaffhausen's instructions to Philippart, and his eventual adjustments to the rendition, reveal a strong temptation to hyperbolically represent a difference – a fixed degree in a gradual sequence designed to fill out a gap – out of which an identity eventually evolves: a face recognizable as our own apart from a glaring dissimilarity.

---

11 Representations of similar creatures, albeit with a less specified anthropological provenance, are found in works of fiction from the same century, such as the geologist Pierre Boitard's posthumously published novel *Paris avant les hommes* (Boitard 1861). The frontispiece depicts a so-called *homme fossile*, all covered in fur except for parts of the face, wearing a skin mantel and loin cloth, and wielding a stone axe outside his cave.

https://doi.org/10.1515/9783110460605-004

Figure 1: Early facial rendition of a Neanderthal man (from Schaffhausen 1888).

The image of the troglodyte as the typical inhabitant of a periphery, both spatial and temporal, was already familiar to the authors of antiquity. Representations of mankind's earliest state thus did not necessarily change in essence by being drawn into the context of historical rationalization and anthropological classification, because these representations had not emerged from the thin air of disinterested inquiry in the first place. Early perceptions of the dumb *Urmensch*, the ulterior other, the primeval giant, and similar liminal beings first grew out of the work of culture itself rather than out of the critical study of culture (Ferguson 1993, 109[12]). In other words, such perceptions are all deeply connected to the human fab-

12 Ferguson makes this point with regard to the speculative rationalization of prehistoric giants in the British Renaissance. I owe the idea of an overlap between the *work* and the study of culture to Jonathan Z. Smith's essay "Differential Equations: On Constructing the Other" (Smith 2004, 246).

rication of otherness. Before beginning to elaborate on this crucial topic from the perspective of prehistoric archaeology, however, I shall pay closer attention to the ways in which notions of spatial and temporal horizons have informed more recent representations of cultural difference.

2.2

Let us begin by considering the notion of spatial periphery. There are some strikingly exaggerated features by which we tend to recognize and represent inhabitants at the outer limits. They dwell in a space with which we cannot claim familiarity other than in terms of a negative correlation, through secondary mediation, and finally in terms of a proximity that has to be distanced because it is initially perceived as too close (Smith 2004, 246).

Herodotus, in the fourth book of his *Histories* (*Hdt.* 4.23–4.25), describes a land beyond that of the easternmost Scythians who drifted away from the royal Scythians on the west coast of the Sea of Azov and the shores of the Don River. He describes a territory beyond that which is already situated beyond more familiar territory, where the soil has hitherto remained deep, but where it has now turned stony and rough. After a long passage through this barren land, one comes across a people inhabiting the foothills of high mountains. They are called, depending on the manuscript reading, either Orgiempeans (*Orgiempaîoi*) or Argippeans (*Argippaîoi*). Not only does this people differ in terms of acquired habits from their western neighbors, who all engage in warfare, but they are also genetically different from both Greeks and Scythians in that they are said to be "bald from birth" (*phalakroì ek genetês*) and "flat-nosed" (*simoí*). They dwell under trees, which they in winter cover with felt cloths. Their language is said to be "peculiar" (*ídios*) in the marked sense of all barbarian customs, that is, on the verge of appearing idiotic and weird, yet significantly uniform between themselves. Because they are peaceful, the Argippeans are also said to be *hiroí*, that is, under some kind of divine protection.[13] They are not to be harmed. Their pristine existence thus makes them

---

Originally published separately in 1992, the essay is referenced here as chapter 11 in *Relating Religion: Essays in the Study of Religion.*

13 Herodotus uses the Ionian form *hirós* – the equivalent of of *hierós* ("sacred") – not the Attic form *hiereús.* Bruce Lincoln seems to sidestep this detail in his otherwise persuasive analysis of the Scythian Enarees (Anarieis). By describing the Argipppeans as "priests" on a par with the Enarees, he assumes that Herodotus refers to a particular social order among the Scythians rather than a specific tribe or ethnic group, (Lincoln 2018, 107 f.). In case Herodotus intended to characterize

suitable to settle disagreements between their neighbors and to provide a safe haven for the banished.

Herodotus' report looks like a typical hearsay in a well-advanced stage of mutation. The more distant the original witness, the more predictable a content according to distinctive rules of genre. The ensuing description of what lies beyond the land of the Argippeans conveys the sense in which credulity in such testimonies – the hearsays (literally "things said" [*legómena*] [*Hdt.* 7.152.3]) on which the bulk of the *Histories* are built – breaks down at a certain point in the narrative. Whereas the land of the Argippeans is said to be known, the territory lying further north can be grasped only in terms of what the Argippeans themselves report. This is the point at which Herodotus has to intervene and announce his disbelief (*emoì mèn ou pistá*), for he cannot accept that there are men with goat's feet and those who hibernate like bears for six months of the year. Still, while we are now asked to leave trustworthy testimony behind and accept the rest as products of fiction, the same logic of differentiation is at work. The same logic is at work, but it ceases to produce valid results. With increasing distance, the gradual mutation of humans into non-humans has eventually turned anthropologically feasible beings into creatures of myth, whose ontological rather than cultural difference is emphasized by their narrator's statement of disbelief.[14]

The troglodytes of Ethiopia fit into the same scheme of spatial differentiation. If in Pliny the Elder's time *Trogdytas* had begun to serve rather as an ethnic label of a distant trading partner (*Plin.* 5.34–5.35), Herodotus is anxious to make the most out of the speaking name (from *trōglodýteō* "dwell in holes") (*Hdt.* 4.183). These cave dwellers are said to be chased in chariots by another tribe, known as the Garamantes. In accordance with their prehuman choice of habitat, furthermore, the troglodytes are reported to feed on reptiles and to speak a strange language comparable to the cry of bats. Once again, something even more unfamiliar lies ahead: men who have no names of their own, and, finally, the so-called Atlantes, who neither eat living things "nor see dreams in their sleep" (*oút' enýpnia horân*) (*Hdt.* 4.184).

If we were to retrace our path back to the position of the narrator, it would be a passage from an eccentric past and yonder, where language and consciousness are still taking shape, towards an epicentral present of relative familiarity. Cultures at the outer limits of the known world are not just unfamiliar relative to the onlooker's lack of knowledge, but positively reaffirm themselves in the mind of the

---

the Argippeans as "priests," however, he would rather have chosen another form (cf. 2.2.5, where the pl. gen. *hiréōn* [sg. *hireús* {?}] signifies the priests of Hephaestus' temple at Memphis).

14 For a discussion of the relationship between ontological cleavage and anthropological distinctions, see Smith (2004, 241).

onlooker as the areas where ignorance resides. All who dwell there are characterized in terms of deficit: lack of technology, lack of distinct human features, lack of a complex language, lack of dreams.

If there is anything virtuous about these ulterior others, anything qualifying as sacred innocence, it is only because they have not yet developed certain malfunctions of civilization. Whereas the bald-headed Argippeans prefer to dwell under trees, the troglodytes dwell in caves like unborn babies in the womb. They exist in a state of postponed emergence, not unlike the first animals – as theorized by Darwin's earliest forerunner, the pre-Socratic philosopher Anaximander – before they broke out of the shell that surrounded them [DK A37]). It appears, even from such early accounts of scholarship, that a perceived distribution of cultural difference in geographic space has informed (and perhaps been informed by) conceptions of cultural origins. Hence, to the same extent that concepts related to space and time show a high degree of mutual translatability in terms of location, movement, and distance; conceptions of cultural self and difference seem equally (and mutually) significant when the ego is spatially framed, by the *here* and the *there*, as when it defines a position in time, in the analogous *now* as opposed to an absent, either past or future, *then.*

This final point, if accentuated to the extreme, also marks the tense of that imperfectly absent yet ideally present state of affairs in which Eliadean scholarship identifies a properly mythical pronouncement: *in illo tempore* ("in that time"). The liturgical locution – a qualifier both of sacred tense and sacred speech – was originally used in the pre-1970 Roman-Catholic mass to introduce readings from the Gospels. Besides its reappraisal in modern quests for Edenic uncontacted peoples, the space-time analogy exerts an influence on a branch of contemporary western folk beliefs still deeply associated with the fabulous aspects of Herodotus' ethnography. I am thinking of how the ancient theme of liminal inhabitants of geographic space helps fostering up-to-date popular conceptions of extraterrestrials, and especially the tenacious pattern of recognition involving so-called Gray (sic!) aliens in post-war western society.

While the genetic alterity of the Grays has likewise resulted in baldness and small or almost absent noses, they preserve, just like the Argippeans, distinctively humanoid physiognomies. Unlike the distant tribes described by Herodotus, however, these creatures are conceivably far more technically advanced than us, for they would otherwise lack the means to traverse deep space. By thus giving us an inkling of what we have not yet become in technological terms, their imaginary world of origin need not only be situated in distant space; it also belongs to the distant future, perhaps even to our own distant future. Still, there is something lacking in them, or, perhaps more accurately, something they have lost.

In his analysis of the role of Grays in American folklore, Jonathan Z. Smith selects a set of traits most clearly distinguishable in the plot of the canonical Abduction Report.[15] Apart from the many deficits associated with the Grays' physical and social appearance, such as their seeming lack of individuality and emotions, Smith also points to a less apparent trait: their silence. The fact that the aliens are unwilling to interrogate the abductees, but instead silently examine their bodies with technologically advanced probes, Smith takes to indicate an underlying problematic of difference (Smith 2004, 308). The aliens disinterestedly dig into everything that is rich in information, variegated, and accidental because they themselves seem to lack those traits of cultural diversity and diversification, that applied logic of othering, with which the fabulous genre of alien abductions is itself indissolubly connected.

Such fantasies continue, even in their quirkiest formulations, to emulate the same cross-cultural tendency towards ulterior otherness. Talking on the popular North American radio show *Coast to Coast AM* in 2006, the self-proclaimed UFO researcher Bill McDonald hypothesized that the increased number of people diagnosed with autism was not due to changes in diagnostic practice, but a consequence of future aliens harvesting genetic material from abductees in order to create a new species.[16] According to McDonald's scenario, aliens are inserting themselves into what we perceive ourselves to be so as to deprive us of ourselves. What better means could there be to negate human self-perception than to adduce a neurodevelopmental disorder defined by the very deficits in being sociable and communicative? Despite its apparent oddity, McDonald's theory neatly exemplifies how ulterior others – apart from inhabiting a distal zone where time and space conflate – stand out as distorted projections of the projectionists themselves; how selves and others become counters in a ceaseless game of identity and difference from which there is no easy escape. It is a game always threatening to interfere with the systems designed to accurately represent culture, but it is also an activity expressing – possibly in a fashion more inscrutable than we like to admit – the veritable work of culture.

Suppose now that every community – both past and present, to some necessary degree, and by virtue of its perceived commonalities – will have engaged in displaying its own outside by hyperbolically reducing and distorting familiar in-group characteristics. We then need to take heed of how such mechanisms keep affecting a community of contemporary scholars theorizing the emergence of culture. To be

15 Originally published in 2001, the essay "Close Encounters of Diverse Kinds" is referenced here as chapter 13 in Smith 2004.

16 The show was broadcast on December 23, 2006, and was still accessible through the audio archive at www.coasttocoastam.com/show/2006/12/23 as of September 2022.

sure, Schaaffhausen and his contemporaries were not the last scholars to imagine prehumans in a fashion less dictated by solid evidence than by habituated means of defamiliarization. No matter how rigid its scientific underpinnings, the question at stake has an unmistakably mythical ring: how did we become what we perceive ourselves to be?

2.3

A key concept in evolutionary anthropology today, behavioral modernity is defined by the universal cultural traits that result from a cross-cultural comparative analysis of various human societies (d'Errico 2003, 189).[17] A list of such traits typically includes abstract thought; the ability to make long term plans; behavioral, economic, and technological innovativeness; and, perhaps most importantly, symbolic behavior, involving "the ability to represent objects, people, and abstract concepts with arbitrary symbols, vocal or visual, and to reify such symbols in cultural practice" (d'Errico 2003, 191; McBrearty and Brooks 2000). The criteria for selecting traits of behavioral modernity, and the archaeological signatures of such traits, are matters of some controversy, but far more controversial is the question as to how, when, and in what hominid group(s) these traits first emerged. Two scenarios – roughly divisible in contradistinction to each other – were at least until fairly recently dominant in the debate about behavioral modernity.[18]

The first and most widely accepted model – the so-called single-species model – links the acquisition of behavioral modernity to the emergence of anatomically modern humans, and hence to the single representative of the subspecies *Homo sapiens* to survive human evolution. Parallel occurrences of personal ornaments, depictions on cave walls, musical instruments, burials, and so forth, all of which have been claimed to roughly coincide with the arrival of anatomical moderns in Europe around 40,000 years ago, are thus frequently conceived as climactic indicators of the single-species model, despite the fact that modern humans started to appear in Africa more than 150,000 years earlier. In order to adjust the apparent contradiction, some scholars even go so far as to introduce a plot device suggestive of a deus ex machina. They argue that modern behavior resulted from a rapid

17 Substantial portions of this chapter (especially sections 2.3 and 2.4) are also found in Jackson Rova 2019a and Jackson Rova 2019b.

18 Whereas this debate is to some extent already overcome by current evidence that all anatomical moderns outside Africa carry Neanderthal genes, as well as by novel views on the emergence of modern humans in Africa, a monogenetic view on the development of modern behavior continues to thrive (Scerri, Thomas et al. 2018, and Kissel and Fuentes 2018).

brain mutation that occurred in Africa around 50,000 years ago without producing any change in skull anatomy (e.g., Klein 2000). The fact that Neanderthal groups in Europe developed similar forms of modern behavior during the transition from Middle to Later Stone Age has often been interpreted as a sign of imitation or acculturation.

The second model – the so-called multi-species model – does not link traits of behavioral modernity with any single subspecies, but rather with a slow and parallel development among different hominid groups causing a drastic intensification of symbolic behavior in the area of their final encounter as a response to the problems of cultural and biological identity (d'Errico 2003, 196). Whereas proponents of the multi-species model are more inclined towards social/demographic explanations for the emergence of symbolism, proponents of the single-species model typically favor genetic/cognitive explanations.

Still, it is difficult to avoid the sense in which the multi-species model seems to reconfirm the persistency of the single-species one. If it holds true that behavioral modernity was not the discrete outcome of unique cognitive abilities, but that it was rather stimulated by a new situation in which similarly able hominid groups encountered and influenced each other, it seems consistent that our self-identification as a species should involve the purported uniqueness of our own kind as opposed to the notion that the human sense of cultural uniqueness may in itself derive some of its continuous pertinence from a multi-species quest for identity. Single-species genetic/cognitive approaches to the emergence of behavioral modernity show an inclination towards exaggerated contradistinction. In the first round, the cognitive abilities of our own species are understood to be dissimilar from those of the other. In the second round, however, the particularities of the modern experience are understood to be essentially different from the universal experience of our anatomically modern predecessors. This self-alienating scholarly impulse is reflected in the two following examples from the volume *Becoming Human*, a collection of fifteen essays from 2009 edited by Colin Renfrew and Iain Morely.

Two of the contributors, Steven Mithen and David Lewis-Williams, are both well-known interlocutors in the debate on prehistoric symbolic behavior. Despite their different points of departure, they share a strong leaning towards the single-species scenario and the employment of models from evolutionary psychology to explain the earliest motivations behind religious behavior. Both authors acknowledge the fact that Neanderthals buried their dead, but they take the absence of grave goods to indicate the absence of a modern conception of burial. According to Mithen's circular argumentation, Neanderthal burials were surely highly emotional events, "but they were not religious *in themselves* (my emphasis), because the Neanderthals had no concept of the supernatural" (Mithen 2009, 126). According to Lewis-Williams, Neanderthals began to bury their dead as a result of the habit's gradual spread in advance of the expanding populations of modern humans (the so-called "bow-wave effect"), or by directly imitating anatomically modern humans in the areas of their final encounter. In both cases, however, Lewis-Williams takes the omission of grave goods to suggest that Neanderthals "could not have entertained any religious concepts of death and burial" (Lewis-Williams 2009, 139).

While initially acknowledging that Neanderthals shared with modern humans the cognitive ability to symbolically differentiate the living from the dead, Mithen and Lewis-Williams move on to stress how Neanderthals must have been cognitively different from us: *their* primary consciousness versus *our* higher-order consciousness (Lewis-Williams 2009, 144), *their* domain-specific thought versus *our* cognitive fluidity (Mithen 2009, 129). First there is proximity, then an inescapable distance. The expected precautions of unprejudiced reasoning now seem increasingly dominated by a forceful imaginary. A next step in the process consists in imagining pre-modern religious experience, including that of our own species, as being trapped in a supernaturalist delusion. Mithen considers the speciation event of *Homo sapiens* to have involved the spontaneous evolution of a fully developed language that allows a flow of knowledge from one cognitive domain to another. Cognitive fluidity supports the ability to infer the intentions behind another person's actions, as well as to imagine entities that do not ostensibly exist in the real world – such as spirits of the dead.

Symbolic thought is, as perceived in such unfamiliar initial stages, never powerful enough to prevent leading its reflecting subject astray. Cognitively modern humans are now predisposed to start wondering about the world, but their sense of wonder is initially framed by a premodern social intelligence destined to render such first-order approximations immature. The decisive moment of religion has arrived: "Once that way of thinking became available, people began to wonder what the intention was behind natural phenomena, such as thunderstorms, earthquakes, and the sight of rare animals" (Mithen 2009, 127). In seeming ignorance of the theory's Aristotelian pedigree, Mithen conceives the earliest form of religion as a primitive theory of the natural world, stimulated by the human bewilderment within that world (cf. Blumenberg 1996, 205, 406). The conclusion leaves us with a predicament, for if religion is reduced by such means to a theory by default, it also begins to look very much like a prefiguration of the theory that now seeks to explain and supersede it.

Where Mithen reveals himself as an undercover Aristotelian, Lewis-Williams rather appears as a Platonist. In the spirit of his famous book *The Mind in the Cave* (Lewis-Williams 2002), he considers the fantastic aspects of Paleolithic paintings and engravings in the caves of southwest Europe to ensue from experiences of altered states of consciousness. The neurologically hardwired character of these states of consciousness explains their seeming conformity around, for example, "floating" imagery, lack of landscape, etc. We easily recognize the mythical setting of this explanation, whether in the Grand Café in Paris (as seen above) or in Plato's allegorical cave:

> Neuropsychological research has shown that hallucinations experienced on the intensified trajectory are projected onto plane surfaces, such as walls or ceilings. [—] First, Upper Paleolithic people did not have to invent two-dimensional imagery. If *some* of them experienced projected imagery under certain circumstances, as they had the neurological capacity to do, two-dimensional "pictures" would already have been part of their world *under certain mental and emotional conditions* (my italics). (Lewis-Williams 2009, 145).

Lewis-Williams seems to infer that the first two-dimensional images on rock walls were nothing but tracings of hallucinatory experiences, and hence that the first painters were no real artists after all, but rather the exponents of a delusion that left them trapped inside the cave of their own minds.

What are we to make of these modern tales of modernity's origin? The archaeological habitus to decipher a fixed script behind early forms of symbolic behavior is characteristically haunted by the spectre of pseudo-representation: we are ourselves represented in the absence of ourselves, transported from a familiar, present-day world of perceived artificiality into a biologically triggered, vanished world of pristine immediacy. The latter is, so it seems, a world potentially both dystopian and utopian. Our point of departure, namely the present, is inherently out of place, because it can only maintain a sense of its own stability in relation to an ever-receding vanishing point at which the duality of dependence and independence – of immanence and transcendence if you will – appears to break down.

The notion of a fully reconciled human consciousness – always postponed, always projected onto an indefinite past or future (differed and deferred) – retrospectively perpetuates the age-old belief in the original iconicity of language. While this belief in pristine immediacy implies a sense of completeness, it inevitably reinforces an imaginary state of captivity beyond, or before, a fully perceptible world of representations.

A case in point is Johann Gottfried Herder's (1744–1803) derivation of the German noun *Blitz* from a primeval poetic idiom of immediate sensation ("Empfindung des Urplötzlichschnellen"), according to which *Blitz* naturally signifies what it sounds like (Herder 1772, 98). In spite of the cross-cultural pertinence of sound symbolism, the fact that phonemes are units of linguistic communication does not imply that they were once all self-contained semantic units. Unsurprisingly, the tendency to argue in such terms prevails in ever shifting scholarly settings to this day.

Regardless of one's choice of model (whether single- or multi-species), any attempt to theorize the evolution of religion also depends on how one chooses to select and scrutinize the evolved abilities that come to count as behaviorally modern. Undeservedly neglected among these abilities are, I submit, the hyperbolic representation of selves and others. For the sake of brevity, I chose to call such representations "hyperboles of identity."

Hyperboles of identity typically imply exaggerations, overstatements, and dissimulations of common perceptions with which human subjects actively engage under the willing suspension of disbelief. If participation in a virtual world of shared hyperboles is considered to be constitutive of behavioral modernity – to count among its necessary ingredients as it were – we should avoid theorizing the origins of religion by disregarding one of its most prominent features of recognition, namely the human willingness to affirm the world *as if* it were, and to do so neither by debunking an apparent illusion nor by self-deceptively immersing oneself in its apparent reality. In the alternative scenarios – whether religion is considered to originate as premature speculation about the natural world, or as a response to the natural workings of the mind (such as dreams and hallucinations) – the implied religious (or proto-religious) subject behind such etiologies always enters credulously into a world that is either falsely construed or deceptively constrained.

Consider, for instance, how Chris Knight and two of his peers (Camilla Power and Ian Watts) chose to interpret the so-called ochre burials at the site of the Qafzeh cave in Israel. A discovery of large amounts of ochre lumps, found in association with hominid remains in a stratigraphic layer with an average date of 92,000 years ago, was reported to the journal *Current Anthropology* by a team of Israeli archaeologists in 2003 (Hovers et al. 2003). Instead of giving way to speculation about the ritual meaning of the Qafzeh record, the Israeli archaeologists justly prefer to discuss the heuristic criteria of distinguishing systems of symbolic behavior from other systems of decision making (Hovers et al. 2003, 507–510). In their cowritten response to the Qafzeh report, however, Knight and his colleagues move in a wholly different direction.

They insist on the proven validity of their hypothesis that such red-ochre burials represent the blood of menstruation or childbirth, which eventually come to suggest conceptions of rebirth or afterlife. Only such a model "can account for such recurrent features as red-ochre burials" on the level of certain time resistant syntactic features (Hovers et al. 2003, 514). Despite superficially abiding by standard methodological assumptions, such as that symbolic sense is always locally constructed and that ritual behavior is non-referential, Knight and Co. still do so on the premise of a deep-seated universal transparency: "In our model, ritually displayed red cosmetics invoke and sustain collective representations translatable not narrowly as 'menstruation' but more broadly as 'fertility,' 'supernatural potency,' etc." (Hovers et al. 2003, 513)

Whence did these deep-seated semantic qualifiers emerge, and how is it that they could once have been universally meaningful just by obeying certain universal rules of syntax? Must one not object that syntax is form and structure, not meaning and content; that phonemes combined according to phonotactic constraints are no less inherently meaningful than a syntactically correct sentence ("For the Snark *was* a Boojum, you see")? Resistance to such queries does not chiefly ensue from accidental evidence, but rather from the absolutizing trend in imagining a past self as other.

If the study of early human ideational culture is to avoid submission to the same logic of defamiliarization as that with which it is ultimately concerned – that is, with culture at work, persistent in its accentuation of identity and difference – it seems necessary to defamiliarize the very habitus in which such quests for cultural origins seem to function. Hence, instead of trying to conceptualize an unfamiliar world of proto-conceptual immediacy from which modern humans eventually broke out in a sudden flash of self-awareness, we should preferably begin with what is always already faintly familiar.

2.4

Symbolic acts are never universally recognizable – neither ethnographically nor in archaeological retrospect – because of what they universally mean, but because of what we can infer about them in their capacity as symbolic acts. A minimal criterion is that they leave behind more or less tangible social artefacts. *Social* because they appear to have been collectively sustained, *artificial* because they neither emerge nor convey information by themselves. Whether palpable or intangible, symbolic artefacts need to be mediated and decoded according to a locally received protocol. Furthermore, symbolic acts are cosmetic. They remain so in the broadest sense of the word (from Greek *kósmēsis* "ordering") because they impose a new and arbitrary order upon the world. Hence, in their capacity as initial and minimal tokens of archaeological recognition, prehistoric symbols do not disclose what they imply outside of themselves, but rather act as cues for the undisclosed network of symbols in which they once participated. They are the perceptible traces of a socially sustained world that remains largely imperceptible.

An intriguing challenge to the single-species scenario, the earliest archaeological evidence of mortuary practice and personal ornaments in southwest Europe does not univocally coincide with the arrival of anatomically modern humans in the area. Whereas the earliest cases of mortuary practice remain ambiguous –

some have even been linked to pre-Neanderthals living in Spain (Sima de los Huesos) as far back as 400,000 years ago (d'Errico et al. 2009, 38) – the earliest unambiguous cases of proper burials from the Near East indicate no differences in funerary practice between Neanderthals and *Homo sapiens*. Furthermore, against the common proposition that cave art and the use of personal ornaments was first uniquely linked to anatomical moderns now speak the approximately 50,000 years old, pigment stained, and perforated marine shells from the Neanderthal-associated Middle-Paleolithic of Iberia reported by João Zilhão et al. in 2010; and the more than 64,000 year old cave paintings from three other sites in Iberia (Hoffmann et al. 2018).

We may thus safely consider burials, the use of personal ornaments, and cave art to fit into a multi-species scenario. This would imply that whatever claims are made to biologically distinguish Neanderthals from the anatomically modern newcomers to Europe in behavioral terms, these groups had already begun to artificially differentiate themselves internally before they eventually came into contact, possibly in the Near East, and before they – as we now know – occasionally interbred (Kuhlwilm et al. 2016). In other words, both groups may have independently developed behavioral traits that, on condition that they can be considered at least vaguely modern, will afford ethnographic generalization.

Taking the case of personal ornaments as a point of departure, I should like to suggest that the perceived sense of non-utilitarian artificiality with which such objects have always been imbued may also apply to funerary practice, that both categories of archaeological data involve hyperboles of identity and difference, and that they may thus provide the earliest visible cues for the human willingness to suspend disbelief.

As has become increasingly clear since the first large-scale diachronic study pursued by Yvette Taborin in the 1990s, prehistoric personal ornaments were not produced or retrieved at random, but by cultural choice. Each Paleolithic so-called techno-complex presents a characteristic variety of primary material for the manufacture of such ornaments (distinct species of marine shells, animal teeth, ivory, horn, etc.), indicating clear-cut in-group preferences specific to relatively small geographic areas, as well as systems of exchange traversing vast areas (Vanhaeren 2010, 4, 288–302). Cross-cultural anthropological data suggest a multitude of integrated functions ascribed to personal ornaments – ranging from aesthetic self-affirmation, social cohesion, the demarcation of ethnic frontiers, exchange value, and so forth – but there are also recurrent aspects of their occurrence that need not be subjected to such functional discriminations: (1) the fact that they are artificial extensions of the body, and (2) that they lack the perceivably utilitarian purpose of other bodily appendages, such as clothes or armor. Regardless of the undisclosed local significance once accompanying artefacts of this kind, they all testify to the cognitive capacity for self-projection, and by doing so they also imply an in-group awareness of their inherent artificiality. Nevertheless, our initial recognition of this fact will not suffice to unlock the virtual world thus artificially sustained.

A certain degree of critical disavowal is required; disbelief in certain invalidated assertions has to be suspended. Such assertions imply the dissimulation of one's biological appearance as opposed to one's appearance in a cosmetic state of alteration. Artificial extensions of the body – say a string of pierced fox teeth around the neck – simultaneously disclose and dissimulate firsthand information about themselves in claiming (1) that they consist of natural objects extracted from a dead animal's jawbone, and (2) that they partake in constituting the body of a person in a specific cultural setting. When such constitutive claims are made, furthermore, they engage hyperboles of identity and difference. A specific in-group identity is enhanced, either within the group or in its relation to another group. Such forms of participation may invite all sorts of psychological and sociological theorizing, but there is always a more fundamental phenomenological sense in which such personal ornaments contribute to the manifestation of what Bernhard Waldenfels has called "hyperphenomena" (including the rhetorical category of hyperbole).

Hyperphenomena are recognized as such by the very fact that, and by means of what, they are something *more* and *other* than what they appear to be, without ever being capable of becoming what they appear to be, or to disappear into what they are not (Waldenfels 2012, 11). For want of all that personal ornaments keep hidden from us in terms of their local significance, this much can at least be conjectured: that they project their owners and onlookers into a virtual world of perceived artificiality in which human subjects stage themselves apart from how they provisionally appear to be. In short, the human subject transcends that which it perceivably is by pretending to be what it perceivably is not.

It now remains to be shown how this fundamental human propensity extends to the area of mortuary practice. It would be premature to infer that the pertinence of burials and other forms of funerary practices, from the Middle Paleolithic onwards, testify to an essential belief in life after death. This way of reasoning reveals an unclear distinction between the exegesis of burial practices and their global raison d'être. Nevertheless, there are some minimal criteria of recognition from which inferences may be drawn without succumbing to such second-order interpretations. Unlike the living members of a society, whether the dead are treated as other than decaying biomass depends entirely on the extent to which their survivors defy treating them as such. If through prescribed actions the dead are converted into the *others within*, into the ontological others of the in-group, it is because they – apart from what they leave behind in the form of incidental recollections and physical traces – have been altogether transformed into artefacts. Their physical bodies, and no longer just the artefacts once attached to them, have become more than what they accidentally appear to be. By being manipulated according to arbitrary, non-utilitarian routines that the surviving members of the in-group have come to define as *their* way of ritually treating their dead – whether through incineration, inhumation, grinding, powdering, or the like – the bodily remains are invested with cultural significance.[19]

A suggestive illustration of how such concatenated motivations manifest themselves is the installation of skeletal remains in the crypt beneath the church of Santa Maria della Concezione dei Cappuccini in Rome. Bones and skulls have been turned into richly ornamented decors on ceilings and walls, some skeletons into statues carrying robes and cowls, and one into an allegorical representation of Death with scales and a scythe. In spite of all that the Capuchin Friars would have thought and taught about the resurrection of the dead, Christian theology is surprisingly absent from the displays themselves, making them perfect representatives of any mortuary monument. A placard at the entrance solemnly declares, in a beautifully devised chiasmus: *Quello che voi siete noi eravamo; quello che noi siamo voi sarete* ("What you are now we used to be; what we are now you will be"). The dead do not only appear before the crypt's visitors in the form of virtual persons, but they are also made to address the living in the first-person plural, thus temporarily setting aside the residual materiality of their current post-mortem status *as if* they still had voices and bodies.

The chiasmus on the placard is strongly reminiscent of a sentence in Epicurus' letter to his disciple Menoecus (*Ep.* III.124): *hótan mèn hēmeîs ômen, ho thánatos ou párestin; hótan d' ho thánatos parê, toth' hēmeîs ouk esmén* ("So long as we exist, death is not with us; but when death comes, then we do not exist"). Whereas likewise situating death in a position of ulterior otherness (where we are not), the two sentences convey radically different yet perfectly tenable messages. The one stresses the fact of biological death, the other the fact of the artefact. If Epicurus urges Menoecus to suspend rash judgement about death as a natural condition, the Capuchin Crypt's installation rather demonstrates how the dead are ontologically made to reappear under the willing suspension of disbelief.

2.5. Claude Lévi-Strauss once pointed out that "man has always been thinking equally well" (Lévi-Strauss 1955, 444). Some might disagree, but those who consider the argument worth pursuing should take heed of the recurrent tendency to underestimate the reality testing abilities of human subjects in the past, to regard

---

19 For a groundbreaking contribution to the hermeneutics of ancient burial practices, see Ruin 2019 (especially ch. 5 [112–147]). See also Schleiter 2022 (on the semiotics of burial and absence).

them as immature theorists, or as unknowing victims of a neurological spectacle. If, on the other hand, our notion of "thinking well" is apprehended in its widest sense, it should also imply that humans have always been engaged in hyperboles of identity and difference, always prepared to test the limits of an intellectual disavowal, and that it is rather *this* ability that makes them uniquely and recognizably human.

If differentiation is the process through which meaning is produced in the first place, hyperbolic differentiation is the process through which the world becomes culturally perceptible to its inhabitants apart from what it appears to be, that is, in a perceived state of contingent human intervention and alteration. If we insist on assigning an exterior purpose to such alterations, we deny them certain ludic, second-order properties without which they cease to function and make sense. Their allocated task thus either becomes wholly meaningless and purposeless (whereby it ceases to be a task), or it ascribes the original logic of the game to the world outside of the game, as if the world had a meaning and purpose wholly distinct from (and prior to) the purpose ascribed to it by humans. Whereas belief in a cosmic purpose has long lost its impact on scholarly discourse, it is still widely held to be a quintessential motivator of religion, that is, not just a secondary trait of whatever one considers religion to be, but its very source and raison d'être. As I have already suggested, and will continue to argue below, this is a far from self-evident conjecture.

3 Fame and Social Eating

3.1

I began my line of argument in the previous chapter by demonstrating how hyperbolic displays of identity and difference tend to instantiate a quintessentially human (and hence cross-cultural) capacity for suspending critical assumptions about selves and others. Indices of this self-projecting capacity pervade all sorts of genres and practices, from scientifically informed conceptions and visualizations of prehumans, to fanciful rumors of bald-headed humanoids inhabiting spatial peripheries, and eventually pointing back to the earliest signatures of behavioral modernity in the form of burials and personal ornaments. A recurrent design behind such genres and practices presumes the claim that first glance similarities and dissimilarities – within, between, beneath, and beyond human populations – occasionally can, and ought, to be exaggerated, artificially enhanced, or staged so as to appear more protrusive than they initially seemed to be.

Proceeding from the final argument regarding the artificial conversion of the dead, I propose to address a related issue in this chapter: hospitality and hostility. The ritual conversion of strangers – of cultural, out-group, or extrafamilial others – into whole or partial, permanent or temporary members of the in-group, constitute a particularly productive social matrix. A great variety of socially sustained propositions can be linked to this ritual setting. They include rules and manners regulating the preparation and sharing of food (what, where, and with whom to eat or not to eat), the courteous exchange of gifts and information as well as a host of mythical extrapolations to such real-life forms of intercourse.

If funerary practice can be roughly categorized as a ritual response to biological death, rites of hospitality respond by similar means to the biogenetic constraints of consanguinity, and they ultimately amount to disinhibiting such constraints by fully perceptible artificial means. Examples abound to illustrate how the sharing of prepared food allegedly induce the consubstantial effects of sexual reproduction (Sahlins 2013, 6). The ontology of kinship (or "mutuality of being" in Marshall Sahlins' phrasing) derives from food sharing the most far-reaching implications of the formula *you are what you eat.*[20]

20 The phrase can be traced back to the gastronomist Jean Anthelme Brillat-Savarin's work *Physiologie du goût* (1825) ("Dis-moi ce que tu manges, je te dirai ce que tu es."), but became proverbial outside France through Ludwig Feuerbach's repeated use of the dictum *Der Mensch ist, was er ißt* (cf. Lemke 2004). Needless to say, none of these authors intended the phrase to be taken literally.

https://doi.org/10.1515/9783110460605-005

Propositions like these need empirical backup. Furthermore, in order to afford non-trivial historical reasoning, our assumptions need to account for the long-term process of cultural mutation from which we eventually derive our data. I will be doing so here by considering the linguistic, poetic, and archaeological imprints of a sacrificial economy assumed to have developed among the prehistoric speakers of Proto-Indo-European (PIE) more than two millennia before the emergence of textual evidence to back it up.[21] As I intend to show in the following, the extended impact of this sacrificial economy may help to explain a set of interconnected phenomena that would otherwise have appeared incommensurable. Questions raised by such otherwise disconnected phenomena include the following: What does it mean to be a god or a monster? On what pretext do high-ranking players engage in costly games of public pretense and expenditure? And, perhaps most importantly, what do notions of fame and social eating add to the social theory of sacrifice?

3.2

Before probing the deeper past of the issues at stake, I shall briefly exemplify how they were conceived in ancient Greek society. A fragment from the proem to Hesiod's *Catalogue of Women* informs us:

> ξυναὶ γὰρ τότε δα͵ῖτες ἔσαν, ξυνοὶ δὲ θόωκοι
> ἀθανάτοις τε θε͵οῖσι καταθνητοῖς τ᾽ ἀνθρώποις.
>
> For at that time feasts were common, and common the seats (of council)
> among immortal gods and mortal humans.
> (Hes. *Fr.* 1.6 – 7)

A state of irrevocable ideality in the past is perceived here against the backdrop of a social factuality in the present, namely animal sacrifice as the epicenter of religious life in the Greek polis. If "at that time" (*tóte*) gods and mortals passed their lives in harmonious coexistence, they no longer eat together on similar terms. According to the same poet, the two groups "reached a crisis point" (*ekrínonto* [←

21 Bewildering as they may appear to the casual passer-by, such conjectures have met with increasing scholarly approval over the last decades due to corroborations from various disciplines. Indicative of this trend are the influences from Calvert Watkins (Watkins 1995) on Martin L. West (West 2007) at the intersection of classics and comparative Indo-European poetics, and the collaboration between David W. Anthony and Don Ringe (e.g., Anthony and Ringe 2015) at the intersection of archaeology and historical linguistics.

krínō[22]) at the ancient city of Mekone (*Th.* 535). The reason for the dispute was a trick played by Prometheus against Zeus during the preparation of a communal meal (*Th.* 535–544). By placing the edible parts of a great ox inside the animal's stomach and smearing its bones in fat, Prometheus violates a fundamental principle of hospitality. While the trick sets the standard for future sacrifices, it also results in the alienation of human society from the community of gods. There is a clear-cut logic at work here. Seen from below, from the perspective of quotidian human life, sacrifice answers to the most refined form of social intercourse. Seen from above, from the imaginary vantage point of divine excellence, it rather instigates the transformation of a once elevated being into a greedy human subject.

The epic treatment of Hermes' invention of sacrifice is another case in point. As the myth unfolds in the *Homeric Hymn to Hermes* (*h. Hom.* 4), the protagonist is seeking recognition as a member of the Olympic family, and eventually achieves "fame" (or "glory") (*kléos*) among the immortal gods (*kléos éstai en athánatoisi theoîsin* [458]) in reward for his technical and ritual skills (his singing and newly invented lyre). Unlike Prometheus, who corrupts a community by trying to deceive his guests, Hermes inverts the program by first committing a crime – stealing fifty cows from Apollo's sacred cattle herd, cunningly driving the animals from Pieria to the Peleponnese, and finally slaughtering two of them by the river Alpheios – and then by exonerating himself through the work of ritual.

A crucial detail in the plot is the fact that Hermes avoids the edible parts of the slaughtered animals, thus affirming his divine status by rejecting the communal meal in which humans take part. In other words, Hermes has to emulate the oblique table manners of the Olympian gods in order to receive a place in their midst. If the two etiologies are analyzed contiguously, they demonstrate how artificial procedures surrounding food sharing – the potentially deceptive "craft" (*tékhnē*) of ritual – define the regulations of communal exclusion and inclusion. The peaceful settlement between Hermes and Apollo – signaled by the verb (*dia*)*krínō* (*h. Hom.* 4.438) – marks the resolution to an original crisis of unfair division caused by Prometheus, and one that was likewise signaled by the verb *krínō* (*Th.* 535).

Whereas the Prometheus narrative revolves around prescribed food sharing among potential equals, the Hermes narrative concerns the restorative power of ritual labor. Hermes achieves rank and glory in terms of what his contrivances afford (they "match the value of fifty cows" [*pentḗkonta boôn antáxia*] [*h.*

22 The verb *krínō* is ambiguously used here to suggest either a spatial separation (at the city of Mekone) or a critical decision resulting in spatial separation. It forestalls the fact that gods and mortals were being separated from one another as the result of Prometheus' transgression. Glenn W. Most translates "reached a settlement" (cf. bibliography under Hes.).

Hom. 4.437]). In order to appreciate the social motivations behind these complementary theories of sacrifice, we need to acknowledge the different procedures by which human relationships are created and sustained, namely (1) through traditions of contractual hospitality conjoining mutually obliged allies, and (2) in an asymmetric relationship between patrons and clients through the exchange of services and commodities. If ties of hospitality are ritually created, ties of patron-clientage are the preconditioned means to such an end. A client skilled in ritual craftsmanship becomes a mediating asset to the community through the patron's expenditure.

Institutions of hospitality and patronage share a deep history of conflation, the full appreciation of which brings acumen to the dynamic interplay between civic and unlicensed forms of religiosity. The comparison of culturally distinct ancient texts and their shared vocabularies allow us to trace the early formation of such institutions.

3.3

Comparative approaches to Indo-European vocabulary pragmatics are based on the assumption that the linguistic reconstruction of PIE enables cultural reconstruction of a native speech community predating the dispersal of the Indo-European language family.[23] Attempts to locate this community in time and space cannot rely solely on the relative chronology of linguistic evidence. Equally important is the combination of data gathered from the proto-lexicon with archaeological evidence.

A collaborative effort to meet such standards univocally points to the Pontic-Caspian steppes during the 5th and 4th millennia BCE (Anthony and Ringe 2015).[24] The archaeology of this region shows that pastoral steppe economies underwent revolutionary changes between 4200–3300 BCE. This period roughly coincides with what linguists have independently come to consider to be the lifespan of

23 A pioneering and still very useful contribution to the topic is Émile Benveniste's *Le vocabulaire des institutions indo-européennes* (1969). Mallory and Adams (2006) add up-to-date knowledge to the relevant vocabulary.

24 Anthony and Ringe (2015) forcefully, and in my view convincingly, argue against the alternative hypothesis that Indo-European languages spread with the advance of farming from Neolithic Anatolia around 7000 BCE. First proposed by Colin Renfrew (1987), the hypothesis has been revisited with support from so-called Bayesian phylogenetic analysis (e.g., Atkinson and Gray 2003).

post-Anatolian and pre-Tocharian PIE.[25] Especially striking is the archeologically attested shift from partial to full dependence on pastoral products, which correlates with new technologies of transport and pastoral herding (wheeled vehicles and horseback riding). These changes very likely conduced to complex migrations out of the steppes beginning with the eastern flow of the so-called Afanasievo culture around 3300 BCE.

Socio-economic particularities of the PIE speech community can also be inferred from textual sources that preserve a concatenated vocabulary of shared institutions. Evidence of inherited Indo-European poetics and anthroponomastics come in handy in this regard to suggest that a variety of widely dispersed tribal groups – ranging from speakers of Iranian and Indo-Aryan during the 2nd millennium BCE to the last pre-Christian populations of Scandinavia by the late 1st millennium CE – maintained sacrificial economies that were continuously resonant with a poetic tradition of naming and heroic praise.

The concept of the good host (the "guests-lord" [PIE *g^h*osti-potis*]) who seeks lasting fame (PIE **k̂léu̯os*), victory (PIE **ség̑*^{h}*os*), and booty (PIE **sóru*) is linked by this tradition with the concept of the sacrificial feast (PIE **dh*$_2$*pn̥óm* [← **deh*$_2$*p-* "to cut up (meat)"]) as a projector of wealth (PIE **h*$_3$*ep-*) and divine servitude (PIE **Hi̯aĝ-* "to sacrifice") (cf. Anthony and Ringe 2015, 212). The image emerges of a pre-ancient herding society in which tribal chieftains are striving to impersonate various, ostensibly conflicting, yet ideologically interdependent roles in the eyes of their minions and allies. A similar logic of contiguity is characteristic of imperial policies to this day. Firstly, chieftains engage in warfare on the pretext of protecting their in-group and exploiting the resources of allegedly savage others. Secondly, they bring back wealth to their people. Thirdly, they act as hosts and patrons so as to turn previous others into allies and clients.[26]

Inasmuch as the contiguous unfolding of such roles reflects the structure of an actual social hierarchy, it is strongly informed by a social rhetoric of hyperbolic

---

25 Shared linguistic features between subgroups of Indo-European can be used to determine in what order the branches separated from each other. There is strong evidence to suggest that the Anatolian branch separated first (around 4200–4000 BCE), and that the protolanguage underwent significant changes previous to the separation of the Tocharian branch around 3300 BCE (references in Ringe and Anthony 2015, 206).

26 A few samples of dithematic names suffice to exemplify how these roles were contiguously conceived: "fame" (PIE **k̂léu̯o-*) + "guest" (PIE *g^h*os-tis*/*g^h*s-enu̯os*) = Runic *Hlewa-gastiz* ("fame-guest" ≈ "having famous guests"), Greek *Kleo-xenos* ("id."); "supreme" (PIE **upm̥mo*) + "fame" = Vedic *Upama-śravas* ("having supreme fame"); "supreme" + "guest" = Lepontic *Uvamo-kozis* ("having supreme guests"); GOD + "guest" = Vedic *Mitrātithi* ("having Mitra as guest"), Greek *Dio-xenos* ("having Zeus as guest"), Runic *Ansu-gastiz* ("having the god [*ansuz*] as guest") (cf. Fortson 2005, 35, and Jackson 2012).

suspense. It reflects ideals transmitted through the medium of commissioned poetry. Chieftains determined to gain reputation and everlasting glory willingly rewarded those skilled in the art of poetry. They knew that a well-crafted poem was capable of doing more than just embellishing a patron's immediate appearance. At best, it could also carry him beyond his corporeal self after death through memorable diction. Still, commissioned poetry did not one-sidedly express the interests of the patron. Ritual professionals had their interests as well, and they knew how to cater these interests through their hymns. This is a pattern still clearly distinguishable in Greek and Vedic poetry.

3.4

An autobiographical hymn from the 10th maṇḍala of the R̥gveda (RV 10.33) amply illustrates of how a poet imagines the equilibrium of a ritual community.[27] The hymn begins and ends in the style of a lament directed at Upamaśravas, the son of the late king Kuruśravaṇa. Due to the death of his former patron and "yokemate" (*yúj-* [9c]) – Kuruśravaṇa, the son of Mitrātithi of Trasadasyu's lineage – the poet (traditionally identified as Kavaṣa Ailūṣa) now lacks protection, esteem, and a source of income. No one tends to his needs any more, and as a consequence his own attention has begun to flutter around like a bird.

He invokes the god Indra in terms that recall the virtues of a caring patron – a "supplier of wealth" (*maghávan-* [3c]) who shows mercy and becomes like a father – and then begins to depict his heyday at the court of Kuruśravaṇa. Kavaṣa significantly shifts to the past tense when he confidently claims to have *chosen* (*āvr̥ṇi* ["I chose"] ← *ā*+√*vr̥* [4a]) his patron owing to the latter's good reputation as a sponsor of poets (4c).

In what looks like the echo of a so-called *dānastuti* (the priestly "praise of the [patron's] gift") once directed at Kuruśravaṇa, the poet metaphorically describes himself as being pulled by the king's horses in a chariot along the straight path (5ab), and expresses anticipation of abundant rewards by using the subjunctive mood ("I shall praise [*stávai* ← √*stu*] [him = Kuruśravaṇa] at [a sacrifice with] a priestly gift of a thousand [cows]" [*sahásradakṣiṇe*] [5c]). Kavaṣa continues to certify that Kuruśravaṇa indeed received sweet songs on a par with a delightful dwelling (6c).

27 A few highly relevant comments about this fascinating hymn are found in Watkins 1995, 245–246.

The next stanza (7) makes the actual errand of the poet explicit: "Beware (*ádhi* [...] *ihi* [7ab]), o son Upamaśravas, o grandson of Mitrātithi, I am the celebrant of your father!" Kavaṣa is apparently seeking to enter a renewed contract with his former patron's son. He has to be self-confident enough to convince Upamaśravas that they, too, will form a union of mutual benefit. There is a limit to what he may achieve as a poet, but nothing seems to prevent his aspirations to extend beyond that limit. The optatives (*ī́śīya* [---] *jī́ved* "If I could be master [---] he would live") in the penultimate stanza are clearly expressive of this bold wishfulness:

8a. *yád ī́śīyāmŕ̥̥tānãm* / b. *utá vā mártiyānãm*
8c. *jī́ved ín maghávā máma*

8a. If I could be master of immortals / b. and mortals,
8c. my bounteous patron would still live.[28]

Kavaṣa's hymn takes its cue from a pattern of triangulation discernible in nearly all aspects of Vedic ritual.[29] The expected behavior towards the gods is matched against the codes of conduct for patrons and poet-priests: gods receive praise and servitude from the poet-priests by analogy with the praise and servitude that patrons can expect from their priestly clients in return for supplying them with bounteous gifts. A typical measure of wealth in Vedic society, cattle and other domesticated animals could be seized in war. Still, competition for success, wealth, and good reputation was as much a concern of ritual specialists seeking wealthy patrons as it involved chieftains seeking recognition for their wealth and generosity.

The royal names evoked in the hymn are in themselves indicative of the ideals that such wealthy chieftains sought to impersonate. Kuruśravaṇa ("glory of the [royal lineage of the] Kurus") is an ancestor of Trasadasyu ("who makes the [occasionally demonized] enemies tremble"), a grandson of Mitrātithi ("having [the god] Mitra as guest") and the father of Upamaśravas ("having supreme fame"). Fame, hospitality, and a fearful appearance on the battlefield are qualities in compliance with the contiguous roles mentioned above.

28 Throughout this book, I rely largely on the new English translation by Stephanie W. Jamison and Joel P. Brereton (henceforth J/B, s.v. RV in the section "Abbreviations, editions, and translations") with the exception of minor deviations intended to emphasize the literal sense of single words. The Vedic text is based on the metrically restored edition by Barend A. van Nooten and Garry B. Holland with the exception of (restored) italicized inserted vowels, all of which are written as subscript letters in order to facilitate italicization of whole stanzas.
29 Cf. the illuminating model used by Almut Hintze to describe the network of relations underlying sacrificial exchange in Indo-Iranian culture (Hintze 2004, 28).

The name Mitrātithi is a particularly telling case. It matches an onomastic tradition reflected both in Slavic, Greek, Celtic, and Germanic, where the PIE element _*g^hos-tis_ "stranger, guest" (with the zero-grade variant _*g^hs-enu̯os_ "id." seen in Greek _xénos_[30]) is likewise preceded by the qualifier GOD (e.g., Greek _Dio-xenos_ ["having Zeus as guest"], Runic _Ansu-gastiz_ ["having the god {_ansuz_} as guest"]) or the qualifier FAME (e.g., Greek _Kleo-xenos_ ["fame-guest" ≈ "having famous guests"], Germanic _Hlewa-gastiz_ "id."). The notion of hospitably serving the gods _as if_ they were human guests to which their hosts were obliged, and from which fame was received in return, has an indisputable common provenance.[31]

Whereas deverbatives from the stem _*g^hos/*g^hs_ are attested in Indo-Iranian, it was rather the noun _*atH-ti-_ "guest" (Vedic _átithi-_, Avestan _asti-)_ that functioned as the direct semantic correlate to the inherited "European" variants _*g^hos-tis/*g^hs-enu̯os._[32] A good example is the parallelism of the Vedic compound _átithipati-_ "host" (literally "guest-lord") and the PIE compound _*g^hosti-potis_ reflected in Latin _hospes_ and Russian _gospodĭ_ (Benveniste 1969, 95; Forssman 1998). Furthermore, the Vedic treatment of the verbal stem √_ghas_ (< PIE _*g^hes_ "to eat") sheds light on the archaic semantics from which the deverbatives _*g^hos-tis/*g^hs-enu̯os_ derived their original sense. The Vedic verb usually conveys the secondary sense "devour, consume destructively" (like predators or fire), but occasionally retains the innocent original sense "to eat" by filling gaps in the conjugation of the commonplace verb √_ad_ (as in Latin _edo_ and Proto-Germanic _*etaną_ [< PIE _*$h_1$ed_]). One such case of suppletion occurs in another hymn from the 10th maṇḍala (10.15) addressed to the male ancestors, or the so-called _pitáras_ ("fathers").

30 For discussions of the etymology, cf. Watkins 1995, 246, Pinault 1998, and Eichner 2002. Neri (2012) proposes an alternative etymology on the basis of the PIE word for "hand" _*$\hat{g}^h$os/*$\hat{g}^h$es_, which renders _*$\hat{g}^h$ós-ti-_ (with a palatal _ĝ_) as "der in der Hand = im Schutz befindliche, Gast." The standard derivation from _g^hes_ ("to eat") seems more compelling on the basis of the philological considerations presented above. Also, this etymology is less costly in that it does not require us to treat the Slavic comparanda (OCS _gostь_ etc.) as reflexes of an early loanword from a (Germanic?) language preserving the root with an initial velar _g_.

31 The so-called Slava feast (from a Proto-Slavic noun _*slovo_ meaning "fame, glory, [heard] word" < PIE _*k̂léu̯os_), celebrated among Orthodox Christians throughout Serbia and Kosovo in honor of the family patron saint, testifies to the unbroken continuity of such traditions in Europe long after the Church's official suppression of pagan rites. The feast includes the ritual cutting up and besprinkling of a cake, toasts asking for the well-being of the family performed by a "wassailer" (_zdravicar_), and numerous other tokens of reciprocity and hospitality. It was inscribed on the UNESCO _Representative List of the Intangible Cultural Heritage of Humanity_ in 2014 (nomination file no. 01010).

32 The reflex of a closely related PIE zero-grade _*sm̥-g^hs-ti-_ is seen in Vedic _ságdhi-_ "eating together, communal meal" (cf. Watkins 1995, 246).

Described as having successively left the earthly realm behind, the forefathers are ritually called back to temporarily join the community of gods and men at the sacrificial ground. A recurrent feature of the hymn is the ritual cry *svadhā́*, which accompanied libations to the forefathers. The apparent gap between the literal sense of *svadhā́* (from an original syntagm *sva-√dhā́-*, *sva-dhā́man*, etc., "*self-establishment" [EWAia, s.v.]) and its technical employment in the hymn suggests an archaic idiom of ritual etiquette. The forefathers are repeatedly invited to "share in the pressed soma and the food through (or at the cry of) *svadhā́*" (3d), "to enjoy the well-performed sacrifice through *svadhā́*-calls" (13d), and "to become exhilarated through *svadhā́*" (14d).

A crucial occurrence in the 12th stanza is the conjoining of *svadhā́* with the suppletive aorist *akṣann* ("they have eaten" [√*ghas* as a substitute for √*ad*]). It testifies to the social event from which deverbatives of the type **g^{h}os-tis/*g^{h}s-enu̯os* must have derived their original sense of a (divine or human) stranger's claim to potential mutuality by means of food sharing. Furthermore, the stanza testifies to the common background of an Indo-European guest/host terminology and the classical notion of "ethos" (literally "self-establishment" [PIE **su̯e-d^{h}eh$_{1}$*]), as seen in Greek *éthos/êthos* ("custom, habit") and Latin *sodālis* ("fellow, comrade"):

12a. *t$_{u}$vám agna īḻitó jātavedo* / b. *ávāḍ ḍhavyā́ni surabhī́ṇi kr̥tvī́*
12c. *prā́dāḥ pitr̥´bhyaḥ svadháyā té aksạ nn* / d. *addhí tvám̩ deva práyatā havī́m̩ sị*

12a. you, Agni Jātavedas (= "[he] who knows the creatures") reverently invoked, / b. have conveyed the oblations, having made them very fragrant.
12c. you have presented them to the forefathers; they have eaten (aksạ nn) them in accordance with custom (svadháyā).[33] / d. Eat (addhí), o god, the oblations set forth!

Pindar's juxtaposition of the cognate Greek terms *xeînos* (< PIE √**g^{h}es*) and (Doric Greek) *ēthaîos* (< PIE **su̯e-d^{h}eh$_{1}$*) in the final verse of *Second Isthmian* (*xeînon emòn ēthaîon* ["my customary guest-friend"] [I. 2.48]) may be derived from the same ritual idiom. Mutual hospitality, or "guest-friendship" (*xenía*), is a recurring theme throughout the whole ode. The customary guest-friend addressed at the end is no other than the poet's patron, Thrasybulos, who has commissioned the poem for a celebration of his dead father's victories, and from whom Pindar is apparently expecting more in recompense (Watkins 1995, 81). Comparable cases of juxtaposition occur in Latin, where *hostis* ("stranger, enemy" [as well as *hospes* in the transferred sense "guest, friend"]) and *sodālis* ("fellow, comrade") underwent a

33 Unlike J/B ("at the cry of '*svadhā́*'"), I have somewhat anachronistically rendered the instrumental *svadháyā* in light of the term's primary sense ("*self-establishment" → "custom") instead of merely implying a secondary reference to a ritual cry.

similar shift in meaning.[34] Although Pindar's locution does not retain the PIE semantics of the collocation – a noun and adjective reflecting a hypothetical syntagm "to eat in accordance with custom" (→ *self-establishment) (PIE *$g^{h}es$ + *su̯e-$d^{h}h_{1}$-eh_{2}-eh_{1}- [instr.]) – the ritual context of commensality remains pertinent to his poetic vocation. Just like the Vedic poets, Pindar shows great ingenuity in exploring the contractual bond between himself and his patron. His claim to be a guest-friend of his host, and not just a temporary client, is a subtle reminder that even the gods may wish to engage in hospitable eating with their human subjects. Pindar is keen to praise Thrasybulus' father – the recently deceased Isthmian victor Xenokrates – for arranging so-called *theôn daîtas* (39) ("feasts for the gods"), never to "furl his sail around his hospitable table (*xenían* [...] *trápezan*)" (39–40).

The purport and context is strongly reminiscent of Kavaṣa's negotiation with Upamaśravas in RV 10.33, where we also noticed a simile linking the hospitable court of the patron to an advancing vehicle. Both Pindar and Kavaṣa take the advantage of praising a dead patron's piety and generosity in order to win the favors of a new one. Furthermore, they both strategically make the royal names – Xenokrates ("guest-friend" [*xénos*] + "strength" [*krátos*]) in the case of Pindar, Mitrātithi and Upamaśravas in the case of Kavaṣa – "speak" to evoke a subtext of ideal hospitality. The poetic evocation of intangible fame and tangible food sharing becomes a means to eradicate borders, both ethnic and ontological, so that participants in the communal drama – whether gods or ancestors, hosts or guests, patrons or clients – all appear to exist on equal terms.

3.5

I have only just begun to indicate the richly layered Indo-European poetics of hospitality and some of the linguistic technicalities that enable us to trace its prehistory. Since all examples have so far only revolved around courteous invitations to

34 Consider, for instance, the contrasting deployment of *sodālis* and *hostis* in Plautus: *estne hic meus sodālis? :: estne hic hostis, quem aspicio, meus?* (*Bacchides*, 534). Another significant passage from the same play combines the nouns *hospitium* ("hospitality"), *cena* ("meal"), and *sodālis* ("fellow, comrade"): *hospitium et cenam pollicere* [...] *salutem tibi ab sodāli solidam nuntio* (*Bacchides*, 185–187). The terms *sodālis* and *hospes* are juxtaposed in Late Latin poetry so as to appear almost synonymous: *sodālis et convinctor, hospes iugiter* ("comrade and table companion, [my] perpetual guest") (Ausonius, *Commemoratio professorum*, 15.14–15). Another telling example is the calendrical occurrence of exclusive meals (so-called *cenae*) that members of the Roman priestly sodalities (*sodales* [cf- *s{u}odālis* above]), such as the Salii and Fratres Arvales had in their assigned sanctuaries.

participate in the life of the community, however, a necessary move towards a fuller understanding of hospitality is to consider measures to the opposite effect. In what terms have hyperboles of ulterior otherness – an issue dealt with more generally in the previous chapter – been creatively adapted to a poetics of hospitality concerned with the limits of friendship, with the forces and beings imagined to violate the foundations of society? As we shall see, these notions have a strong bearing on a circular rhetoric of fame and social eating, according to which a community facing the outside threat of consumption can only succeed in coming full circle back to its original state of equilibrium through an act of heroic intervention.

Odysseus' first and final speeches to the Cyclops Polyphemus in the 9th book of the *Odyssey* (Hom. *Od.* 9.266–271, 9.475–479) are clearly imbued with such fears and anticipations. Whereas the first speech (answering to the Cyclops' blunt question "Who are you, strangers?" [*ô xeînoi, tínes estè* {9.252}]) resounds with the obligation to respect the gods and a repetitive deployment of *xeînos* (+ derivatives), the final speech condemns the disruption of sacred commensality:

> [...] ἡμεῖς δ' αὖτε κιχανόμενοι τὰ σὰ γοῦνα
> ἱκόμεθ', εἴ τι πορoίς ξεινήιον ἠὲ καὶ ἄλλως
> δοίης δωτίνην, ἥ τε ξείνων θέμις ἐστίν.
> ἀλλ' αἰδεῖο, φέριστε, θεούς· ἱκέται δέ τοί εἰμεν.
> Ζεὺς δ' ἐπιτιμήτωρ ἱκετάων τε ξείνων τε,
> ξείνιος, ὃς ξείνοισιν ἅμ' αἰδοίοισιν ὀπηδεῖ.
> [---]
> Κύκλωψ, οὐκ ἄρ' ἔμελλες ἀνάλκιδος ἀνδρὸς ἑταίρους
> ἔδεμεναι ἐν σπῆι γλαφυρῷ κρατερῆφι βίηφι.
> Καὶ λίμην σεγ' ἔμελλε κιχήσεσθαι κακὰ ἔργα,
> σχέτλι', ἐπεὶ ξείνους οὐχ ἅζεο σῷ ἐνὶ οἴκῳ
> ἐσθέμεναι
>
> [...] We come to you on our knees, as suppliants
> in the hope that you might give us a host's gift or some other
> present, as is the custom among strangers. Respect the gods,
> O mighty man! We are your suppliants, and Zeus
> is the avenger of suppliants and strangers – Zeus the god
> of strangers, who always stands by respectable strangers.
> [---]
> Cyclops, it turns out that you did not eat
> the companions of a man without strength in your hollow cave,
> taking them by might and by violence. Surely your evil
> deeds were bound to come back to you, wretch! You did not
> show holy fear of eating strangers in your own house.[35]

35 I am following Barry B. Powell's translation (s.v. Hom.) with the exception of a few details emphasizing the links between notions of hospitality, hostility, and eating. Powell accurately remarks

I am quoting from both speeches (*Od.* 9.266–271 and 475–479) in order to emphasize the contrasts between hospitality and hostility. These contrasts are brought out in the first speech by evoking a host's expected entertainment of foreigners, and in the last speech by recalling how these expectations have been violated by the Cyclops to the extreme: instead of having fed his guests in his home, he has feasted on them in his cave. Once again, the gods (and preferably Zeus) serve as exemplars of the good host. They protect their suppliants and take revenge on those violating the commandments of hospitality.

The god's antithesis in this regard is the monster. It represents the inverse of a hospitable being, hindered by the dialectic of imagination to appear simply as an innocent beast satisfying its natural desires. Instead, the monster characteristically mimics traits of human culture so as to evoke the false impression of civility. In spite of his preternatural facial appearance and cannibalistic predilections, the troglodyte Polyphemus is also a shepherd and a dairy farmer.

The depiction of the Cyclops as a partly savage, partly cultivated being on the threshold of civilization is expressive of an institution that necessarily entails risk and indeterminacy. If hospitable trust derives its hope from the sanctity of divine law (*thémis* [268]), its outbalancing of risk implies fear of the indeterminate stranger who fearlessly profanes the sacred commandments of hospitality. Odysseus' accusation against Polyphemus – "you did not show holy fear" (*oukh házeo* [*házomai* < PIE **Hi̯aĝ-* "to sacrifice"]) [478]) – is clearly an accusation of sacrilege. Hence, hospitality does not merely involve transient phenomena in the lucid sense of a guest/host reciprocity, but also in the ambiguous sense that its focal agent – the eponymous "stranger" (**g^{h}os-tis/*g^{h}s-enu̯os*) – can be either hostile or benevolent. This original connotation of inherent unfamiliarity is usually taken to account for a semantic development that eventually yielded "favorable stranger" in some languages (modern English *guest*) and "hostile stranger" in others (Latin *hostis* [with the original sense preserved in the compound *hospes* {Proto-Italic < **hosti-pets*} "guest-lord"]) (Benveniste 1969, 92).

in a footnote to verse 9.236 (9.252 in the Greek text), 177, that Polyphemus "inverts all rules of *xenia*," which the Cyclops already starts doing by asking the strangers to identify themselves instead of first feeding them. Cf. also Calvert Watkins' perceptive analysis of the passage, which further links it to Odysseus' triumph over the suitors (the non- or anti-guests) in his own house (*Od.* 24) (Watkins 1995, 402–403).

3.6

Two further examples – both linked to the survival of pagan Germanic lore in medieval literature – suffice to show how the mythical rhetoric of hostility has kept informing the Indo-European institution of hospitality.[36] While in these cases the scenario of the Cyclops story is inversed so as to portray a hostile guest in the house of the favorable host, the purport and moral remains the same. Once again, the covenant of hospitality is being exploited by the stranger through various forms of violation (gluttony, insult, threat), culminating in an open confrontation or even – just as in the case of the Cyclops story – plain cannibalism.

Both examples involve a being referred to in Proto-Germanic as **etunaz* (Old Norse *jǫtunn* [pl. *jǫtnar*] and Old English *eoten* [pl. *eotenas*]). I am avoiding the common translation "giant" here, because the Germanic noun is not unambiguously associated with a being distinguishable by size in the colloquial sense of a "gigantic being." Despite a continuous disagreement regarding formation and semantics, the standard procedure in contemporary scholarship is to derive the noun from the verb **etaną* "eat," which in its turn developed from the commonplace PIE stem **$h_1$ed* seen in Latin *edo* and Vedic √*ad* (Petzold 2003). The etymology finds its best textual justification in an unconnected stanza (Lv 5^{II}) composed by the eleventh-century skald Þjóðólfr Arnórsson, where it is apparently used as an agent noun to denote "eater" ("*jǫtunn* of goats' flesh" [*hafra kjǫts* {*at*} *jǫtni* {dat.}] as a kenning for "tanner") (Whaley 2009, 169–171).[37] As I shall argue here, it is only by taking into account the wider implications of this semantic sense in a context of precarious commensality that we can begin to appreciate the ambiguous role of the **etunaz* in Germanic myth.

Snorri Sturluson's thirteenth-century *Edda* (*Skáldskaparmál* 3) contains a systematic prose account of a myth, the final section of which is also alluded to in pagan skaldic poetry. It relates how the god Odin races on horseback with a *jǫtunn* called Hrungnir in order to test the strength of their horses. When they reach the abode of the gods (Ásgarðr), Hrungnir is received as a guest in the hall. He drinks abundantly and starts to insult the gods, threatening to drink all their ale and destroy their community. The god Thor is called upon and enters the hall, wielding his hammer, but Hrungnir invokes the "covenant" (*grið*) preventing a host from attacking an unarmed guest. As a final challenge to the patience of his host, the *jǫtunn* asks to be championed on just terms in a single combat. Thor

36 This section is a slightly modified rewriting of passages from Jackson 2014, 95–99. An exploration of the passages from *Beowulf* along similar lines is found in Lincoln 2012, 124–130.
37 The *u*-stem is also seen in the Latin agent noun *edulus* "eater" (as in *ficedula* "fig-pecker").

accepts the challenge and eventually defeats Hrungnir in an arranged meeting beyond the borders of Ásgarðr.

A similar plot is found in the first episode of the Old English poem *Beowulf.* Hrothgar, the king of the Danes, has reached the peak of his power and fortune. He decides to build a great mead-hall (or "guest-hall" [*gestsele*]) called Heorot, which is described as the epicenter of his power and a locus of redistributing wealth among his allies. A creature called Grendel, an inhabitant of the desolate marches beyond Heorot, begins to attack the hall at night. Unable to defend himself against the intruder, Hrothgar suffers devastating losses every night. When the news of Hrothgar's misery reaches the court of the Geats, one of king Hygelac's thanes decides to rescue the Danish king in order to promote his career as a young warrior. Beowulf is hospitably received in Heorot, declares his determination to fight Grendel, and eventually succeeds in defeating the unarmed creature with his bare hands. No sooner is Beowulf honored in Hrothgar's hall than the Danes have to face yet another threat. Grendel's mother is desperate to avenge her son. She attacks the hall when Beowulf is absent, creating havoc and sorrow in the hall, not least by killing Hrothgar's best warrior, Æscere. Beowulf is summoned by the king, sets out for the underwater abode (or "lair") of Grendel's mother, and defeats the creature in a context mirroring that of Grendel's intrusion into Heorot: the hero as anti-guest in the house of the anti-host. Before embarking on his expedition, Beowulf addresses the sorrowful king with a plea to the aristocratic ideal of undying fame:

> Ne sorga, snotor guma;   selre bið æghwæm
> þæt he his freond wrece,   þonne he fela murne.
> Ure æghwylc sceal   ende gebidan
> worolde lifes;   wyrce se þe mote
> domes ær deaþe;   þæt bið drihtguman
> unlifgendum   æfter selest.[38]

> Do not mourn, wise man;   it is better for each (man)
> to avenge his friend,   than to lament greatly.
> Each of us shall   await the end
> of (this) worldly life;   achieve let the one who may
> fame before death;   this remains for a warrior
> (when) no longer alive   afterwards the best.

38 I am using the edition by Dobbie, s.v. *Beowulf* in the section "Abbreviations, editions, and translations."

Snorri's rendition of the Hrungnir myth and the current episodes from *Beowulf* continuously explore the limits of hospitality by hyperbolically conveying (1) the shortcomings of the good host (Hrothgar) or the sacred covenant (*grið*) to provide sufficient protection, (2) the unwillingness of a bad guest (Grendel, Grendel's mother, Hrungnir) to abide by the covenant, and (3) the willingness of a good guest (Beowulf) to heroically assist his host. Furthermore, the *Beowulf* poet emphasizes the structural affinity between a guest/host and a hero/monster relationship by reassigning the roles of hero and monster to those of guest and anti-guest.

Calvert Watkins has discussed numerous variations on this theme in Indo-European poetic traditions (see, especially, Watkins 1995), but it was Joyce Tally Lionarons who first demonstrated its strong bearing on the mythical elements of *Beowulf* in her 1996 paper "Beowulf: Myth and Monsters" (Lionarons 1996). A key to understanding the impact of the theme is the scribe's ambiguous usage of the spelling *gæst* to denote either *gist* ("guest, stranger") or *gast* ("spirit, demon"), which is paralleled by the unambiguous usage of the spelling *gist* to denote either "favorable guest" or "stranger, foe" (Lionarons 1996, 9). Lionarons argues that this ambiguity was deliberately explored by both poet and scribe for the purpose of paronomasia:

> [T]he poet's usage of the variants *gast* and *gǣst/gæst* to refer to his monsters carries with it the punning sense of "(monstrous) guest." Conversely, in the second part of the poem, the traditional Christian association of the dragon with the devil would make the explicit designation of the monster as a *gast*, "spirit, demon," unnecessarily and perhaps undesirably specific, while the dragon's metaphoric role as *gist* or "guest" is less self-evident and needs pointing out in specific usages of the word. (Lionarons 1996, 11)

Lionarons links the figures of Grendel and his mother to the theme of scapegoating, associating the scapegoat with a figure removed from the position of the included other to the position of the excluded other (Lionarons 1996, 12). I prefer a less distinctive concept of social rejection in this regard, precisely because we are dealing with a reversal of the means by which rites of hospitality secure symbolic consanguinity. In the widest sense of an out-group subject, the "stranger" or "outsider" should rather be conceived as someone who is not yet (or no longer) recognized as an insider by the in-group. The bidirectional means to regulate such social transgressions do not necessarily include scapegoating, but rather the mutually opposed procedures of ostracism and hospitality. There are certainly hints of such themes in *Beowulf*, not least the premise that the very source of Grendel's grievance is the sound of convivial feasting in Heorot (lines 89–90).

The characterization of Grendel as *eoten* (e.g., line 761) is usually understood as a token of monstrosity. We are told in an early section of the poem (102–113) that the *eotenas* belong to Cain's bloodline, which has produced preternatural propagation (*untýdras ealle onwócom* [111]) as a result of Cain's ungodly fratricide. This biblical insertion into the framework of an otherwise indigenous heroic tradition effectively emphasizes Grendel's monstrosity as a sign of social stigma. His mark of disgrace recalls a primeval event of rejection from the community that he now seeks to destroy. There is consequently little to suggest that the designation of Grendel as *eoten* served the ad hoc purpose of distinguishing a monster who seeks to "devour" his involuntary host. This seems especially unlikely when we consider the only safe basis for locating the Germanic **etunaz* in a wider narrative framework, namely the complex epic function of the *jǫtnar* in Old Norse mythology. In the same ambiguous vein as Grendel is referred to as *gast*, he is apparently called *eoten* with reference to an old treaty of commensality.

Just as the earliest attestations of Germanic **gastiz* seem to suggest, the noun **etunaz* was especially used to designate a class of beings marked by distance and difference in terms of kinship, time, and space. To be sure, this difference was not always considered insurmountable, for it also implied potential physical contact, shared social characteristics, and even original consanguinity. Such implicit assumptions are variously employed to distinguish Grendel as "Cain's (and thus ultimately Adam's) offspring," the *jǫtunn* Bǫlþorn as the grandfather of the all-father Odin (*Hávamál* 140), Grendel as the intruding *ellorgæst* ("alien *gæst*" [line 1617]) inhabiting the moors beyond Heorot, and the *jǫtnar* as inhabitants of Útgarðr (an area specified as lying "outside" [*út, útan*] of the "enclosed habitation" [*garðr*]). It is also significant that the *Beowulf* poet employs the plural *eotenas* as a pun to characterize the Jutes (or Jutelanders) (e.g., lines 1072, 2180), which calls to mind similar instances in Old Norse poetry where specific ethnonyms are employed as a generalized characterization of the *jǫtnar* (e.g., *berg-Danir* "mountain-Danes" [*Hymiskviða* 17, *Haustlǫng* 18]).

If we render **etunaz* in the exclusively asocial sense of "devourer" ("Vielfresser, Menchenfresser") along the lines of earlier interpretations, we fail to grasp the full semantic spectrum of the noun (Falk and Torp 1907–1911 and Fick 1909, 24). One would, then, rather expect such a being to be called **fretunaz* ("glutton, devourer" [< **fra-* +**-etanq*] as in Old English *freoten*]). We need to recognize that the Old Norse *jǫtnar*, apart from their occasional sensitivity to shared rules of conduct, even appear alongside the gods in situations of overt commensality. This is particularly evident from the pivotal story of the feast in Ægir's hall (the so-called *Ægisdrekka*), the location of which is even referred to as a "place of covenant" (*griðastaðr*) (*Lokasenna* 141–143). What brings an end to the convivial atmosphere in the hall is not a transgression on behalf of the *jǫtunn* host Ægir, but rather the uninvited trickster Loki, a treacherous member of the gods' community, who engages in a so-called flyting against both Ægir and the gods.

Since we do not expect an inherently beastly being to be hospitable, nor to be embraced by any preliminary observations of hospitality, it is arguably rather the ambiguity of the stranger as a potential friend-fiend that allows the **etunaz* to take on such shifting roles in Germanic lore. Just as the sense of Latin *hostis* developed into "enemy" from the more general sense "stranger," the notion of a "devouring" and inherently hostile **etunaz* is more likely to reflect a similar semantic development along the lines of defunct hospitality.

3.7

As I have sought to demonstrate in the last two sections, violent acts of prevention and exploit ascribed to a ruling warrior elite are characteristically reinterpreted in poetic terms as actions of heroic virtue. Under such showcased circumstances, heroism is conceived as the corrective to a state of violated hospitality, restoring a community to its ideal state of equilibrium, and eventually securing eternal glory for its poetically embellished protagonist. The ideal of heroic intervention can thus roughly be seen to anticipate the Clausewitzian principle of war as an extension of policy by other means. A crucial factor to account for in this regard is that messages linking the function of heroism with those of festive eating, sacrificial exposures of abundance, and the poetic promise of fame, cannot be separated from the situation in which such messages were commissioned and composed. In order for such messages to resonate with a living community, it had to be a community in which notions of wealth, ownership, and fame would have included domesticated animals, and in which ritual professionals could be hired by tribal chiefs to communicate such notions in hyperbolic fashion.

It is against this backdrop that I hesitate to accept Walter Burkert's famous derivation of Greek blood sacrifice from the hunting rituals of prehistoric hunter-gatherer societies. Whereas the hunter interacts through experienced skill with an indeterminate resource of game, the herder slaughters systematically in order to protect a perpetual resource of moveable wealth. Furthermore, if the hunter's inability to "own" game is most glaringly echoed in the notion of supernatural ownership (e.g., the figure of the "Master of Animals"), the herder's sense of extended ownership rather works inversely to elicit notions of the preternatural thief (e.g., the figures of Geryon and Cacus in classical tradition, or the demonic cattle-thieves [Vala and/or the Paṇis] in ancient Indian tradition). The two scenarios, or matrices, appear particularly cogent in contradistinction to each other; much less so, in fact, if the one is conceived as the formative antecedent of the other. Their most apparent feature of coordination is that of inversion, not that of continuity. By following Jonathan Z. Smith's lead in considering sacrifice as "an elaboration of the selective kill," and "the artificial (i.e., ritualized) killing of an artificial (i.e., domesticated) animal" (Smith 1987, 200–201), one may continue the analysis by regarding the acquisition of animals from the outside as a source of wealth and prestige that requires warlike confrontations with an artificial (i.e., demonized, dehumanized) proprietor who illegitimately claims to own it.

3.8

The principal aim of this chapter has been to trace an emergent logic of civic religiosity through a sacrificial ideology of hospitality and fame, and to seek a possible source of this ideology in a tribal society of rivalling cattle herders identified as the prehistoric speakers of Proto-Indo-European and Proto-Indo-Iranian. Especially pertinent to this logic are the means by which a stratified tribal community (or perhaps rather *chiefdom*) invents and imagines itself through the medium of poetically affirmed hyperboles, and the sense in which such affirmations require a willing suspension of disbelief to gain momentum. I shall now turn in a different direction to explore how the antecedents of unlicensed religiosity begin to emerge in a similar tribal context, informed by the same sacrificial ideology, yet with a focus on the salvific aspirations of clients and patrons rather than on the heroism and hospitality of the good host.

4 Itinerancy and Afterlife

4.1

"To what land shall I go to graze my cattle? Where shall I go to graze them?"[39] The poet of the so-called *Kamnamaēzā Hāiti* (Y 46) begins his composition in a tone of despair and isolation.[40] Zarathushtra, the alleged author of the hymn, is identified in younger tradition as a prophet and founder of the Mazdayasnian religion. Nevertheless, such secondary attributions should not mislead us to consider the *Hāiti* (a portion of the Old Avestan *Gāthās*) as the unprecedented testimony of a proselyte. Despite its ellipses and idiosyncrasies, it is a hymn steeped in the poetics of fame and social eating that I have tried to sketch out in the previous chapter.

The poet introduces himself to us in the narrative present as a wandering priest in search of a patron's support. Excluded from clan and community, he traverses a land of deceitful rulers (Y 46.1) where the only remaining hope for future success thrives on the imagery of a still unrevealed host with good intents and gifts in plenty (3). In other words, the fact of the poet's material poverty ("having few cattle" [*kamnafšuua-]* [2]) does not discount him as a spiritual bringer of prosperity. He then goes on to ponder the mutual obligations of poet and patron, bound by the stipulations of a "contract" (*miϑra-)* according to the model of a guest-host relationship (5). He stresses the importance of exposing deceitful clients, but also points out that these are ultimately fooling themselves as they "shall go to the bonds of deceit's captivity" (*drūjō* [...] *dāmąn haēϑahiiā gāṯ* [6]). The latter theme is further emphasized in stanza 11, where the malevolent poet-priests – collectively referred to as Kavis and Karapans – are said to have "yoked (us) with evil actions" (*yūjə̄n* [...] *akāiš ś̌iiaoϑa-*

39 The rest of the verse runs (in the translation of HES [see below]): "[—] They keep (me) away from (their) family and tribe. / The community which I wish to join does not satisfy me / nor (do) the deceitful tyrants of the land. / How shall I satisfy Thee, O Wise Ahura?"

40 The seventeen hymns (or "chapters" [*hāitis*]) of the five *Gāthās* were composed in an East Iranian dialect, possibly towards the end of the 2nd millennium BCE and are still acknowledged by practicing Zoroastrians as the constitutive core of the Mazdayasnian "liturgy" (*yasna* [henceforth Y]). While linguistically close to the Vedic hymns, their elliptic and idiosyncratic idiom make them extremely difficult to untangle. In order to provide a reasonably well-poised rendering of the content, I am always following interpretations in line with at least one of the modern translations by Stanley Insler (henceforth I), Kellens-Pirart (henceforth KP), and Humbach-Elfenbein-Skjærvø (henceforth HES). Full references to editions and translations are given in the bibliography under Y (= Yasna). The bulk of the material discussed in this chapter has been outlined in greater detail elsewhere (Jackson 2016). I am reproducing some passages from this publication verbatim here. A slightly abbreviated version of the chapter is also found in Jackson Rova 2021b.

https://doi.org/10.1515/9783110460605-006

nāiš) and hence shall become "guests in the House of Deceit forever" (*yauuōi vīspāi / drūjō dəmānāi astaiiō*). This unpleasant dwelling – conceivably the hellish terminus of sinister traffickers in ritual patron-clientage – stands in stark contrast to the elsewhere attested so-called *garō dəmāna-* ("House of Laudation"), the eschatological implications of which I intend to pursue further below.

In the second half (13 ff.) of the hymn, the poet reappears in his new status as a recognized client under the patronage of Vištāspa. The generous patron has become a "truthful ally for the great offering" (*aṣ̌auuā uruuaϑō / mazōi magāi* [14]). Both poet and patron are said to be worthy of "fame" (or "to be heard") (*fərasrūidiiāi* [13–14]), but it is lastly only on account of the sacrificial "fee" (or "prize" [*mīžda-*]) – more specifically "by means of two fertile cows" (*gāuuā azī*) – that the latter's "higher existence" (*parāhū-* [19]) gets realized in the poet's imagination. The last stanza develops and derives its new meaning from the traditional Indo-Iranian genre of *dānastuti* ("praise of the gift"), an inserted coda through which the poet addresses his patron in praise of experienced or expected opendhandedness (see above, ch. 3) (HES I, 91 f.).

A distrustful reader of the *Kamnamaēzā Hāiti* might dismiss the whole composition as an elaborate plea for ritual remuneration: a ritual performance designed to secure its inherent value by evoking the mysterious blessings of ritual. It is easy to perceive why the marketing of such a craft occasionally attracts scorn and incredulity. Immediate enthusiasm cannot be expected from those asked to give hard currency in exchange for delayed and intangible gifts of postmortem elevation, let alone from those competing for the same ritual appointments. Wandering sages have therefore always incurred accusations of being charlatans and malicious practitioners of magic, both in their contemporary environment and in retrospect. Hence, the Gāthic Zarathushtra's characterization of deceitful clients does not differ much from how his pseudo-epigraphical counterpart Zoroaster gets characterized by Pliny the Elder, namely as the inventor of monstruous impostures of magic (*Nat.* 30.1–2). But there is more to be drawn from this game of advanced ritual bargaining than cynical conclusions.

The precarious condition of ritual vagrancy was also an incentive for being conceptually inventive. Extending and examining the meaning of ritual exchange, and doing so in a manner persuasive enough to win a patron's liking and financial support, was the ritual professional's best insurance against destitution. As I shall try to demonstrate below, the poetic skills involved in fashioning a patron's lasting fame were contiguous with the ritual invention of transfigured immutability. I intend to show that this supposedly "ritual" invention emerges both in the Greek and Indo-Iranian world out of a common tribal past, and that the new sense of self and knowledge to which it was conducive – including phenomena such as sacrificial exegesis and ascetic practices of self-control – took independent share in a process much less evasive and enigmatic than theoreticians of axiality (Karl Jaspers' *Achsenzeit* [Jaspers 1949]) have so far been prone to admit.

A first step in elucidating key moments in this process is to consider the various disguises of the itinerant ritual client, both in his role of a speaking poetic subject and as an idealized projection of that same subject. The apparent realism of Zarathushtra's address in the *Kamnamaēzā Hāiti* can be balanced against an inherited mythical framework of itinerant ritual specialists. Evidence to support their pertinence include traditions linked to the Greek figure of Orpheus and a triad of semidivine travelling craftsmen addressed in Vedic poetry with a cognate appellative, the R̥bhus (pl. *r̥bhávas*, sg. *r̥bhú-* < PIE *$^*h_3erb^h$-*). I first turn to the more familiar example.

4.2

The postclassical artistic reception of Orpheus has somewhat obscured the big picture of this complex personality in antiquity. Apart from his roles as a wonderworking minstrel and the victim of tragic love, he was also perceived as a founder of mysteries and the author of salvific doctrines that attracted sectarian activities all over the Greek-speaking world. While a great deal of controversy exists today over the proper definition and delineation of Orphism, there can be little doubt that Orpheus was already conceived as a religious authority among independent purveyors of ritual (so-called Orphics [*orphikoí*] or Orpheotelests [*orpheotelestaí*]) by the late archaic period.[41] An early witness to this phenomenon is Plato.

A key passage occurs in the second book of *Republic* (*R.* 363c–365a) wherein Socrates engages the brothers Adeimantus and Glaucon in a conversation about the true sense of justice. A distinction is made throughout the dialogue between being truly righteous and merely appearing to be so on account of commended "rewards and reputations" (*misthoùs dè kaì dóxas* [367d]). Such rewards may also, Adeimantus contends, extend into the poetically crafted promise of a blissful afterlife. A first example concerns the two legendary ("Orphic") figures Musaeus and Eumolpus, who are said to "extol" (*egkōmiázō*) justice, bringing their righteous benefactors down to Hades so as to let them enjoy eternal drunkenness at a symposium, whereas the unjust are buried in mud and forced to carry water in a sieve (363c-d). Poetic "praise" (*épainos*) and "blame" (*psógos*) can be claimed here to falsely determine virtues and vices in terms of mere appearances (363e).

41 A good overview of the scholarly currents regarding Orpheus and Orphism is found in Graf and Johnston 2013, 50–65.

The ensuing passage gives an early testimony to the actual experience of itinerant mystagogues (364b–e). Adeimantus complains about "begging-priests and seers" (*agýrtai dè kaì mánteis*) who arrive at the doors of the wealthy – some even try to win whole cities over to their cause – with persuasive promises of atonement and purification through the arrangement of sacrificial feasts. Indulgence in the childish delight of their "initiation rites" (*teletás*) is supposed to prevail after death, but those who neglect them are threatened with suffering in the afterlife. The priests and seers are said to use books by Musaeus and Orpheus from which they confusingly chant (producing "noise" [*hómados*]). A denigration, no doubt, since adherence to doctrines encoded in privately acquired scriptures (as opposed to the public inscription of sacred law) was a sign of heterodoxy in Athens during this period (Parker 1996, 55).

The passage gives a deterrent account of priestly self-marketing in accordance with the strategy of the *Kamnamaēzā Hāiti*. In its essence, it implies that the bond of allegiance with an awarding patron is presented by the client as a warrant for an elevated existence, whereas breach of a contract on either side of the bargain is severely reciprocated in the afterlife. The repudiation of such activities on Plato's behalf should not divert attention from his own share in the same spiritual legacy.[42] It was apparently against those competing for similar claims to truth and deliverance – whether sophists, poets, or initiators into the mysteries – that Plato raised his case. The *agýrtai* may be accused of persuading whole cities, but what about the city that Plato envisions in the same dialogue? Is it not just another theoretical construct meant to persuade a city?[43]

A particularly telling case of Plato's Orphic inclinations, furthermore, is the Socratic account of the souls of the wise and virtuous who, purified by philosophy, arrive at beautiful abodes in the afterlife (*Phd.* 114c). Philosophy is conceived here as a purificatory way of life that secures a "prize of contest" (*âthlon*) after death.[44] We have here an obvious case of intersecting frameworks, the mutual implications of which enforces both the novelty and familarity of the message: the celebratory context of athletic contest on the one hand, and the initiatory context of the mys-

42 HWPh 6, 1397 (with references to passages in Plato concerning the soul and the afterlife clearly resonant with Orphic notions).

43 Socrates considers this city to be a theoretical construct designed to identify the principle of justice (369a), but he also emphasizes that our need for it will build it for us (the verb used here is *poiéō* [369d]). The philosophical capacity to build a city out of pure reason is in itself an argument in favor of the philosopher as the most capable ruler of the city.

44 Regarding Plato's notion of purity and its conceptual links to Bacchic/Orphic initiations, see Graf and Johnson 2013, 122. A discussion of archaic philosophical references to athletics and eschatology with particular regard to Parmenides is found in Jackson Rova 2021a.

teries on the other. The pre-Platonic legacy and Aristotelean continuity of such thematics will be further explored in the following chapter.

What, then, can the legendary appearance of Orpheus teach us about the conceptual heritage associated with his name? Let us begin with a comparatively late datum: a fresco from one of the houses on the Vicolo dell'anfiteatro in Pompeii (Helbig 1868, 893; see fig. 2 below). Orpheus is seen seated in the middle of the image, facing the viewer. Dressed in a long, yellow garb with a blue hem – the typical outfit of a kitharode – he holds a lyre and a plectrum. Around him are seen seated or standing females, five of which are labelled as muses (Euterpe, Thaleia, Urania, Terpsichore, and Melpomene). A damaged figure on a cliff in the far back of the fresco probably represents Eurydice. In the foreground on the left, Hercules is seen seated on a lionskin with his back turned against the viewer. He listens attentively to the music with his head resting on his right hand. Clues to the narrative subtext of the scene are found in the preface to the second book of Claudian's *De raptu Proserpinae* ("The Abduction of Proserpina"), which the poet dedicated to the Urban prefect of Rome, Florentinus, during his time in office between 395 and 397 CE. Despite its late date, both the content and context of the preface allow us to identify a series of essentials in the transmission of Orphic lore.

We are told that Orpheus has for a long while refused to sing, neglecting his required task, which brings the land of Thrace into turmoil. Heifers fear the lion, mountains and woods lament his silence, but as soon as the happy news of Hercules' capturing of the man-eating mares of the Thracian king Diomedes, the "famed ivory" (*nobile ebur* [16]) touches once more the strings of the lyre. Winds and waves are stilled; Hebrus flows more sluggishly; popplar, pine, and oak are allured by his song. A crucial detail in the description is that Orpheus performs his miraculous task in a context of heroic fame. He is encouraged to resume his art (29) in order to extol the labors of Hercules (*actusque cenebat / Herculis* [29–30]). This circumstance has immediate bearing on the final address of the preface, in which Claudian brings his model narrative to the fore: So Orpheus, so I (Claudian); so Hercules, so you (Florentinus) (*Thracius haec vates – sed tu Tirynthius alter, / Florentine, mihi* [49–50]). It is the fortitude of Florentinus that incites Claudian to sing, but the mutual excellence of their labors (both the poet's and the prefect's) secures fame for them both (51–52).

Whereas Hercules sides with Orpheus in this scene by analogy of the patronizing aristocrat, he is recurrently seen to do so in his capacity as a prototypal Eleusinian initiate (Graf and Johnston 2013, 170, 202). In his capacity as initiate, the patron becomes a client of the ritual specialist, who in his turn takes over the role of the patron as a spiritual supporter of his master. Ties of patron-clientage were thus not merely hierarchical in the sense that the *patronus* was more resourceful than

Figure 2: Orpheus extolling the labors of Hercules. Fresco from the House of M. Epidi Sabini, Pompeii (tracing from Helbig 1868, 893).

his *cliens*, but always inherently ambiguous in the sense that the *cliens* had the capacity to persuade his *patronus* to the contrary.[45]

It has been misleadingly claimed that Orpheus is a singer not of *kleós*, but of *pénthos* ("grief") (Freiert 1991, 46). Quite on the contrary, the intangible force by which to extol fame is not just a means of honoring the living, but of keeping them alive after death. The notion of fame was equally present in the so-called "dirges" (*thrênoi*) composed by Pindar and Simonides as in their epinician poems. Furthermore, the concept of a song that mysteriously moves the world to such an extent that it beguiles death (Eur., *Alc.* 357–359) seems indistinguishable from the concept of undying fame that the same poets developed in a tradition said to ensue from Orpheus, the "father of songs" (*aoidân patêr*) (e.g., *Pyth.* 4.176).

Although Orpheus is absent from Homeric epic, the extant traditions associated with his name in post-Homeric lore are likely to reflect an ancient melic genre that was perhaps already considered distinct from the topics of epic song by the poets of the Dark Age (Wilson 2009, 55–56).[46] In its developed melic sense, as it were, a hero's *kleós* could be conceived as *áphthiton* ("undecaying") and *ásbeston* ("inextinguishable") according to the same logic of privation – that is, irresistable to decay and forgetfulness in a poet's memorable song – as its philosophical continuator was thought to be "uncausing forgetfulness": *alêtheia* (Dor. *alátheia*).

---

45 I will henceforth consider such relationships according to the familiar model of plebeians and patricians operating within systems of servitude in ancient Roman society. Ties of patron-clientage were usually hierarchical in the sense that the *patronus* possesed greater wealth than the *cliens*. The *patronus* was the benefactor of the *cliens*, who in his turn was expected to offer his services to the *patronus*. The English word "client," in its developed sense of someone who rather *uses* the service of a professional, can be said to reflect a relation that is always inherently reciprocal. As will become apparent in the following pages, the role of the ritual client may lend some of its social characteristics to the patron. In his role as initiate, the patron becomes the client of the ritual specialist, who in his turn takes over the role of the patron as a spiritual supporter of his master. While it is only in the latter, modern sense of the term "client" that contemporary scholars speak of "ritual clients," I anticipate that my choice of words will appear idiosyncratic to some.
46 In addition to the distinction between an archaic Orphic/melic and a Homeric/epic tradition, Wilson (2009, 55–56) makes the following perceptive remark regarding Thamyris the Thracian, an apparent representative of Orphic ("melic") lore *avant la lettre:* "If we [...] admit the possibility that Thamyris in the *Iliad* may have presented a tradition of religious song that proferred the hope of an afterlife radically different from that implied by the *Iliad*, the passing story of his encounter with the Muses takes on a very different character. [...] Like Orpheus, Thamyris was not merely a rival to the singers of Homeric poetry, or to their authority figures in myth, be they an archetypal Homeros, or the Muses of Olympos. Early music and poetry did not form an autonomous sphere of artistic excellence and competition. Differences in music implied differences in world view, and in particular, in religious outlook."

Philosophers from Thales onwards were prone to associate the global substance of all that appears and disappears with an indestructible force of mind and memory, whether stable or ever-flowing (Thales [HWPh, s.v. Seele]), that clearly hearkens back to the tradition of poetic praise. Simonides perhaps came closest to linking these concepts together. Firstly, in his eulogy to those who fell at Thermopylae, wherein the Spartan king Leonidas is said to have left behind an "ever-flowing glory" (*aénaon* [...] *kléos* [PMG 531.9]) – an epithet of *kléos* likewise employed by Simonides' Ionian contemporary Heraclitus (DK B29). Secondly, by treating "valour" (*áretê*) and "inextinguishable glory" (*ásbeston kléos*) as the intangible forces by means of which the dead are brought back "from the house of Hades" (*dômatos ex Aídeô* [LG 126]). Finally, in an isolated fragment virtually rephrasing Heraclitus' aphrorism "nature loves to hide" (*phýsis krýptesthai phileî* [DK B123]): "appearance even constrains truth" (*tò dokeîn kaì tàn alátheian biâtai* [PMG 598]). The constitutive force of nature is likewise the undying principle of truth beyond fleeting appearances.

In addition to being considered a father of songs, Orpheus was thought to embody the very principle of undying fame by virtue of his name. He was the one "with famous name" (*onomáklytos* [Ibycus, PMG 306]), that is, both a provider and receiver of the gift that made him a prototype of his guild. His inert strangeness and propensity to leave and reappear, moving disruptively from city to city, was a feature that he shared with the god most strongly tied to his name and alleged country of origin: Dionysos, the veritable "stranger within" (*l'étranger de l'intérieur* [Detienne 1989, 33]).

This was also a feature that he shared with the first Greek philosophers, both the truly itinerant ones (such as Xenophanes) and those merely metaphorically "roaming" (*plânē*) so as to challenge commonsensical wisdom (as in the case Socrates) (Montiglio 2005, 152). Their concept of immutable truth and excellence no longer served the sole purpose of ritual persuasion, but had begun to gravitate towards a new sense of politics. The true philsopher of the new polis must begin his precarious career as a figure of ridicule. Steering beyond the hyperboles of local politics with his cosmopolitics, he is allegorized by Plato as a "stargazer and babbler" (*meteōroskópon te kaì adoléskhēn* [*Rep.* 488e–489a]) of little apparent use to the self-indulgent citizen (a theme to be further explored in the following chapter). A contrast is created through such an imagery between a local politics of civic pretense and a global politics of antinomian attention. Nevertheless, the transgressive and subversive aspects of the latter will merely appear threatening from within the bounds of the temporary pact, whereas the travelling supplicant carries a message of otherworldly liberation.

4.3

Simplistic solutions to the puzzle of Orphic origins have typically consisted in taking the foreign appearance of Orpheus in ancient art and literature at face value. His appearance in myth is thus reduced to the distorted version of a real-life Thracian "shaman," whose foreign ways earned him the reputation as seer and magician, and the salvific doctrines associated with his name to some alien substance sprung from an exotic (whether Thracian, Phrygian, or Iranian) source.[47] Such habits of theoretical procrastination deflect attention from the inner dynamics of ritual life and mythical imagination. Greek religion owed much of its peculiarity to the symbolic vacillations between "foreign" (*xeînos*) and "homely" (*oikeîos*) aspects of life, between gods who arrive and those already at home. If the citizens of Athens or Thebes conceived Dionysus as the personification of a liberating force arriving from the outside, it was not because the god was an import, but because these were his hereditary characteristics.[48] He was, in Walter Otto's wording, the "the coming god" (*der kommende Gott*). The inherent strangeness of Orpheus would make equal sense in this regard. His Thracian appearance could be perceived more loosely as a sign of eccentricity, sufficient to mark out the itinerant client's aptitude for ritual innovation.[49] Evidence of this original ("pre-Thracian") trait can be obtained by considering the etymology of the proper name, which links the secondary appearance of Orpheus in Greek myth to a native tradition of considerable depth and consistency.

The Greek name is likely to have developed from an inherited PIE noun (< *h_3r̥bhéu-)* retained in Vedic *r̥bhú-* to denote a "(skilled) craftsman" (→ "ritual specialist").[50] The complex semantics of the underlying verbal stem can be traced through its usage in Anatolian, where it expressed the quality of someone (or something) voluntarily moving between different groups: the case of a domestic animal that voluntarily "strays" (*ḫarapta*) into another fold, thus im-

---

47 Cf. DNP (s.v. Orpheus): "O[rpheus"] Rolle als Seher, Arzt und Zauberer und der Inhalt der frühesten orphischen Texte legen die Existentz eines realen histor[ischen] Vorbildes, vielleicht eines thrakischen 'Schamanen', nahe."

48 The god's foreign appearance testifies to the fact that his cult was not primarily concerned with the life of the city, but rather with the life of each individual. Cf. Jaccottet 1990, 156.

49 The status of Thrace as "a land of promise and peril," "a savage country [...] but one with which it was indispensable for economic and strategic reasons to constantly grapple" fits well with what Greek citizens in the 5th century would have conceived as the origin of a new religious sensibility (Parker 1996, 174).

50 Cf, for instance, RV 9.21.6 (of Soma): "Like a craftsman a new chariot (wheel)" (*r̥bhúr ná ráthi̯aṃ návaṃ*); and 9.87.3 (of Soma): "an insightful craftsman, Uśanā in poetic skill" (*r̥bhúr dhī́ra uśánā kā́vi̯ena*).

plying the specified sense "change herds," or of deities asked to "ally themselves" with their human hosts in a cultic context of commensality ("Come, eat and drink! *Ally yourselves with me!* [*nu=mu=ššan ḫarapdumati*]") (Melchert 2010). The quality of moving between different groups (in search of a new ally) makes a feasible semantic basis of the Vedic noun *r̥bhú-*. It may originally have signified any kind of travelling professional, but, as suggested by the secondary adjectival sense "skillful, ingenuous" (seen in Ved. *ŕ̥bhva-* [from a virtual **h_3ŕ̥b^h-u̯-o-]* and *ŕ̥bhvan-* ["the skilled one"] [PIE < **h_3ŕ̥b^h-u̯-o-n-]*), especially recalled the "fashioning" (Ved. √*takṣ* < PIE √**tetk̂*) skills of a carpenter.

It deserves paranthetical notice that a similar logic of manual professionalism applies to the social world of Homeric epic, where the skills of a travelling craftsman could inform a contiguous whole of itinerant professionals (including seers, healers, and poets). In the seventeenth book of the *Odyssey*, Odysseus turns up at his own court in the undercover appearance of a wandering beggar. He is urged by Athena to collect bread among the wooers as a means to distinguish the righteous from the unlawful ones (17.361). The wooer Antinoos delivers an angry speech against dinner-spoiling beggars, but the swineherd Eumaios replies that invited strangers (as opposed to uninvited ones) usually belong to one of the four types of "craftsmen" (*dēmioergoí* [383]):

> τίς γὰρ δὴ ξεῖνον καλεῖ ἄλλοθεν αὐτὸς ἐπελθὼν
> ἄλλον γ', εἰ μὴ τῶν, οἳ δημιοεργοὶ ἔασι,
> μάντιν ἢ ἰητῆρα κακῶν ἢ τέκτονα δούρων
> ἢ καὶ θέσπιν ἀοιδόν, ὅ κεν τέρπῃσιν ἀείδων;
> οὗτοι γὰρ κλητοί γε βροτῶν ἐπ' ἀπείρονα γαῖαν·
> πτωχὸν δ' οὐκ ἄν τις καλέοι τρύξοντα ἓ αὐτόν.
>
> For who comes up to invite a stranger from abroad
> unless it be one of those craftsmen,
> whether a seer, a healer of ills, a carpenter,
> or an inspired poet, who brings delight with (his) song?
> These mortals are called upon all over the boundless earth.
> But no one would invite a beggar just to get himself consumed.

The passage reveals a lot about the Homeric perception of wandering professionals: (1) The term *dēmioergós*, which was especially associated with "manual skills" (*tekhnḗmata*), could designate any professional invited from abroad to perform work for the community (Hunter and Rutherford 2009, 10). (2) The co-occurrence of *téktōn* and *aoidós* clearly indicates that the work of the poet was not just conceived as "skilful" by analogy with that of the craftsman, but that the poet and the craftsman are also in a relation of contiguity. In other words, their skills may be related to each other both in a paradigmatic, *metaphorical* sense, and in a syntagmatic, *metonymical* sense.[51] The hereditary Indo-European characterization of poetry as "verbal craftsmanship" (PIE **u̯ék$^{u̯}$os* + √**tetḱ*), first identified by James Darmesteter in 1878, thus possibly entails more than a grammatical metaphor (Schmitt 1968, 26 ff). (3) Despite the positive sense attached to the noun *dēmioergós*, it is only the poet who qualifies for being called "inspired, divine" (lit. "filled with the [words of] God" [cf. LSJ]) (*théspis*). Whereas the profession of the craftsman sets a paradigmatic example of the skills of seers, healers, and poets, it is clearly the poet who occupies the marked position in the sequence. It is he, the noblest of the four *dēmioergoí*, who speaks to us through these lines.

The definitie uncovering of Orpheus' pre-Greek past hinges on the identification of a proper noun **H_3r̥b^{h}éu̯s* that developed (supposedly in late-PIE) from a honorific title "the **h_3r̥b^{h}éu̯s* par excellence," "who excels in wondrous crafts," or something equivalent. Both the noun and the proper noun appear side by side in Vedic, with the developed adjectival sense still attached to the noun, while Greek evidence merely leaves us with an opaque proper noun. Unlike Orpheus, however, Vedic R̥bhu does not operate alone. Rather, he is conceived as the leading member of a triad, the so-called R̥bhus (pl. *r̥bhávas*), whose mythical deeds and characteristics prompted the poets of the R̥gveda to contemplate and advertise the achievements of their own guild.[52] Just like Orpheus in his capacity as the fountainhead of melic poetry, the R̥bhus are represented as prototypes of the ritual clientele. It will thus prove suggestive to examine the parallell lives of Orpheus and the R̥bhus in pursuit of the real-life concerns that fostered such mythical extrapolations.

Prime events in the R̥bhus' mythical biography are the five canonical deeds of excellence for which they became famed and attained immortality: (1) multiplying Tvaṣṭar's soma cup into four, (2) fashioning the chariot (sometimes said to belong to the Aśvins), (3) fashioning the fallow bay horses of Indra, (4) fashioning a cow (carving it up or making it to give milk), and (5) rejuvenating their parents.[53] The following verse (3.60.3c-d) provides a summarizing moral of the five deeds:

c. *saudhanvanā́so amr̥tatvám érire* / d. *viṣṭvī́ śamībhiḥ sukŕ̥taḥ sukr̥táyā*

---

51 Cf. Roman Jakobson's analysis of metaphor and metonymy according to a linguistic model of intersecting axes (cf. Jakobson 1971, 241–259).

52 The other members of the triad are named Vibhvan and Vāja (e.g., RV 1.161.6). In fact, the trio could be invoked by the name of any member in the form of elliptic plurals (e.g., 7.48.1).

53 J/B (vol 1, 51).

c. The sons of Sudhanvan [= the Ṛbhus] rose to immortality / d. by applying themselves to their labors, ritually acting well by good ritual action.[54]

The wondrous deeds themselves suffice to suggest that the crafts of the Ṛbhus were modelled after ritual acts. In less specific terms, the three brothers are also said to "have fashioned sacrifice" ("In company with Pūṣan, o Ṛbhus [...] you have fashioned the ceremony" [*pūṣanvánta ṛbhavo {...} adhvarám ataṣṭa*] [3.54.12]), "clear away paths to sacrifice"[55] (*patháś citana yáṣṭave* [4.37.7]), "fashion fame" for the priests ("fashion here for us the fame that heroes accompany" [*ihá śrávo vīrávat takṣatā naḥ*] [4.36.9]), and themselves to be "seeking fame among the immortals" (*ámartiyeṣu śrava ichámānāḥ* [1.110.5]).

While the Vedic poets apparently represented the Ṛbhus as idealized members of their own guild, they were also keen to emphasize the Ṛbhus' divinely authorized promotion to permanent members of the divine community.[56] This change of status also meant that they could appear in the roles of patrons (sg. *sūrí-)* receiving priestly praise (√*stav*) ("[clear away paths to sacrifice {see above}] [...] since you are praised, o patrons" [*sūraya stutā́*] [4.37.7]). In so far as the Ṛbhus can be understood to impersonate ideals incumbent on any priestly lineage, we need to consider the possibility that the triad's eponymous "change of allegiance" also echoed the ritual client's innate propensity to surrender his current patron and seek out a more beneficent ally.

There is another story hinted at in some of the hymns that, despite its notorious obscurity (Geldner called it a "Dunkler Sagenzug"), appears particularly relevant to our current investigation. It might be referred to provisionally as the "Story of the Ṛbhus and Agohya," but it should be kept in mind that Agohya (lit. "Unconcealable"[57]) may be just another appellation of a more familiar figure,

54 The verb *su-kṛt-* (lit. "acting well" [cf. Lat. *bene facere*]) had an unmistakeable ritual ring. Cf. also OAv. *hū.kərəta-* (Y 34.13).

55 The same hymn (4.37) begins with an address to the Ṛbhus, asserting that they "established the sacrifice for [themselves] among these clans of Manu [i. e., among early mankind] on a clear day of days" (*yajñám mánuṣo vikṣú āsú / dadhidhvé* [...] *sudineṣu áhnām*).

56 Witzel and Gotō (2007, 722) stress the fact that the Ṛbhus are apotheosized to the same extent as they seem to be joining a new sacrificial community.

57 Besides the passages associated with the current story, the epithet *ágohya-* occurs twice in the RV. Once as a characterization of Indra (8.98.4), once in an enumeration of divine names and epithets preceded by Narāśaṃsa (an epithet of either Agni or Pūṣan), Pūṣan, and followed by Agni (10.64.3). According to Yāska's *Nirukta* (11.16), the oldest surviving etymological treatise on the Vedic language, Agohya should be identified as an Āditya, i. e., as a son of the goddess Aditi, because "he is not concealed" (*agūhanīyaḥ*). Yāska probably intends either Sūrya or Savitar, who are both characterized by this epithet in Vedic poetry (cf. Brereton 1981, 308 ff. and 314 ff.).

namely the god Savitar (lit. "Impeller"[58]). Regardless if we chose to associate the two appellations with the same figure, or with distinct figures performing equal functions in the same dramatic plot, the story is overtly paraphrased in at least three different hymns, twice in the first Maṇḍala (1.110.2–3; 1.161.11–13) and once in the fourth (4.33.7). By comparing these stanzas, we may single out four significant moments in the storyline: (1) The R̥bhus wander about in search for custody; (2) they arrive at the house of Agohya/Savitar and enjoy his hospitality; (3) they sleep in the house of their host for either twelve days or a whole year; (4) during (or in direct adjacency to) this transitional state, they exert the force of their wondrous skills on nature.

The theme of itinerancy is highlighted in 1.110.2. In sudden recognition of his "own comrades" [*máma* {...} *āpáyaḥ*]), the poet Kutsa imagines the former situation of the R̥bhus by analogy with the present hardships of unemployed poet-priests. The theme of the distressed vagrant ("in search of daily bread" [*ābhogáyam* {...} *ichánta*]) is thus employed by the poet to fulfil his own hope for future immortalization.[59] We noticed above how the poet of the *Kamnamaēzā Hāiti* recalled, in a similar fashion, his former calamities on the road as a foil for his eventual rise to excellence under the patronage of Vištāspa.

1.110.2a. *ābhogáyam prá yád ichánta aítana* / b. *ápākāḥ práñco mama ké cid āpáyaḥ*
2c. *saúdhavanāsaś caritásya bhūmánā* / d. *ágachata savitúr dāśúṣo gr̥hám*

2a. When, [both in east and west→[60], you went forth in search of your daily bread, / b. as certain comrades of mine[61],
2c. o sons of Sudhanvan, after your fill of roaming / d. you came to the house of Savitar the pious.

The next stanza informs us that Savitar, in accordance with the impelling power inherent in his name, "impelled [them] to immortality" (*'mr̥tatvám ā́suvad*). The reason for their promotion is, however, not explicitly expressed. They went, it sim-

58 The name (or rather epithet) is a fully transparent agent noun formed with √*sav* ["to impel"] to indicate the god in his capacity as "impeller" of the sun and all living beings.
59 Cf. the introduction to the hymn in J/B: "thus perhaps holding out the hope that immortality will come to them [i.e., the poet and his comrades] as well."
60 I have indicated with a single square bracket and an adjacent arrow the words retracted from (or protracted to) the following hemistich in the English translation (e.g., [RETRACTED FROM←, [PROTRACTED TO→).
61 I chose to deviate from the markedly colloquial rendering in J/B ("kind of like my pals"), for which I see no justification. I have made a few further alterations in order to convey a more literal sense of the verse.

ply says, "to make Agohya heed" (*ágoh$_{i}$yam* [...] *chraváyanta* [√*śrav*]).[62] Hence, we need to consult two other hymns in order to learn more about the R̥bhus' laudable service at Aghoya's. One cryptic stanza (1.161.12) apparently refers to something that the R̥bhus did while asleep ("having shut your eyes, you crept around the living worlds" [*sammīlya* {...} *bhúvanā paryásarpata*]), whereas another (4.33.7) seems to hint at the same event in more explicit terms:

> a. *d$_{u}$vā́daśa dyū́n yád ágoh$_{i}$yasya* / b. *atithyé ráṇann r̥bhávaḥ sasántaḥ*
> c. *sukṣétrākr̥ṇvann ánayanta síndhūn* / d. *dhánvā́tiṣṭhann óṣadhīr nimnám ā́paḥ*
>
> a. When [the R̥bhus enjoyed the hospitality→ of Agohya / b. [for twelve days← sleeping (there), c. (then) they made the fields good and led the rivers; / d. plants arose upon the dry land and waters upon the low ground.

The interposed "then" at the beginning of the second verse should not be taken to imply that the R̥bhus were already awake while exerting their mysterious force on plants and rivers.[63] This would have made perfect sense had it not been for the information provided by 1.161.12–13, which clearly implies an intermediary period of sleeping (and dreaming?) distinguished by the contrasting absolutive *sammīlya* (√*mīl*) (12a) ("having shut your eyes") and the perfect participle *suṣupvā́ṃsa* (√*svap*) (13d) ("after you slept") (cf. Geldner 1951[i], 221). We need to assume that the actions referred to in 12a-d denote wondrous deeds performed during sleep. The motif alluded to here thus very likely belonged to the catalogue celebrating the accomplishments of the R̥bhus' ritual craft. In fact, the phrasing in 1.110.3 ("Savitar impelled you to immortality") suggests that it was the triumphant culmination of their career. The R̥bhus prove themselves worthy of immortalization because they are already behaving like immortals.

Another piece of the puzzle is supplied by the imperfect *parysárpata* (lit. "you crept around") in 1.161.12, because the same verb (√*sarp* ["crawling, sneaking"]) is elsewhere used to indicate misinformed or mischievous actions (sg. *māyā́-* ["wonderworking, deception" etc.]) – the Greek term γοητεία ("witchcraft, jugglery") comes to mind – in a statement treated as a veritable corrective to the laudable

62 The first hemistich of the second stanza (2a) and the second hemistich of the third stanza (3b) form a ring: *ābhogáyam prá yád ichánta aítana* [—] *ágoh$_{i}$yam yác chraváyanta aítana.* This is probably the poet's way of indicating closure of the mythical allusion introduced in the previous verse.
63 The interposition is rather motivated by the relative conjunction *yád* in 7a, which is typically found at the beginning of a determinative clause ("when..., then...").

deeds of the Ṛbhus. It concerns the quintessential "(ungodly) aliens" (sg. *dásyu-*) who instead perform unholy rituals for which they are punished by the gods:[64]

8.14.14a. *māyā́bhir utsísr̥psata* / b. *índra dyā́m ārúrukṣataḥ*
c. *áva dásyūm̐r adhūnuthāḥ*

a. They who, through their viles, / b. were trying to [creep up← and mount to heaven, Indra,
c. those Dasyus did you send tumbling down.

The alternating connotations of √*sarp* in stanzas 1.161.12 and 8.14.14 seem to have covered both malicious and beneficial aspects of a ritual performance in its extended sense of thaumaturgy. Whereas the Dasyus try to reach heaven by force of their outlandish machinations, the Ṛbhus are rewarded with immortality for their ritual correctness. We are witnessing yet another example of the poet's elaborate means of self-promotion in contradistinction to the slandering ways of his ritual competitors.

4.4

There are obvious comparative benefits to be drawn from this Vedic excursus. Just like his namesakes in the Ṛgveda, Orpheus performs transfiguratively, that is, not merely by relating a topic of song, but by mysteriously moving nature on a par with a divinity. The motif is first attested in a fragment from Simonides (PMG 567), which describes how countless birds fly over Orpheus' head and fish jump straight out of the sea *in accordance with his beautiful song* (*kalâi sỳn aoidâi*).[65] Echoing a focal point in postclassical Orphic mythology, this early testimony reflects Orpheus in a role once indistinguishable from that of the quasi-historical mystagogue.

64 The same theme is elaborated in RV 4.16.9: "In your dominance you [= Agni] came here to the poet in need [= Kutsa?] at the winning of the sun, o bounteous one (*maghavan*) with your mind on men. With your help you urged him on *at the invocation to heavenly brilliance* (*dyumnáhūtau* [cf. OAv. *diuuamna-* above]); but the Dasyu, *possessing magic arts* (*māyā́vān*) but *no sacred formulation* (*ábrahmā*), sank down." The loc.sg. *dyumnáhūtau* (*dyumná-* ["heavenly brilliance"] + *-hūti* ["invocation"]) is grammatically and thematically suggestive of OAv. *garō dəmānē* (see below). A particularly noteworthy parallel is Y 51.15, which also contains the cognate dat.pl. *magauuabiiō* (sg. *magauuan-* ["benefactor"]) in the previous hemistich.

65 The summoning force of Orpheus' music is also attested in Euripides (*Bacch.* 560 ff.), who likewise employs the preposition *sýn* (*sunágō*) to characterize the performative vigour of the citharode.

In his joint role of a prototypal wandering singer, inventor, and initiator, Orpheus is the ultimate jack-of-all-trades. By tuning the cosmos to his all-embracing organon, he excels in a craft lacking in immediate gain, yet rhetorically equiped to supersede all other crafts through its power over matter and mortality. His example thus belongs to a narrative framework within which the promulgations of latter-day religion and rarefied autotelic art had not yet begun to develop distinctive features of their own.[66] It is also within this framework that one must seek the eschatological foundations of the philosopher's *bíos* ("mode of life"). As touched upon above, the distinctly ritual notion of a life in purity – of ending up "purified" (*kathērámenos*) in a "pure dwelling" (*katharà oíkēsis*) (*Phd.* 114c) – was a legacy shared between Plato and his contemporary Orpheotelests. It traces a discourse impelled by the existential concerns of ritual specialists in a distant tribal past, structured around the prize and lasting value of ritual, and ultimately designed to a life perfectly at rest in its state of being thus ritually informed.

Gāthic poetry, once again, gives a succinct testimony to the early emergence of such a discourse. In addition to the abovementioned thematics of the *Kamnamaēzā Hāiti* (Y 46), Zarathushtra's eschatological intimations are centered around a fixed figure of speech that brings the theme of laudation to the fore: *garō dəmānē* (or *dəmānē garō*). The figure combines two transparent Indo-Iranian nouns (OAv. *gar-*, Ved. *gír-* ["{song of} praise"] and OAv. *dəmāna-*, Ved. *mā́na-* ["house, dwelling" {< PIE **dm-eh$_2$-no-*[67]}]) to suggest something like "in(to) the House of Laudation"[68] (*-ō* and *-ē* are clearly genitive and locative markers). The fact that many modern translators chose to render *gar-* as "welcome" might convey the wrong impression that the concept of song was occasionally absent in the concept of welcome.[69] A closer look at the pragmatics of Vedic √*gar* (pr. *gṛ̥ṇā́ti*) and the deverbative

66 The different (and partly anomalous) roles of Orpheus in classical tradition already caused puzzlement among ancient authors, such as Herodorus (FGrHist 31 F 42), who speculated that there must have been two different Orpheis (*dýo eínai Orpheîs*) (Cf Karanika 2010, 393f.). Karanika also points to significant parallels between the representation of Orpheus as *oikistḗs* ("colonizer, founder of a city") and *keleustḗs* ("bootswain") in the *Argonautika*, emphasizing the invigorating force of his song, and the double role of the Orphic song to *present* a cosmogony and to *encapsulate* the beginning of a new cosmos.

67 The PIE root for "to build" contained the laryngeal h_2 (pace Nikolaev 2010).

68 For the sake of congruity, I shall systematically employ the term House of Laudation, even when following translations that are otherwise quoted verbatim. Semantically adjacent variants are Insler's "House of Song" and Nyberg's "Haus des Gesanges" (1938, 161).

69 Cf. Hintze 2000 ("ins Haus des Willkommens"), H/E/S ("into the house of welcome"), and K/P(i) ("dans la maison de la bienvenue" [but cf. K/P(ii) "chant de bienvenue").

noun *gír-* confirms that the two concepts in fact conditioned each other.[70] The song of praise was a gesture of welcome enacted in typical guest-host situations on which the cultic invocations and invitations of gods were modelled.[71]

An eschatological interpretation of the Gāthic *garō dəmāna-* has been endorsed by many influential Iranists, who usually consider it the model of the eschatological concept of *Garōdmān* in Sassanian Pahlavi literature.[72] According to a text completing the scanty information in Bundahišn XXX, it is imagined as a region stretching beyond the stars and transfiguring everything into a pure state of youthful bliss.[73] H. S. Nyberg, in his comprehensive treatise on Iranian religion, concluded that the *garō dəmāna-* was the heavenly dwelling towards which the hymns of praise ascended. He adduced Y 34.2 to suggest that it was through the mediation of Ahura Mazdā's "thought" (*manaŋhā* [instr.sg.]) and the poet's "songs of praise" (*garōbīš* [instr.pl.] *stūtąm*) that the "sacred actions of a man" (*nərəš śiiaoϑanā* [nom.pl.]) were brought up to that place.[74] In the meantime, other scholars have grown sceptical about the evidence for such notions in the Gāthās. Jean Kellens, perhaps the most persistent of the sceptics, argued in an article from 1987:

> There is no word in Old Avestan for reward or punishment after death. The hereafter is present: here and there the singer threatens his enemies with hell and promises his followers heaven, but that is all. The idea of a last judgement is most certainly absent, and eschatology not only does not play a central role in moral thinking, it has not even produced an abstract specialized vocabulary. (Kellens 1987, 248)

While the Gāthās do not present a fully developed eschatological system, it seems inconclusive to argue that a terminology marked by the present situation of ritual exchange fail to accomodate notions of an afterlife. Consider, for instance, the following stanza from the last hymn in the fourth Gāthā (Y 51.15):

---

70 Note, for instance, *figurae etymologicae* of the kind *gīrbhír gr̥̄ṇati* (RV 8.46.3 [= 8.54.1]) and *girā́ gr̥ṇīhi* (RV 5.53.16). An unmistakable PIIr. inheritance lingers behind formulations such as Ved. *gīrbhí* (instr.pl.) *stotr̥̄ṇā́m* ("through praises [...] of the praise singers" [Jamison and Brereton 2014 {Henceforth J/B}]) (RV 3.5.2) ≈ OAv. *garōbiš* (instr.pl.) *stūtąm* ("by songs of praise" [Insler]) (Y 34.2 [see also below]) (cf. K/P[iii]).

71 This pattern is not only seen in Indo-Iranian, but is reflected in the use and sense of other derivatives of PIE √*g^u*erH* (LIV²), such as Lith. *giriù* ("to fame, to praise") and OCS *žьrjǫ, žrьti* ("to sacrifice").

72 See, for instance, Bartholomae 1904 (s.v. ⁵*gar:* "als Bezeichnung für den Aufenthalt *Mazdāhs* und der Seligen, sva. Paradies"), Lommel 1930, 211, and Nyberg 1938, 160 f.

73 The title of the text is merely paraphrased by Darmesteter (Z. ii, 640, footnote 138).

74 "Diese 'Taten' [i. e., die sakralen Handlungen] sind durch Vermittlung von Ahura Mazdās Manah unter den Sängen und Hymnen der Mysterienteilnehmer zur Himmelswohnung hinaufgefürt worden." (Nyberg 1938, 161).

1a. *hiiat̰ mīždəm zaraϑuštrō* / b. *magauuabiiō cōiš parā*
2a. *garō dəmānē ahurō* / b. *mazdå jasat̰ paouruiiō*
3a. *tā vā vohū manaŋhā* / b. *aṣ̌āicā sauuāiš cəuuīšī*

1a. What prize Zarathushtra / b. previously promised to his adherents,
2a. into that House of Laudation [did the Wise→ Lord / b. come as the first one.
3a. Through good thought these (offerings) / b. are committed to You, and to Truth, with benefits.[75]

It is conceivable that the notion of the "House of Laudation" occurred to the poet and his auditor not just as a house *in* which praise is sung, but as a dwelling forged by the poet's song. Ahura Mazdā enters into it "as the first one" by first being subjected to poetic praise, and it is along the same itinerary that the openhanded patron (the "adherent" or "benefactor" [*magauuan-* {cf. 1b}]) will finally receive the reward of joining his supreme lord as a guest. [76]

The poet himself is sure of following along on that route, treading on the "path of invigoration," and presenting himself as someone who, depending on our interpretation of *səraošānē* (< PIE √**k̑leu̯s* ← √**k̑leu̯*[77]) in 4b, either wishes to "hearken" or to "be heard" in the House of Laudation (50.4, 3–4). If the poet indeed expresses a wish to become transfigured by fame, it makes perfect sense that his course of self-fulfilment (scil. "path of invigoration" [**īšō paϑ-*]) is suffused with a quality (*īš-* ["vigour"]) on a par with that fame. His Vedic congeners employed a similar idiom to express their wish for "fame and refreshment" (*śrávas-* + *íṣ-*) in recognition of cultic servitude ("place in us lofty fame and splendour [*asmé dhehi śrávo br̥had / dyumnáṃ*[78]] [...] and refreshments by the cartload" [*rathínīr íṣaḥ*] [RV 1.9.8] [J/B]).[79] Not unlike the bacchic initiates described in the poetry of the Orphic gold tablets as

75 I follow Insler with the exception of 3a–b. While the referent of the dem.pron.pl. *tā* in 3a is not supplied by the stanza, it is plausible that it was intended to denote the totality of the hymn. It is not clear to me why Insler renders "This prize..." as if the pronoun referred back to 1a. K/P(i) renders "Ces (eloges)..." in vague accordance with H/E/S. The co-occurrence of Ved. *śávas-* (cf. the instr.pl. *sauuāiš* in 3b) and √*gar* is quite common in RV (especially in stanzas praising Indra) (cf. Lubotsky 1997 [s.v. *śávas-*]), where the intended sense is occasionally that the god is made strong though the poet's song (6.44.4: "I will sing for you to this lord of power [Indra]" [*tyám* {...} *gr̥̥ṇīṣé śávasas pátim*] [...] 5: "He whom songs make strong" [*yáṃ vardháyantī́d gíraḥ*] [J/B]).
76 Cf. the preceding footnote.
77 The root **k̑leu̯s-* is abstracted from the desiderative stem **k̑léu̯-/*k̑lu-s-* seen in the Gr. fut. *kleusómetha* ("we will hear") (cf. LIV², 298, 299).
78 Cf. the employment of the Av. cognate *diuuamna-* "id." in Y 31.20 (see below).
79 Cf. also RV 1.165.12: "receiving fame and refreshment" (*śráva éṣo dádhānāḥ* [J/B]).

treading "gloriously" (*kle‹e›inoí*[80]) on a sacred road in the afterlife, the Gāthic poet reinvents himself as a future subject of poetic praise:

3a. *xšaϑrācā yā* / b. *īšō stå̄ŋhaṯ ā paiϑī*
4a. *ākå̄ arədrə̄ṇg* / b. *dəmānē garō sərаošānē*

3a. and with the power by which / b. one shall tread the path of invigoration,
4a. in the face of the zestful, / b. I wish to be heard in the House of Laudation.[81]

The theme of divine hospitality is invoked in other stanzas lacking overt references to the House of Laudation, yet clearly revolving around the same notion of the good patron's future reward (Y 31.20–22). Such a person shall achieve "splendour"[82] (*diuuamna-*) and become Ahura Mazdā's "well-provided guest"[83] (*vāzištō* [...] *astiš*) (22), but those who are deceitful will end up in that awful abode of which we got a glimpse above. This time, however, the poet supplies a more graphic description of their misery (20):

3a. *darəgə̄m āiiū təmaŋhō* / b. *duš.xvarəϑə̄m auuaētās vāco*
4a. *tə̄m* ⁺*vå̄ ahūm drəguuaṇtō* / b. *š́iiaoϑanāiš* x^v*āiš daēnā naēšaṯ*

---

80 I follow the reading in Alberto Bernabé's restored edition of the Hipponion tablet in *Orphicorum et Orphicis similium testimonia et fragmenta* (OF). The tablet is indexed 474 F (4 [A 62] C).
81 I follow H/E/S in order to indicate the alternative interpretation of *səraošānē* (II,216) as "I wish to be heard." Insler has "I shall always obey" and K/P "en faveur de l'obéissant."
82 Insler emphasizes the equivalence to Ved. *dyumná-* by rendering "Heavenliness," whereas H/E/S prefers the more straightforward "splendour." K/P(ii) seems to posit the same etymology, but curiously render "sort" (or "lot") with reference in the commentary (K/P[iii]) to Ved. √*dīv* ("to game] [cf. EWAia]).
83 K/P(ii) take the superlative adjective *vāzišta-* as an equivalent to Ved. *vā́hiṣṭa-*/*váhiṣṭa-* ("le plus convoyer"). H/E/S and others (including Hintze 2000, 68; and Hintze 2007, 133–144) proceed from OAv. *vāza-* ("gift of hospitality") and Ved. *vā́ja-* ("prize [of victory]," etc.) to suggest "most well-provided." Ved. *átithi-* is also seen in the context of *vā́ja-* (cf. RV 8.74.1). The final line (22a. *ahurā* [...] b. *astiš*) nicely captures the hereditary notion of a human being as "(a) GOD's guest" (or, vice versa, "having [a] GOD as guest"), which is an otherwise conspicuous feature of Indo-European onomastics. A possible match is the Old Scandinavian (Runic) name *Asugasdiz* (= *A*[*n*]*sugastiz*). The initial element *A(n)su-* (PGmc. **ansuz* ["god"]) is possibly cognate with OAv. *ahura-*/Ved. *ásura-* (< PIE **h_2n̥su*[*ro*]-) (cf. also Hittite *hassu-* ["king"]), as hesitatingly acknowledged by Manfred Mayrhofer in EWAia ("nicht primär auszuschließen"), and the second element (*-gastiz* [PIE < **g^hosti-* {"guest, stranger"}]) is functionally fully compatible with PIIr. **átHti-* (> OAv. *asti-*/Ved. *átithi-*). If the recurrent Mitanni-Aryan onomastic element *-atti* really does reflect PIIr. **átHti-* (> OAv. *asti-*) (pace Kammenhuber 1968, 168 ff.), the name *Ašuratti* would belong to the same tradition (cf. Pinault 1998, 454 [with reference to a series of studies on the topic by Mayrhofer {e.g., Mayrhofer 1960, 137 ff.}]), reflecting either a late-PIE proper noun **H_2n̥su(ro)g^hosti* realized as PIIr. **AsurātHti*, or a pre-Germanic calque of the PIIr. name.

3a. (But) a long lifetime in darkness, / b. foul food, the word woe —
4a. to such an existence shall [your conception→, / b. along with its (corresponding) actions, lead you, ye [deceitful ones←.[84]

Could a poetic invention such as the House of Laudation perhaps be considered an enhanced projection of the poet's present locus of performance? Was the poet in fact modelling his prospect of a happy afterlife after the solemn occasion in his master's house, imagining the patron to be sitting once again among his gods, once again becoming the subject of praise alongside his gods? Such conjectures do merit consideration in view of the hints supplied by other traditions.[85] In any case, there is ample evidence in the Gāthās of a contiguous relationship between the poet's praise and the patron's happy afterlife. While still unconditioned by a set of fully developed eschatological doctrines, it was apparently an eventual urge to inoculate such notions into a coherent system, or program, that emerged from the flashing images of poetic immediacy.

Offshoots of a similar development in Greek culture likewise appear in contexts of poetic praise. The doctrine of the three "ways" of the postmortem soul, as envisaged by Pindar in *Second Olympian* (*O.* 2.68–70), is a much debated example that need not concern us further here.[86] Another example can be adduced to illustrate how an eschatological device continues, beyond its proper encomiastic context of lyric poetry, to inform philosophical self-understaning. Plato, in *Phaedrus* (*Phdr.* 247c–248b), evokes a region above the heavens with which true knowledge is concerned. It is a region that, *unlike* (yet still by analogy with) those "sung by the poets" (*hymnēsé tôn poiētès* [247c]), presents itself to the sole receptacle of the mind's eye as a colorless, formless, and intangible "plain of truth" (*alētheías pedión* [248b]) (the opposite of the canonical "plain of oblivion" [*Lḗthēs pedíon*] in the netherworld). We are witnessing how the philosopher's heuristic technique

84 I follow Insler's translation verbatim.
85 I can think of no better indicator of such a poetic strategy than the notion of Valhǫll ("the hall of fallen warriors") in Old Norse poetry, which clearly emulates the festive occasion in the guest-hall of the chief. Such events were not only popular topics of epic song – as seen, for instance, in *Beowulf* – but the typical setting of their performance. The epic strategy of the paradigmatic banquet usually marks a turning point in the storyline, but it can also function as a window on other topics of song – much in the style of the classical rhetorical figure known as *ékphrasis* – through the medium of the imaginary bard in the hall. The banquet represents an idealized image of social intercourse according to the expected standards of good food, plenty of drink, and poetic performance. For an exhaustive treatment of Valhǫll in Old Norse poetry, prose, and iconography, see Dillmann in RGA[35] [s.v. Valhǫll]).
86 Cf. the summary in Willcock (1995, 171–172), which draws much from the analyzes in Willamowitz-Moellendorff (1922, 249–252; 298–500).

asserts itself by at once interrupting and dissimulating a poet's technique for fashioning a patron's lasting fame. If the latter appeals to a ludic spirit of local self-confidence, however, the former requires an arduous dismantling of accepted experience by directing one's mind towards a solid state of true being.

The philosopher and the encomiast would seem to have little in common had it not been for the ritual legacy that so neatly ties them together. It is this deep-seated legacy that I have sought to unravel here, and by doing so I have also tried to elucidate how the predicaments of ritual professionalism gave incentive to new means of ontological reasoning. It was arguably, and ironically, among itinerant traders in ritual, decisively in need of what they were able to create, that the notion of a life at rest in deathless purity received its first and most pregnant formulations. This conclusion would be consistent with what Wallace Stevens, in his essay *The Figure of the Youth as Virile Poet* (1944), once considered to be the ultimate achievement of poetry:

> [I]f we say that the idea of God is merely a poetic idea, even if the supreme poetic idea, and that our notion of heaven and hell are merely poetry not so called, even if poetry that involves us vitally, the feeling of deliverance, of a release, of a perfection touched, of a vocation so that all men may know the truth and that the truth will set them free – if we say these things, and if we are able to see the poet who achieved God and placed Him in His seat in heaven in all His glory, the poet himself, still in the ecstasy of the poem that completely accomplished his purpose, would have seemed, whether young or old, whether in rags or ceremonial robe, a man who needed what he had created, uttering the hymns of joy that followed his creation.[87]

4.5

The area from which the Mazdaysnian religion supposedly spread – the old land known to the Greeks as Arachosia (Hoffmann and Narten 1989, 87) – was one of the first to witness a confluence of ascetic currents that apparently emerged independently in India and Greece during the mid-1st millennium BCE. Centered around ascetics and itinerant sages, such as Pythagoras from Samos in the West and the historical founders of Jainism and Buddhism (Vardhamāna and Siddhārtha Gautama) in the East, they mark out the first historically tangible sects and schools of philosophy to challenge the established ways of religious life. By "established ways" I aim broadly at various forms of public worship in the Greek city states,

87 First published in *The Sewanee Review*, Autumn 1944, the essay was included in the book *The Necessary Angel* (1951). It is quoted here from The Library of America edition of Wallace Stevens collected poetry and prose (Stevens 1997, 674).

and the traditional Vedic ritual system expected to thrive on the mutual commitment of priestly lineages and local warrior-elites in Indo-Aryan society.

The renegotiation of such prescribed forms of ritual life would come out differently depending on the periods and parties involved: in some cases by causing violent uprising and civic antipathy (as exemplified by the anti-Pythagorean revolts in Magna Graecia, and public attitudes towards the so-called "*bacchanalia* sacrilege" in Rome), in others by gaining support in imperial policies (as exemplified by Aśoka's decrees against animal sacrifice, and Constantine's legalization of Christianity).[88]

Especially relevant to the understanding of this dynamic, however, is that it occurred in parallel among groups who initially would have had only vague notions about each other. Nevertheless, when Greeks became more permanently exposed to Indian culture in the settlements established by Alexander the Great and the Seleucids, they seem to have received the antinomian lifestyle of wandering ascetics as a sign of recognition. The terms unambiguously used in the Greek and Prakrit versions of Aśoka's edicts (3rd century BCE) to capture such circles of like-minded wanderers (Gr. *diatribḗ*, Pkt. *pāsaṃḍa*) indicate social phenomena that had long been familiar to Greeks and Indians alike (Schlumberger 1964, 133; Norman 1972, 113). So strong were the ascetics' similarities in appearance and outlook that writers from the Roman-Hellenistic period considered Greek philosophers, such as Pythagoras and Democritus, to have come under the direct influence of the "naked wise men" (*Gymnosophistaí*) of India long before the campaigns of Alexander.

Contrary to this anachronistic view, the ritual legacy shared between speakers of Greek and Indo-Iranian has given us sufficient cues for attributing certain secondary similarities to the social forces inherently at work within these communities. It was a legacy that these speakers, in enduring unawareness of each other and their common linguistic ancestry, would have claimed as their own, but one that we are now able to retroject into the pre-ancient past of Indo-European pastoral societies. Exerting its influence long after the migrations out of the Pontic-Caspian steppes, it remained a characteristic means of communication between aspiring warrior elites and professional suppliers of ritual in archaic Greek, Iranian,

88 Schlumberger (1964, 136) noticed the philosophical, and specifically Pythagorean, character of the formula *apékhesthai tôn empsýkhōn* in the Greek rendition of Aśoka's Rock Edict XIII (from Kandahar [Alexandria in Arachosia]). Cf. the title of Porphyry's *On abstinence* (*Perì apokhês empsýkhōn*). The Greek translator does not even seem to have paraphrased a Prakrit original in this case, but presumaby intended to summarize the practice of Buddhist *dhaṃma* in a way that would have resonated with a philosophically inclined reader (Norman 1972, 115).

and Vedic societies.[89] If we can accept that this social formation had developed at least some of its rudimentary characteristics in a pre-ancient tribal past, it becomes less of a bewilderment to trace the parallel moves towards its gradual reformation.

89 I am, of course, aware of the apparent links between this general assumption and Georges Dumézil's (1898–1986) trifunctional hypothesis. Contrary to Dumézil, however, I take the Indian *varṇa* system to be a reformulation of a more primitive system, predating the emergence of a hereditary priestly class in India. Hence, it is not a preferable point of departure in analyzing systems of patron-clientage in prehistoric Indo-Iranian, and ultimately Indo-European societies.

II Ancient Themes (Confluence)

Resumé and Preamble

The outline of the previous section can be envisaged in dramaturgical terms as a three-act structure. In the first act, the characters of the play introduced themselves to us through their ability to recognize, and actively participate in, a virtual world determined by cultural choice. General attention was drawn to the human disposition towards hyperphenomenal displays of identity and difference, and especially to the earliest signatures of behavioral modernity by which awareness of such phenomena affords archaeological identification. Two categories of data lend particular credence to such abilities in the absence of written records, namely the manufacture of personal ornaments and the ritual treatment of mortal remains. For the sake of argument, we may imagine the protagonists of this act as the hunter-gatherers of the Middle to Upper Paleolithic transition. In their decipherable modern appearance, they have broken the boundaries of necessity through the means by which they redundantly create social bodies apart from what they biogenetically appear to be, that is, in a perceived state of cosmetic alteration.[90]

The second act brought attention to the means by which such social perceptions might inform the raison d'être of a stratified sacrificial community in a relatively late prehistoric (pre-ancient) past. Comparative textual (mainly Vedic, Greek, and Germanic) evidence was adduced to exemplify how rituals of commensality create a counterpoise to the epic event of heroic confrontation. Discursive claims on social cohesion typically conform to this logic in the interest of privileged insiders, who willingly sponsor spectacular events of momentary suspense in order to maintain the status quo. It is in this mold that day-to-day civic religiosity continuously thrives.

In the third, and final, act a different approach to such civic games of pretense was introduced by shifting perspective from the stationary employer to the itinerant employee. The former's reliance on the ritual expertise of professional outsiders can be seen here to foster an emergent spirit of inventive ritual rhetoric, whereby global conceptions of truth and afterlife pose challenges to local cultic concerns. This is the point at which the plot reaches its climax. It is also the point at which the different perspectives begin to conflate.

90 I proceed here from Bernhard Waldenfels' phenomenological analysis of the adornment, which distinguishes a thing in its recognizable property of having broken the boundaries of necessity without attracting critical scrutiny as to its redundancy (Waldenfels 2012, 204–211).

https://doi.org/10.1515/9783110460605-007

5 The Stargazer's Sacrifice

5.1

An extract from the lost treatise *Perì eusebeías* ("On piety") by the peripatetic philosopher Theophrastus (*c.*371/0–*c.*287/6 BCE) informs us about the sacrificial customs of the Jews (Porph., *Abst.* 2.26). Identified as the hereditary praxis of a caste among the Syrians, it is said to revolve around the nightly immolation of animal victims. These the Jews "do not feast on" (*ou* [...] *hestiṓmenoi*) in the usual manner of the Greeks, but instead have them burnt whole along with large quantities of honey and wine. The rite is swiftly executed during the night in order to keep it hidden from the "All-Seeing One" (*hó panóptēs*) (= the Sun[91]), whereas fasting, prayers, theological reasoning, and a dedication to the "theory of stars" (*ástrōn* [...] *tḕn theōrían*) are matters of greater confidence to this alleged "race of philosophers" (*philósophoi tò génos*). They are said to maintain this ancestral praxis *perforce* (*anángkēi*), that is, not *with appetite* (*epithymíai*) in the implied manner of Greek citizens. To sacrifice without a sacrificial meal in the extraordinary fashion of a so-called *holókaútōma*, which would only take place intermittently in the life of Greek society, is inaccurately described here as the sole form of sacrifice practiced among the Jews (cf. ThesCRA I 2a Sacrifices, Gr.[92]). Equally inadequate, of course, is the presumption that the Jews represented a priestly caste among the Syrians.

While the extract from Theophrastus is preserved in a work composed only a few decades before the initial stages of imperial Christianity, it stems from a period during which the cultural exchange between Greeks and Jews is otherwise weakly documented. Whatever scant information about Jewish tradition – including the echo from *Leviticus* 6:8–13[93] – that Theophrastus could have received in his time is of little concern here. The issue at stake is rather the generic model according to which the philosopher-sage keeps reappearing, again and again, behind the superficial guise of ethnic eccentricity so as to reflect an ideal among philosophi-

---

91 The epithet can be safely attributed to the sun (cf. S. *Ant.* 1045). Among the few cases of holocaustic sacrifices mentioned in the sacred laws, one (from Erchia) is significantly said to belong to Zeus *Epōpetḗs* ("Zeus the *over-seer*") (LSCG 18 Γ, 20–23). Is Theophrastus hereby seeking to introduce yet another sense of contrast between the pious burnt offerings of the Jews ("hidden from the All-Seeing One") and their extravagant counterparts among the Greeks?

92 See also footnote above.

93 A possible source of such indirect information is the work *Aegyptiaca* by Hecataeus of Abdera, a contemporary of Theophrastus.

https://doi.org/10.1515/9783110460605-008

cally inclined Greeks. It makes no substantial difference if such an idealizing stance on the progenitors of wisdom identifies Egypt, Syria, Persia, or India as their country of origin. If once expected to arrive from regions such as Thrace (Orpheus) and Hyperborea (Abaris), the barbarian sage preferably reappears within the broadened cultural horizon of the Hellenistic period as the member of a priestly caste or religious confraternity (Festugière 1971, 443). What really matters is that the source of wisdom is situated outside of the Greek *oîkos*. It matters because of the genre's underlying purport, that is, not an ethnographic concern with the varieties of cultural influence, but to invert the initial values of the *oîkos*.

Phenomena seen to result from such a reprogramming of values are oblique ritualism (= an overestimation of ritual), vegetarianism, sectarianism, and an underestimation of time-honored local affairs. One suspects, therefore, that a similar logic of correlation brought the themes of sacrifice and stargazing together in Theophrastus' description of the Jews. Despite representing separate undertakings at first sight – the ritual slaughter of animals on the one hand, and astronomy on the other – they may, on closer consideration, appear contiguously reunited from two different analytical angles. The first of these angles I shall call *mantic*, the second *antinomian*. I intend to pursue these two lines of inquiry here by first briefly considering the mantic angle.

5.2

The stargazer's sacrifice can be considered a mantic affair in the sense that it evokes related techniques of interpretation. Among the various techniques of deductive divination practiced throughout the Near East and the Mediterranean, extispicy (and especially hepatoscopy) enjoyed particular antiquity and esteem. Ever since its earliest attestation in the urban centers of ancient Mesopotamia, it was a technique carried out within the confines of ritual slaughter. An extispicy could only be performed on the entrails of a sacrificed animal.

The task of a professional "diviner" (*bārû*) is reported in a single source to include, among other things, the so-called "touch of the hand" (= "ritual act"), offering of the sacrifice, and the performance of extispicy (Jeyes 1991–1992, 23). He belonged to an establishment of learned experts who were employed by the kings of Babylonia and Assyria to engage in the recording and interpretation of omens, the eventual result of which was an immense corpus of scribal lore concerning the interconnection of signs and events. An ancient division of responsibilities entrusted to the *bārû* the interpretation of so-called "provoked omens" actively sought by ritual (such as extispicy and lecanomancy), whereas the interpretation of "unprovoked omens" (such as astrology) was entrusted to the *ṭupšarru* ("scribe"/"scholar") (Koch-Westenholz 1995, 10–17). Nevertheless, the basic theory behind such practices remained essentially the same. Its implied logic of conditionality can be grasped both from within the divinatory genres themselves (if *x* appears [if the planet so-and-so is present in the eclipse], then *y* is its correlate [e.g., a noble dignitary will die in the king's place]) and through the proposition rendering the genres mutually compatible. As implied by the latter, all events were thought to have correlates somewhere else in the world, and since the correlations were considered to be encoded in divinely engendered signs, it followed that the different divinatory genres could themselves be conceived as mirroring each other.

In a mythological fragment possibly originating in the reign of Nebuchadnezzar I (*c.*1120–*c.*1104 BCE), the legendary king Enmeduranki of Sippar is said to have been instructed in the art of divination by the gods Šamaš and Adad. The "liver" (?) (*takāltu*) is referred to here as a "tablet of the gods" (*ṭuppi ilāni*) (Lambert 1967, 132). Šamaš is accordingly said in an Akkadian prayer to be inscribing his oracles into the sheep's liver (Bottéro 1987, 164). While such means of reasoning are consistent with how the scholarly elite understood natural occurrences to represent a deducible script, they attest as well to the notion that occurrences in the terrestrial world are analogously linked to those in the heavens. Celestial phenomena could be expressed to represent a "heavenly writing" comparable with signs on the exta (Rochberg 2004, 2). A particularly striking outcome of this vertical analogy is a catchline from the 1st millennium extispicy treatise known as the *Bārûtu* ("The Art of the Diviner"): "if the liver mirrors the sky" (*šumma amūtu maṭṭalat šamê*). Identified as a direct quote from one of the treatise's ten "chapters" (the so-called *Mutābiltu* ["The One Who Interprets"]), it occurs in an autobiographical passage ascribed to Aššurbanipal. The king speaks of the never-failing craft of divination that was entrusted to him by Šamaš and Adad, and how he learned the secrets of scribal lore in the gathering of scholars:

> I understood the signs of Heaven and Earth, I discussed in the gathering of scholars, I pondered "If the liver is like a mirror of the sky" with the learned experts of lecanomancy [...] (Trans. Koch 2005, 28–29).

As suggested by the quoted catchline (a topic to be *pondered* with the experts), the liver of a sacrificed animal was occasionally held to convey a visible impression of heaven. The presumption that it was exclusively *sacrificial* exta that could "mirror" (or appear in the "image" [*maṭṭalātu*] of) celestial events implies, furthermore, that the reading of internal organs only becomes contiguous with the reading of heavenly signs during certain ritually provoked circumstances. Sacrifice, in this regard, transcends the space of civic feasting to become a scholarly site of reading and speculation. What enters into it from above (e.g., in the form of encoded messages on the entrails) may retroject into the celestial world from below (e.g., Babylonian scholia referring to Jupiter and Mars respectively as "Spleen" and "Kidney-star" [Koch-Westenholz 1995, 179]).

To judge from its absence in Homeric epic, the art of extispicy is likely to have spread from the Near East to the Greeks via Asia Minor during the Archaic period (Bachvarova 2012 and Rollinger 2017). Tacitus (*Hist.* 2.3) significantly labels it a *borrowed science* (*scientiam* [*artemque haruspicium*] *accitam*) first incorporated into the cult of Aphrodite at Paphos by the wandering seer Tamiras from Cilicia. Notwithstanding its nature of standard procedure by the Late Archaic period, however, the performance of extispicy could also represent an unwanted supplement to the communal proceedings of sacrifice.

A case in point is Aristophanes' derisory portrayal of the diviner Hierocles, who arrives out of the blue to meddle with a sacrifice to the goddess Eirene ("Peace") (*Pax*, 1039 ff.).[94] He is supposedly attracted by the odor of fat, engages in all sorts of ritual quiddities with the patron, and is eventually driven off with a stick – without a share in the "inward parts" ([*splágkhnon*] 1012) – as a sign of final relief. Hierocles is depicted in the familiar terms of a travelling charlatan (*alazṓn* [1120]). His costly claim to knowledge about the divine decrees makes him an ominous presence and a threat to the city's peace. Still, a trace of the diviner's legacy had found a different path into Athenian society. Much in the fashion already witnessed in the case of Plato's redeployment of Orphic eschatology, it was a legacy encrypted in philosophical discourse.

Plato, in the *Timaios* (70d–71d), expounds on the divinatory properties of the liver in terms that recall the phraseology of the Mesopotamian diviners. Most strikingly in this regard, he describes the liver as a "mirror" (*kátoptron*) of the soul (71b). Divinely inspired thoughts are imprinted on its many-colored surface in the form of visible images, but these cannot intelligibly account for themselves as they appear to the mind's eye in an obscured state of sleep or frenzy (71d). Plato thus advances his plea for philosophical reasoning by reinterpreting traditional means of seeking divine guidance in the context of animal sacrifice. If the animal liver could be held in such a context to effectively encode divine dispositions towards the sacrificial offering, the human soul is far better disposed to catalyze that encounter through its compliance with reason.

The positive re-evaluation of divinatory cognizance against this specifically Platonic backdrop will be dealt with more thoroughly in chapter 6. For the time being, however, it suffices to say that divination – though apparently not a "science" in the strict modern sense of the word – can be understood to interfere scru-

94 An almost identical scene occurs in *Birds* 848–1057.

pulously with the festive, make-believe aspects of civic worship. While this oblique aspect of sacrifice is not explicitly addressed in Theophrastus' account of the Jews, it adds consistency to an otherwise less clear-cut conclusion: that the Jews sacrifice in a decidedly un-Greek fashion (i. e., "without feasting") precisely *because* they are philosophers, *because* they are devoted to theology and the theory of stars. The scholarly devotion to theory (whether of the sacrificial *exta* or of the stars) becomes a factor in explaining the logic of correlation that brought the themes of ritual slaughter and astronomy together, but it has also given us an inkling as to why the scholar is prone to become an antinomian figure. If an outsider, like Hierocles, his arrival is understood in invasive terms; if an insider, like Socrates, as an out-of-place figure corrupting his host from within. It is to this latter aspect that we shall now turn.

5.3

In an incisive study, Hans Blumenberg probes deep into the implications and repercussions of an ancient anecdote – first attested in Plato's *Theaetetus* (174a) and in Aesop's corpus of fables – concerning a stargazer who falls into a well (Blumenberg 1987). Whereas the key player in Aesop's fable remains anonymous (an unidentified "astronomer" [*astrológos*]), he is identified in Plato's version as the Milesian proto-philosopher Thales. Blumenberg gathers from this seeming piece of passing fancy the long-term impact of a philosophical foundation myth, of a "proto-history of theory" (*Urgeschichte der Theorie*), in which the far-sighted theoretician is variously reimagined as the original subject of mundane scorn. The anecdote makes a proper myth in the topical sense that it covertly substitutes philosophy's obscure beginnings with an always imaginable position outside of philosophy.

Although the archaic collection of *Aesopica* that was circulating in Athens in Plato's time has not survived, it is likely that the gist of the original story of the stargazer's plummet was preserved in the later collections now forming the basis of the *Corpus Fabularum Aesopicarum* (see CFA, no. 40). According to this version, an astronomer was in the habit of leaving his house every night in order to observe the stars. Once when he was walking on the outskirts of the city, directing his mind's full attention to the skies, he unobservantly fell into a cistern. An unidentified passerby, who had heard his cry for help, stopped by the edge of the cistern and said to him: "you wish to pierce through the things in the sky, but fail to see that which is on earth." The concluding moral (or so-called *epimýthion*) states that the fable applies to those falsely pretending to know (*alazoneúontes* [from *alazṓn* {see above}]) things contrary to opinion (*paradóxōs*) while being incapacitated to serve the common good.

Plato's adaptation of the fable is designed to evoke the legacy and tragic fate of his teacher. First, by linking the story to one of the earliest historically tangible figures considered (in Plato's own view) to have passed a life in philosophy. Secondly, by putting the anecdote in the mouth of Socrates shortly before he goes to answer to the suit brought against him (210d). Socrates is ingeniously made to predict his own end – that which lies "before his feet" (*parà pódas*) – in retrospect of his forerunner's mishap, and to be doing so in the style of a genre particularly dear to him.[95] The readjusted version of the fable now runs:

> Ὥσπερ καὶ Θαλῆν ἀστρονομοῦντα [...] καὶ ἄνω βλέποντα, πεσόντα εἰς φρέαρ, Θρᾷττά τις ἐμμελὴς καὶ χαρίεσσα θεραπαινὶς ἀποσκῶψαι λέγεται ὡς τὰ μὲν ἐν οὐρανῷ προθυμοῖτο εἰδέναι, τὰ δ' ἔμπροσθεν αὐτοῦ καὶ παρὰ πόδας λανθάνοι αὐτόν.
>
> While Thales was studying the stars and looking upwards, he fell into a cistern, and a neat, witty Thracian servant girl jeered at him, they say, because he was so eager to know the things in the sky that he could not see what was there before him at his feet.[96]
> (*Theaet.* 174a)

The ensuing passage of the dialogue makes extended use of an alternative *epimýthion* ("this jest applies to all those...") designed to save the honor of Aesop's ridiculous stargazer by having him laugh back at the truly laughable presumptions of civic life from the elevated position of philosophy. Socrates begins by recounting the immediate disadvantages of exerting oneself to a life in which nothing eludes scrutiny, not even one's own sense of being. Such a person is declared a fool and a nuisance in the popular assemblies, he falls "into pits and all sorts of perplexities" (174c) out of failure to join in the game of civic pageantry. The laudations of kings and nobility must appear futile and mendacious to him, both in their claims and choice of imagery, by representing the ruler as a milking shepherd or some proud citizen as the twenty-fifth ancestor of Amphitryon. The philosopher dismisses such "absurdities" (*átopoi* [175a]) in the same terms as he is himself dismissed by the crowd, namely as a figure literally "out of place" (*átopos* [cf. *Prt.* 361a]). Aloof from the commonalities of regular practice, he is only bodily present in the city. His intelligence, on the other hand, is borne in every direction ("both below the

---

95 Socrates is said to have composed metrical versions of Aesop's fables during his imprisonment (*Phaed.* 60d).

96 I am following Harold North Fowler's translation in all essentials (see the bibliography under *Theaet.*).

earth and above the sky" [173e]) in search of a stable reference and, hence, the ultimate means of godlike self-realization (*homoíōsis theôi* [176b]).

The opening anecdote is creatively misread by Plato as the incomplete representation of an ideal. A life devoted to the contemplation of uncreated essences – represented here by the regular movements of heavenly bodies – is the only truly desirable way of life, but one that is constantly endangered by the habitual activities of non-philosophical others. Instead of setting a terrible example, cisterns and laughing Thracian maids are periphrastically taken to represent inevitable disjunctions and humiliations along the superior course of life in philosophy. While the so-called contemplative life (*bíos theoretikós*) remains, in Aristotle's retrospect, the *only activity loved for its own sake* (*autḕ mónē di' hautḕn agapâsthai*), it cannot be accommodated to the civic pursuits (including the so-called *bíos politikós*) considered to produce gratifications distinct from the activities themselves (*EN* 10.5. 1177b).

True symbiosis can only occur, as it were, in the event of a radical transposition, when the true art of politics is either equated with philosophy; or when the promotion of noble (yet impracticable) leisure activities for citizens is embraced by the good constitution.[97] Until then, as Blumenberg puts it, the Thracian maid is justified in her malicious joy (Blumenberg 1987, 12). The tables are turned. She, the uneducated barbarian, stands in for the exemplary citizen, whereas Thales, the Milesian noble, has become a stranger in his own house.

5.3.1

Plato's account of the philosopher's political incommensurability is an exaggeration used to make a point. There is enough material in his personal biography to prove the contrary. Nevertheless, young Plato had indeed witnessed the fatal consequences of an influential citizen's uncompromising lifestyle. Regardless of the hidden reasons for putting Socrates on trial, he was clearly a figure at odds with the public discourse of Athenian self-understanding.

We need only consider the scurrilous portrait of the philosopher in Aristophanes' *Clouds* (originally performed in 423 BCE) to realize that the official charges laid against him more than two decades later – not least that of impiety against the gods of Athens – were deeply rooted in popular opinion. Socrates is described in the comedy as the leader of a secret fraternity gathered inside a "thinking-shop"

97 Plato and Aristotle are clearly not in agreement on this point (Nightingale 2004, 6).

(*phrontistérion*) to engage in the contemplation of celestial matters (225–229), to call down false divinities (i.e., the Clouds) with promises of sacrificial appeasement (269–274), and to forswear all other gods except those of Chaos, the Clouds, and the Tongue (423–426).

The theoretical contemplative is clearly on display here, much in the fashion of the diviner Hierocles touched upon above, as an obstacle to the cultic institutions of civic patronage with which Attic comedy was itself indissolubly connected. Yet, whereas Hierocles obtrudes from the outside with bogus claims to a share in the communal meal, the insider Socrates has given up civic piety for the sake of idiosyncratic speculation. Despite its comic distortions, Aristophanes' portrayal of Socrates attests to the pre-Platonic perception of a tension between active citizenship and the private pursuit of theory as an end in itself.

Another early exponent of this perceived tension is Euripides, who (contrary to Aristophanes) repeatedly elaborates on the superiority of a quietist life over a life in politics. Significant representatives of the two types are Antiope's twin sons Amphion and Zethys in the fragmentary drama *Antiope.* Amphion, the "Orphic" singer-musician, is typecast to defend the unpolitical life against the active life of the hunter-herdsman Zethys. The fact that such distinctions were already being made in fifth-century Athens does not imply that a figure like Amphion can be squared with the theoretical philosopher in Plato's and Aristotle's revisionist accounts of philosophy's past. It would be likewise misleading to assume that the perceived lives of the so-called pre-Socratics – none of which would have labeled themselves philosophers – were really as unpolitical as they have been made to appear in retrospect (Nightingale 2004, 25–26). The apophthegmatic traditions, such as the ones collected by Diogenes Laertius in the 3rd century CE, are often strongly marked by a Platonic ethos. Figures like Pythagoras, Anaxagoras, Democritus, and Thales may thus come to appear less involved in the politics of their time than they assumedly were, and if their active involvement with others is emphasized it is rather done to include them in a perennial lineage of ancient wisdom.

The priestly communities of Egypt and Chaldaea, from which men like Pythagoras and Democritus are said to have acquired instruction, are evoked by Aristotle and other early members of the Academy as the direct precursors of an ideal *bíos.*[98] This is also the implicit assumption behind Theophrastus' depiction of the Jews. If there is anything that such accounts pass on from the sages of Ionia and Magna Graecia, it is neither the unpolitical ideal nor its exotic pedigree, but rather

98 This strategy of the early Academy in creating a suitable historical framework for its own ideal of life is discussed in a groundbreaking study by Werner Jaeger (Jaeger 1928, 9–10).

the notion of a life officially unbound by (yet conceptually linked to) certain public institutions of cultural discourse and practice.[99]

The public institutions at stake can be roughly subsumed under the category of "sacred spectacle" (*theṓrēma*) to include a variety of sponsored occasions for civic and private participation: joint prayers and sacrifices, athletic and musical contests, lyric and epic performances, oracular consultations, and so on. Whether locally confined to city-states or globally attuned to Panhellenic gatherings, such events enabled the temporary visitor (the "envoy" or "spectator" [*theōrós*]) to dwell within ritually enhanced horizons of expectation. A spectator at such cultic events was, as once suggested by André-Jean Festugière, momentarily distracted by the happy illusion of living the life of the gods (Festugière 1950, 57). More importantly, however, the sacred spectacle functioned within a system of exchange between agents of patronage and appointed suppliers of ritual service.

It is precisely within this system of exchange and expenditure that the figure of the philosopher-sage ceases to function. He is not a recipient of encomiastic poetry, not a priest or poet taking fees, not a visiting spectator at a festival. Nevertheless, he can still be held to incorporate and cross-correlate crucial aspects of these roles so as to enable the self's complete transformation of (and by) itself. In order to backtrack the notion of such an all-encompassing, self-fulfilling art of living beyond the legacy of the fourth-century philosophers, it is particularly illuminating to consider the paradigmatic case of Pythagoras and the early Pythagoreans.

5.3.2

Despite the difficulty in producing a reliable account of Pythagoras' political activities in Magna Graecia (especially in Croton) during the late 6th and early 5th century BCE, the ensuing impact of the Pythagorean society in that region inevitably makes him stand out as a political figure. His failure to match the image of the unpolitical, quietist sage does not, however, make Pythagoras less of an antinomian figure. This impression pertains not so much to the conceivable content of his doc-

99 The complex transfer from traditional cultic spectatorship to philosophical theorizing (the primary and secondary sense of *theōría*) has been explored at length by others. Most recently, and forcefully, by Andrea Wilson Nightingale in *Spectacles of Truth in Classical Greek Philosophy* (Nightingale 2004). A precursory statement along similar lines is found in A.-J. Festugière's *Contemplation et vie contemplative selon Platon* (Festugière 1950).

trines, but rather to their ritualized mode of containment, that is, a *bíos* virtually designed to short-circuit the basic components of public worship.[100]

The oldest tangible evidence of the Pythagorean life consists in the so-called *akoúsmata* ("heard things"), or *sýmbola* ("tokens"), that start to appear in writing from around 400 BCE.[101] It is safe to assume that these maxims and sayings belonged to a genuinely pre-Platonic oral tradition, for they were already in need of an explanation when Anaximander of Miletus (the younger) wrote his now lost treatise on their hidden meaning (*Symbólon Pythagoereíōn exḗgēsis*). Another early collection of *akoúsmata* appeared in a now likewise lost book on the Pythagoreans by Aristotle, which was a prime source of the extant material gathered by Diogenes Laertius, Porphyry, and Iamblichus in the 3rd century CE.

The largest group of *akóusmata* fall into the category of *tí praktéon* ("what is [or is not] to be done?"). They take the form of minutely designed behavioral precepts with a strong leaning towards sacrificial ritual (e.g., *not to* dip one's hand in holy water, pour libations over the handle of the cup, sacrifice a white cock, enter the temple barefoot etc.). In an attempt to capture the gist of the acousmatic message, Walter Burkert observed that many of the precepts were modelled after generally acknowledged ritual prescriptions (such as the preparation for initiations and incubations), but whereas the latter only came into force at certain demarcated phases and places, they were turned by the Pythagoreans into permanent rules of life:

> He [the Pythagorean] lives every day of his life as though he were preparing for initiation at Eleusis, for incubation at Asclepius' temple, or for the journey to Trophonius. He follows not the cult rules of a certain holy site, but those of a βίος which he has personally and consciously chosen. (Burkert 1972, 190 f.)

While such prescriptive *akoúsmata* were purposely designed to cancel the periodicity of civic worship, they would also have implied an aberrant attitude towards its most prominent expression of communal participation: animal sacrifice. The earliest, explicitly Pythagorean, testimonies do not support complete renunciation of the eating and killing of animals. Nevertheless, the ideal of bloodless ritualism

---

100 Interestingly, Plato contrasts Pythagoras with Homer by emphasizing the former's achievement of having passed on a "(mode of) life" (*bíos*) to his successors (*Rep.* 600a-b), and himself (?) (in the possibly spurious 7th letter) distinguishes between the "doctrine and life" (*lógon kaì bíon*) of his own teaching (328a). André Laks, in a compelling effort to rectify (or, more specifically, "dearistotelize") the category of "pre-Socratic philosophy," draws attention to the importance of distinguishing philosophy's content from its form (Laks 2006, 56).

101 I rely in what follows on Walter Burkert's groundbreaking treatment of ancient Pythagoreanism (Burkert 1971, 166–192 [concerning the evidence of *akoúsmata*]).

was apparently close at hand. We encounter it, for instance, in Empedocles' *Purifications* (*Katharmoí* [D24–29]) and in Plato's account of initiates into the Orphic life (the so-called *Orphikoì bíoi* [see below]).

The early Pythagoreans may have manifested a similar ethos by choosing *only* to eat what had been sacrificed, and to do so under certain dietary constrictions. Such aberrations from the civic norm were not necessarily meant to violate sacred law, but to render it valid at all times. It is presumably in such a radically reformed sense that "to sacrifice" (*thýein*), according to one of the *akoúsmata* gathered by Iamblichus (VP 82), is defined as the "most just" (*dikaiótataos*) action of all. Ostensibly, the Pythagoreans sought to dissolve sacrifice in its familiar context of public feasting. In reality, however, they may have conceived of their own conduct as the fulfillment of sacrifice. They had, to quote a more familiar example, "not come to destroy [scil. The Law] but to fulfill" (Matt. 5:7).

The ascetic lifestyle of the early Pythagoreans correlated strongly with a set of doctrinal add-ons often classified as "Orphic" in modern scholarship. Their joint message involved a drastic requalification of the human soul with insistence on its immortality, transmigration into animals, and reunification with the gods at a banquet in the netherworld.[102] A motivating force behind such insistencies was the implicit hope of being set free from the obligation to sacrifice, in the style of mortal citizens, according to the opposite principle: that of being separated from the gods, leaving the handling of sacrificial animals to hired cult officials, and momentarily suspending disbelief in a real communion with the gods (as the foundational "trick" of Prometheus had suggested [*Th.* 535–44]).

If early Pythagoreanism is to be heuristically differentiated from the scholarly category of Orphism, emphasis should rather be placed on sociopolitical factors than on theological doctrine. Orphism stricto sensu can thus be held to reflect the activities of wandering mendicants (so-called *agýrtai*) who perform salvific rituals on demand, whereas Pythagoreanism represents a gentrified version of Orphism in the hands of propertied citizens who aspire to transform themselves and their world *by themselves* and *from within.*[103]

---

102 Such requalifications of the soul are widely represented in sources that, more or less explicitly, attest to an Orphic-Pythagorean tradition. Most conspicuously, descriptions of a banquet in the netherworld occur in Empedocles' *Purifications* (D40), Plato's *Republic* (363c–d), the gold tablet from Pelinna (4th century BCE), and in the fourth-century comic poet Aristophon (fr. 12 [cf. Burkert 1971, 199]).

103 For discussions of the sociopolitical differentiation between Orphism and early Pythagoreanism, see Burkert 1971, 132–133 (with references to earlier scholarship) and Detienne 1977, 167. Fritz Graf's *Appendix 1* ("Orphism in the Twenty-First Century") adds further substance to the issue in view of more recent findings and scholarly trends (Graf and Johnston 2017, 187–194); see also Jan

Despite circulating oral instructions derived from a historically tangible founding figure, as well as constituting a sort of guild, they rely less on the traditional strictures of patron-clientage. The Pythagorean bears a closer resemblance to an aristocrat who, eschewing the role of ritual patron, seeks to incorporate the function of client in order to become the architect of his own spiritual fortune. Such a laicized understanding of ritual craftsmanship among the early Pythagoreans is faintly outlined in Diogenes Laertius' *Lives.*

Laertius quotes Heraclitus (DK B129) in stating that Pythagoras "made a *sophíē* (= '[poetic] skill' [?]) of his own" (*epoiḗsato heautoû sophíēn*). Despite the sense of rebuke implicit in the complete quote, it is significant that Laertius takes the notion of self-fashioning to echo the beginning of an ancient treatise, and hence to favor the contested claim that Pythagoras left behind writings:

> οὐ μὰ τὸν ἀέρα, τὸν ἀναπνέω,
> οὐ μὰ τὸ ὕδωρ, τὸ πίνω,
> οὔ κοτ' οἴσω ψόγον περὶ τοῦ λόγου τοῦδε.
>
> No, by the air I breathe,
> no, by the water I drink,
> never will I bear blame for this account.
> (D. L. 8.6)

While the conjecture is almost certainly false, the incentive for deriving the oath from a genuinely Pythagorean treatise is nonetheless noteworthy: the emphasis on an "I" swearing not to bear any blame (*psógos*) for the ensuing discourse. Laertius takes this to imply that Heraclitus must have had the epigraph in mind when characterizing Pythagoras as a self-proclaimed deviser of his own *sophíē*, that is, as someone independent of the poetic skills of others. The author of the epigraph can thus be held to cancel the traditional rules of encomiastic performance according to which, as perhaps best seen in the case of Pindar, the exoneration from blame is always incumbent on a hired poet. For Pindar, the gloom of *psógos* is simply the conceptual inverse of the genuine (or truthful) glory that the encomiast proffers to his patron in anticipation of a fee (*Nem.* 7.61–63):

> ξεῖνός εἰμι: σκοτεινὸν ἀπέχων ψόγον,
> ὕδατος ὥτε ῥοὰς φίλον ἐς ἄνδρ' ἄγων
> κλέος ἐτήτυμον αἰνέσω: ποτίφορος δ' ἀγαθοῖσι μισθὸς οὗτος.

Bremmer's "Rationalization and Disenchantment in Ancient Greece: Max Weber among the Pythagoreans and Orphics?" (Bremmer 1999).

> I am (your) guest-friend. Keeping away dark blame,
> like streams of water with my praises to the man who is my friend,
> I shall bring true fame: for that is the proper reward for good men.

As exemplified here, the notion of *psógos* operates smoothly within the system of exchange brought to attention in the two previous chapters. The poet's work upon the aspiring patron is determined by a suitable "fee" (*misthós* [cf. Av. *mīžda-*]), and hence would seem consistent with the less respectable work of Plato's *agýrtai kaì mánteis.* Yet the two kinds of work do not differ significantly in terms of their putative logic of functioning. In both cases, namely, it takes a worker in a skilled trade to fulfill the task.

Laura Gemelli Marciano has convincingly argued that it was precisely against such socially opposed (yet functionally analogous) forces of ritual craftsmanship – the illegitimate work of self-appointed religious experts (typically labeled "magicians" [*mágoi*] and "stargazers" [*meteōrológoi*]), and that of legitimate cult officials – that the pre-Platonic intellectuals (to be subsequently labeled "philosophers") had sought to strike a double-edged blow. They did so by means of distancing themselves, on the one hand, from the alleged charlatanry of the former group and, on the other, from the claim among appointed cult officials to exclusively inhabit the religious sphere (Gemelli Marciano 2006, 230).

In order to conclude this brief exercise in tracing the Pythagorean origins of the philosopher's *bíos,* I draw attention to what Aristotle takes to be the philosopher's superior *misthós.* Philosophical theorizing is by no means an activity "without reward" (*amisthí*), but the recompense for its pursuit comes at no expense (*Protrepticus* [B44]). Unlike the *theōrós* at a theatrical performance, however, the philosopher needs no hired intermediary to indulge in the always superior spectacle of truth.

It is perhaps in this rudimentary sense of being a "philosopher" that Pythagoras can be reclaimed as a real precursor, that is, without being retrofitted into the fourth-century image of the quietist sage. He stands out as an early version of the Greek man who disembeds himself by "opting out of traditional civic systems of exchange" (Nightingale 2004, 91). At a time when Pindar excelled in his intellectually challenging artistry to defend such a system of exchange – possibly under the influence of some Italian variety of Orphism – there were apparently others who had begun to radically rethink it under a similar influence.

5.4. Despite its elusive historicity, Pythagoras' example points to the gradual emergence of an aristocratic counterculture at odds with traditional institutions of patron-clientage. This new spirit of independent self-fashioning – emerging in the early 6th century BCE and continuing throughout the 5th century BCE – may help to explain why figures like Parmenides and Empedocles chose to retain the traditional medium of dactylic hexameter in an idiosyncratic style distinct from the expectations of epic and lyric performance. The countermoves resulted in various efforts to simultaneously opt out and blend in.

Xenophanes appears under the familiar guise of a wandering rhapsode, but calls the traditional topics of myth the "inventions of earlier men" (*plásmata tôn protérōn* [D59.21]) and urges the primacy of wisdom over athletic displays of wealth and glory (D61). Parmenides, in a similar vein, combines Homeric cosmology with epinician visions of the charioteer on the pretext of exploring the foundations of being. Empedocles, lastly, begins his *Purifications* with a dauntless claim to divinity ("I [am] for you [scil. Citizens of Acragas] an immortal god" [*egṑ d' hymîn theòs ámbrotos* {D4.4}]), proceeds by rejecting theological doctrines in favor of divine mental powers (D8), and concludes by condemning the atrocities of blood sacrifice (D25–29).

Plato's invention of philosophical *theōría* marks a seeming end to such experiments in performative wisdom. We need only consider the impact of an institution that (from the 4th century BCE onwards) remains tied to his intellectual legacy to this day: the Academy. Plato's preference for literary prose – albeit in the dramatized, ventriloquizing style of Socratic dialogue – might nonetheless convey the false impression that an entirely new form of knowledge was thereby finally cut loose from its poetically obfuscating beginnings in myth.

In terms of its epistemic techniques and soteriological aspirations, however, philosophy formed a continuity with earlier tenets of thought and practice. The eventual success of philosophical *theōría* – in its updated, Aristotelean version of contemplative life – consisted rather of its ability to accommodate itself to a world of cultural practice (not least that of civic religion) by insisting on being a self-sufficient, leisured, and hence politically harmless pursuit.

I began this chapter by exemplifying how an early member of the Peripatetic school represented the origins of theory as an unrealized ideal in the present: Theophrastus' account of the stargazing Jews, at pains to maintain their ritual obligations ("without appetite") in order to find true food for thought in the revolving skies. Plato had already begun to sketch out this storyline. He did so by creatively misreading the fable of the astronomer's plummet. He also did so by anachronistically representing the bloodless rites of the *Orphikoì bíoi* – those "abstainers from animals" (*empsýkhōn* [...] *apekhómenoi*) who appease the gods with offerings of cakes of meal and grain in order not to stain the altars with blood – as an ideal thing of the past (among "those of us who existed then" [*egígnonto hēmôn toîs tóte*]) (*Laws* 782c-d).

The description looks like a recap of Empedocles' account in *Purifications* (D25).[104] Unlike Empedocles, however, Plato did not evoke the myth of bloodless origins as a pretext for nonparticipation in the public rites of the polis. Instead, the spiritualization of the stargazer's sacrifice was to re-emerge as a theoretical construct; it was to remain the unrealized ideal by which philosophers would abide for many centuries to come. Their universalizing means of seeking solace for the soul through the suspension of rash judgement did little to obstruct traditional forms of cult. Prominent philosophers (such as Cicero, Plutarch, and the Stoic *hieropoioí*) were even invited to hold religious offices.

When, in the 4th century CE, the model of a "bloodless and rational sacrifice" had finally become so enmeshed in imperial policies as to foster a ban on public animal sacrifice in the Roman Empire, Christians were already beginning to dissociate themselves from the philosophical discourse in which that model first took shape (Eckhardt 2014). The traditional figure of the stargazing sage from the East, who Aristotle and others had identified as a kind of proto-philosopher, was now rather expected to kneel in obeisance, bringing bloodless offerings of gold, frankincense, and myrrh to the Christ Child under a new lodestar of faith.[105] In order to appreciate this unprecedented synthesis of two once distinct yet fully compatible religious orientations – that of civic allegiance on the one hand, and that of a self-chosen *bíos* on the other – we first need to delve further into their pre-Christian particulars.

---

104 Considering that the passage from *Purifications* derives from the abovementioned treatise by Theophrastus, it may very well have formed a part of the curriculum in Plato's school. Before joining Aristotle to become his eventual successor, young Theophrastus is reported to have studied with the ageing Plato, that is, by the time of the composition of *Laws*.

105 The nativity scene in the Gospel of Matthew (Matt. 2:1–12) explicitly identifies the vernacular "wise men from the East" as *mágoi*, i.e., as members of the Persian priestly caste.

6 Apparitions and Apparatuses

6.1

The terms *thaûma* ("wonder") and *mēkhanḗ* ("machination, contrivance") are occasionally used alternately by ancient authors in reference to an apparent failure to distinguish perceptions of reality from its contrived representations.[106] A sense of uncanny artificiality is conveyed by these terms through the implied sense of realism that they invoke. We, the readers, are given the impression that the credulous participants are *really* deceived, and that they would never have acted accordingly in appreciation of the theatricality at work.

Herodotus, one of the first Greek authors to express such inclinations, marvels at the foolish plan of Megacles and Pisistratus to deceive the (assumedly even more foolish) Athenian populace in order to secure Pisistratus' reestablishment as tyrant of Athens in the year 550 BCE (*Hdt.* 1.60.2–5). The two men are said to have selected the tall and beautiful woman Phye from an outlying district of Athens, equipped her in full armor, placed her in a chariot next to Pisistratus, and instructed heralds to run in front of the chariot when they came driving into the city, proclaiming: "Athenians, kindly accept Pisistratus, whom Athena herself honors the most among men when she brings him home to her own citadel." Herodotus calls the operation a *skhêma* (in the sense of "show" or "pretense") that Megacles and Pisistratus "devise (by cunning)" (*mēkhanôntai*). Nevertheless, the citizens are reported to have been so persuaded by the contrivance that they began to worship the woman.

This last, and crucial, point in the description has caused disagreement among modern scholars. Many dismiss the historicity of the episode as a whole, whereas those who accept its accuracy characteristically marvel at the blatancy of the propagandistic charade.[107] In an essay from 1987, W. R. Connor calls attention to the false dichotomy that such dissentient readings reinforce out of failure to rightly distinguish the anecdotal nature of the report from the conceivable element of

106 The noun *mēkhanḗ* may refer to any artificial means for doing (*mēkhanáomai*) a thing. Its primary (and neutral) sense is that of a *crane* used for lifting weights, from which we get the secondary sense (as exemplified by the familiar [latinized] Aristotelean coinage *deus ex machina*) of a *theatrical machine* by which gods, etc., were made to appear in the air (LSJ). Substantial portions of this chapter (especially 6.2–6.3) are based on a paper referenced in the bibliography as Jackson 2012.

107 References to earlier scholarship (before 1987) expressive of such views are found in the groundbreaking essay by W. R. Connor 1987, 42.

https://doi.org/10.1515/9783110460605-009

shared drama involved in the event as (or rather *if*) it occurred. Parallel examples, such as the description of a similar procession in a novel by Xenophon of Ephesus (*The Ephesian Tale* [mid-2nd century CE]), suggest that the interaction between the contrivers and their supposedly credulous onlookers had in fact been far more ambiguous than Herodotus was prone to admit (Connor 1987, 44). If Pisistratus really did enter Athens in the company of a tall woman dressed as the city's patron goddess, we have no reason to assume that the Athenians approved of this maneuver in a state of delusion. It seems more likely that they (or at least some of them) were simply expressing delight in an overtly theatrical event as a sign of public consent.

The impulse to resist such perfectly feasible assumptions is indicative of the habituated means by which conceivably archaic, exotic, infantile, or vulgar responses to organized ritual are understood to ensue from defective reality testing. Herodotus' reported version of how an undisclosed political sham could effectively beguile the masses in the relatively recent and familiar setting of sixth-century Athens is good evidence of the remarkably fast pace at which such tendencies begin to dominate popular imagination. It is also an early testimony to a dominant trope – distinguishable in a variety of postclassical genres, including the Judeo-Christian discourse on pagan idolatry and psychoanalytic film theory (so-called apparatus theory) – whereby an implied lack of reality testing invalidates the games that people willingly play in momentary states of inhibition. Designed to shockingly disclose a falsely perceived reality, the trope begins to exert its rhetorical force in a purely fictitious narrative that postdates Herodotus' historicizing anecdote with but a few decades: the famous parable of the cave in the seventh book of Plato's *Republic* (514a–519a).

6.1.1

It would be foolhardy to revisit this thrashed out passage without first making a reservation. I am not seeking new means to elucidate the parable's philosophical subtext (whether it be epistemological, political, or both), suffice it to say that Plato must have intended the depiction of humans in bonds as the all-inclusive inverse of an unrealizable ideal (Hall 1980).[108] My concern is rather (and therefore!) the misleading distinction between blindness and insight – between the captivating mechanics of wonder and the philosopher's aporetic vision – in the extended con-

108 This is a crucial point, since the "strange prisoners" (*desmṓtas atópous*) are explicitly claimed by Socrates to be "like us" (*homoíous hēmîn*), that is, including the speaking philosopher who would otherwise have seemed best equipped to escape the category of prisoner (515a).

text of cultural theory. Here, the question of the parable's applicability works better in reverse: is there an anthropologically feasible corrective to the imaginary state of affairs in which Plato's troglodytes seem to dwell, as it were, in a likewise captivated state of allegorical reduction? A preliminary survey of the parable's most apparent narrative features is in order before we can move on.

A first striking feature of the prisoners in the cave is their lack of awareness and volition *qua* prisoners. With their legs and necks fettered from childhood, unable to perceive anything but the shadows and echoes of an ongoing machinery behind their backs, they show no awareness of having entered into a condition from which they consequently cannot seek to escape. Even in the hypothetical scenario of a single prisoner's rescue, release from the bonds comes as an unrequested force majeure (*ei phýsei* [515c). He is *compelled* (*anagkázō*) to stand up, turn around, walk, and look into the fire by which shadows of various props are thrown onto the wall of the cave. He is then *forcibly* (*dià trakheías*) *dragged out* (*exélkō*) into the light of the sun.

Secondly, the parable presents an incommensurably bifurcated world: an inside world of becoming (a perceived reality represented, for the sake of argument, by the work of airy-fairy artifice [*phlyaría* {515d}]), and an outside world of uncreated being (a reality that we cannot immediately perceive). Whereas the inside world can be dismantled further into that of the contriver's "implement" (*skeuḗ*) and the prisoner's misinformed perception of its "shadow" (*skiá*), there is nothing factual to connect the inside world with the outside, no residual contiguity, only a vague iconic agreement (fire ≈ sun). The cave dwellers are thus not just spatially cut-off from a world which they cannot perceive, but entirely bereft of a will to attentively observe and pretend to believe in circumstances beyond their own precipitate judgements and convictions. We do not know of such caves or shadows, of not knowing what a cave or a shadow is, precisely because of the power of deduction and symbolic action that, by the willing suspension of judgement and disbelief, enable us to perceive the world differently.[109] If such inaccuracies are typically pointed out in order to downplay the allegorical imagination of a fully accomplished ascent to the intelligible realm, however, they should also pertain reversely to the state of total captivation in which the cave dwellers are said to exist.

Interestingly, Plato refers to the parable as an *eikṓn* (515a), that is, in the same terms that he has previously (towards the end of the sixth book) used to characterize the least trustworthy condition of the soul: apprehension by images (*eikasiá*

109 *Nicht zu wissen, was eine Höhle ist* ("Not knowing what a cave is") is the title of a chapter in Hans Blumenberg's *Höhlenausgänge*, possibly the most exhaustive source of inquiry into Plato's parable and its continuous impact on western thought (Blumenberg 1996, 185–192).

[511e]). We may thus begin to rethink the circumstances of which the parable speaks as an *eikṓn* by examining the real-life props that Plato selects for his allegorical purpose. One such point of reference is that of *thaumatopoiía* (literally "wonderwork") used, in particular, to characterize various mimetic arts in the tenth book, and as a general characterization of a misconceived reality in the parable of the cave.

As a generic term in fourth-century Athens for a particularly unrefined form of entertainment – including jugglery, acrobatics, and possibly some archaic precursor of the Turkish *karagöz* shadow theater – the art of *thaumatopoiía* was not merely known for causing public amazement, but also for its immediate gratification through violent impulses of laughter (the so-called "Megarian laughter") (Gocer 1999–2000). A conclusion to be drawn from this frequently overlooked detail is that Plato seems to count inducement to uncontrolled laughter among the most mischievous artistic means to exploit the human soul.

Hence, when the alluring forces of *thaûma* and *mēkhanḗ* are juxtaposed in the tenth book so as to convey the hyperbolic sense of total delusion, we need to assume that more delicate aspects of polis mentality are in fact being aimed at:

> ...καὶ πᾶσά τις ταραχὴ δήλη ἡμῖν ἐνοῦσα αὕτη ἐν τῇ ψυχῇ: ᾧ δὴ ἡμῶν τῷ παθήματι τῆς φύσεως ἡ σκιαγραφία ἐπιθεμένη γοητείας οὐδὲν ἀπολείπει, καὶ ἡ θαματοποιία καὶ αἱ ἄλλαι πολλαὶ τοιαῦται μηχαναί.
>
> ...and every kind of confusion like this [e.g., bent objects seen in water etc.,] is clearly present in our soul. So scene-painting, by exploiting our natural affections, is nothing else but witchcraft, likewise *wonder-work* (*thaumatopoiía*) and many other such *contrivances* (*mēkhanai*). (*R.* 602d., trans. Henderson [s.v. Pl. *R*])

The allurements of visual art and poetry with which Plato periphrastically grapples in this passage need not be taken literally to cause false beliefs, nor need the ploys of magicians and puppeteers. What these techniques evidently do share, however, is an ability to induce habits of false pleasure. By giving in to laughter and the raptures of trickery, we commit ourselves to violent changes of mood, making us decidedly unlike the unchanging god-like beings that Plato believes we should aspire to become through the exercise of reason (cf. *R.* 388e4–5).

Civic religiosity certainly had a stake in this critique. Intimately connected as it was to the volatile pleasures of public spectacle, it could be likewise criticized for disfiguring cultic participants through the distractions of a happy illusion (apropos of the reference to Festugière in the previous chapter [5.3.1]). Plato would never have expressed himself by such impiously direct means, but it is an inevitable consequence of his critique.

It is noticeable how the negative sense of childish laughter and wonder-struck rapture is positively brought to bear on the release of the involuntary pilgrim in the parable of the cave, for it is now rather *he* who is forcefully changed by "being at loss" (*aporéō*) about true reality (or the "more real" [*alēthéstera*]) (515d). It is *he* who changes and marvels, not the abulic captives in the cave. Here, the experiences of *thaûma* and *aporía* ("puzzlement") are irrevocably opposed (through the split between paideutic *thaumatopoiía* on the one hand, and philosophical *aporía* on the other), whereas the same terms are used interchangeably elsewhere to describe a precursory condition of the soul (that of being "puzzled" [*aporôn*] and "wondering" [*thaumázōn*]) from which philosophical reasoning eventually ensues.

In the first book of *Metaphysics*, Aristotle elaborates on the Platonic idea that it was indeed by exposure to the wonders of myth that human beings, thinking themselves ignorant, began (and still continue) to philosophize about the wonders of nature (*Met.* 1.982b10–20).[110] A similar notion recurs in the pseudo-Aristotelean treatise *Mēkhaniká* (possibly composed during the 3rd century BC), which begins with a brief meditation on the wonderful effects of mechanics. Amazing things are said to occur (*thaumázetai tôn* [...] *symbainóntōn*) either "in accordance with nature" (*katà phýsin*) while their causes are unknown, or "contrary to nature" (*parà phýsin*) because they are produced "by skill" (*dià tékhnēn*) to various human advantages.

A *mēkhanḗ* is hence no longer referred to as such because it deludes us, but because it saves us from the difficulty of being "at loss" (*aporía*) by virtue of our skills (*Mech.* 847a). The conceptual redeployment of *thaûma* and *mēkhanḗ* has suddenly come to define circumstances entirely opposed to the *captivating mechanics of wonder* with which I began this inquiry. We are now rather facing what could perhaps best be referred to as the *liberating wonders of mechanics.* How are we to circumvent this apparent contradiction?

6.1.2

As indicated above, Plato did not hesitate to assess philosophy against an inferior sense of *thaûma* that either restrains rational judgement (through the impact of sly politics, paideutics, entertainment, etc.) or progressively forestalls it. What the first model thus critically rejects as an irrational response to the malfunctions of art

---

110 The idea is first attested in Plato's *Theaetetus* (*Tht.* 155d).

and politics, the second model reaffirms as a prerequisite for emergent rationality. It would, however, be misleading to consider such alternative explanations incompatible.

Whereas a pessimistic vision of misguided politics defines the first statement, the second statement derives its Aristotelean appeal from a less political stance on the nature and development of knowledge. Today, we are still able to recognize the long-term impact of these models on two dominant etiologies of religion. The first recurs in various strands of cultural critique seeking to decipher the means by which religious discourse strategically mystifies asymmetrical relations of power; the second in an intellectualist tradition seeking to explain religion in terms of faulty reasoning.[111] Religious subjects are always bound by such etiologies to enter credulously into a world that is either deceptively constrained or prematurely construed (cf. the discussion above, ch. 2.3).

This overarching problematic comes to a head in Giorgio Agamben's essay *Che cos'è un dispositivo* ("What is an apparatus?") from 2006.[112] A core concern in this text is the genealogy and extended application of a theological concept (Lat. *dispositio*, Gr. *oikonomía*) that Agamben now somewhat alarmingly brings to bear on the machinations of high-tech capitalism. Michel Foucault used the term *dispositif* ("device" or "apparatus"[113]) from the mid-1970s to describe the heterogeneous network that, at a given historical moment, strategically relates the elements (discourses, institutions, laws, moral propositions, etc.,) that support, and are supported by, certain types of knowledge. To the same extent that the apparatus always acts within a play of power, it is also linked to certain limits of knowledge.[114]

Agamben traces the origin of the Foucauldian concept through Jean Hyppolite (from whom Foucault apparently borrowed it), Hegel, and all the way back to early

---

111 One way of identifying such competing etiologies in the present-day academic study of religion (excluding theology) would be to trace the first trend back to Marx via figures such as Lukács, and the second back to Darwin via figures such as Frazer. Whereas proponents of the cognitive science of religion characteristically respond to the second trend by seeking explanations to cultural delusions in the natural workings of the mind, scholars associated with the relatively loosely structured Marxist camp typically engage in what Paul Ricœur labelled "hermeneutics of suspicion."

112 All references in the following are to the English translation from 2009. The remaining part of this chapter closely follows (with minor alterations) the text referenced as Jackson 2012 in the bibliography.

113 Agamben himself, in a lecture held at the European Graduate School, suggests the alternative English translation *dispositor*, an obsolete astrological term signifying a planet ruling the sign in which another planet is located (https://www.youtube.com/watch?v=ua7ElsQFZPo, last accessed on November 5, 2018).

114 Foucault elaborates on his own use of the term *dispositif* in an interview from 1977 (quoted in Agamben 2009, 2).

Christian theology. In the trinitarian expositions of the Latin church fathers, *dispositio* (a derivative of *dis* + *pono* "to arrange") or *dispensatio* (from *dis* + *penso* "to adjust") signified the means by which God administers his creation through the agency of the Son. In the world of appearance, God's being is always separated from the historical contingencies of action and praxis that ensue from providential governance. In other words: action has no foundation in being. The concept of *dispositio/dispensatio* was apparently calqued on the Greek concept of *oikonomía* (lit. "management of a household") in a Christian theological tradition that, via figures like Irenaeus and Justin the Martyr, ultimately got its conceptual input from the metaphysics of Plato.[115] Agamben now goes on to show how this deep-rooted theological legacy eventually finds a path into the post-Enlightenment critique of religion and western subjectivity.

Young Hegel regarded the historical element of Christianity, its so-called "positivity" (*Positivität* [another derivative from Latin *pono*]), as that which keeps obfuscating the purity of reason until the abstract character of reason is dialectically reconciled with the concrete aspects of life (Agamben 2009, 4–5).[116] The apparatus thus implies a state of captivation that, since it simultaneously restricts and preconditions human knowledge, installs the curse and blessing of the human condition. Without such artificial preconditions, there can be neither insight nor delusion. It is not the apparatus as such, however, but rather the accumulation of dispositors in the current phase of capitalism that worries Agamben:

> Rather than the proclaimed end of history, we are, in fact, witnessing the incessant though aimless motion of this *machine* (*machina*), which, in a sort of colossal parody of theological *oikonomia*, has assumed the legacy of the providential governance of the world; yet instead of redeeming the world, this machine (true to the original vocation of Providence) is leading us to catastrophe. (Agamben 2009, 23–24)

If we are to proceed in this fashion of critical inquiry initiated by Foucault and some of his compatriots during the 1960s and 70s, it is necessary to consider another concept that brings the force of the apparatus into a state of opposition: indeterminacy. While the singular apparatus has the capacity to direct and stabilize certain aspects of human knowledge and behavior, the multitude of conflicting

---

115 A telling case is Justin's *Dialogue with Trypho* (supposedly composed around 155 CE) which draws extensively on Platonic metaphysics.

116 Agamben refers to Jean Hyppolite's interpretation of Hegel's idea of positivity in *Introduction à la philosophie de l'histoire de Hegel* (1968) which seems to underlie Foucault's use of the terms *positivité* and *dispositif.* Hegel advanced his concept in an early work entitled *Die Poistivität der Christlischen Religion* (1795).

apparatuses inevitably causes instability of meaning and knowledge.[117] The indeterminacy of meaning is an unrequested source of confusion to the same extent as the captivating force of the apparatus that seeks to invalidate it.

Although irresistible to a certain degree, this conclusion presents us with a paradox. The critical examination of apparatuses and indeterminacies presupposes a rational emancipation from certain culturally imposed inhibitors that cannot itself be likewise inhibited. Taken to its extreme, the conclusion may reactivate some of the misconceptions for which it was originally considered a remedy. In so far as the falsely dichotomized concepts of apparatus and indeterminacy are concerned, one such lapse consists in denying human agents the willingness to overlook the limitations of a medium, so that these limitations do not interfere with the acceptance of the premises given by that medium. The other lapse, which needs to be balanced against the former, consists in denying the same agents a willingness to surrender certain choices to an indeterminate response. I refer to such dispositions, elsewhere and above, as the means by which mental rejections (= disbeliefs) and preconceived notions (= judgements) are repeatedly being held in check by human agents as they willingly enter into various pre-arranged states of affair.

Without contesting the assumption that there are apparatuses (such as language or culture) in which humans are to some extent captured, or that fuzzy conceptual boundaries must imply a certain indeterminacy of meaning, we should not allow such inevitable cognitive obstacles to outweigh the deliberate staging and triggering of events and processes – both bounded and boundless, inhibited and disinhibited – as an incessant modality of human culture in general, and of religious participation in particular. This stipulation brings me to the next issue of this chapter, which essentially aims at breaking a conceptual deadlock – between the determinate force of the apparatus on the one hand, and the indeterminate force of truth and reality (in the Platonic sense of *aporía*) on the other – by reconsidering testimonies to the general practice of divination (Cicero and Plutarch) and oracular consultations (Pausanias) in the Roman-Hellenistic world.

117 Two familiar cases of purported indeterminacy are the term *phármakon* in Jacques Derrida's essay *La pharmacie de Platon* (1968), and the concept of insanity in Foucault's early writings on the history of madness and the clinic (roughly between 1954 and 1963).

6.2

In one of the most extensive philosophical treatises on the subject still extant, Cicero emphatically calls in question the utility and rational basis for those various methods of divinely inspired foresight referred to in his time as *vis divinandi.*[118] His arguments are directed against the Stoics, who are said to have been such insistent proponents of divination as to jeopardize the confidence of their most eminent adherents (Cic., *Div.* 1.6.). Cicero approaches his topic through the consistent exercise of doubt and surmise, which leads him to the conclusion that things either happen by chance, and hence cannot be foretold since they must remain uncertain, or they are certain to take place, in which case it would be pointless to know them in advance since they cannot be avoided (*Div.* 1.6). He also ridicules the various methods of divination (such as hepatoscopy or ornithomancy), considering these as being unsuited for the lofty nature of the gods. Why would gods stoop so low as to employ chickens when addressing a mighty state, and why would the gods insist on using such obscure means to communicate instead of stating things clearly (*Div.* 2.24)?

It is important to notice that Cicero's philosophy of doubt did not always amount to a meddling in public affairs. The virtues to which he willingly adhered as a Roman citizen (such as loyalty and justice) required diligence and restraint to the same extent as a successful philosophical investigation. Though himself a member of the so-called augural college, he does not hesitate to refute the doctrine of augury as being scientifically unfounded while still asserting that the practice is doing great service to the state (2.70). The ancestors once believed in it, we do not. He advances a similar argument in an earlier work (*De natura deorum*, 1.3), namely that the gods may lack the power or the will to influence our lives, but the sincerity with which they ought to be worshiped is a precondition for the virtues on which society is founded.

As a result, the suspension of judgement endemic to some of the executive functions of society (such as forensics and science) need not interfere with the momentary suspension of disbelief required of educated citizens in the context of traditional worship. Cicero thus firmly endorses an attitude of pious restraint in the context of worship and divination, yet not in the interest of direct intellectual gain, but rather in the interest of maintaining social virtues from which the arts and sciences may ultimately benefit.

Cicero's scathing critique of divination did not prevent others from revisiting the subject in a more affirmative spirit. While officiating as a priest of Apollo at

---

118 *De divinatione ad M. Brutum.* Henceforth *Div.*

Delphi sometime after 90 CE, Plutarch composed a philosophical treatise apparently designed as an elaborate response to Cicero's *De divinatione.* The Greek title of the treatise, *Perì tôn ekleloipótōn khrēstēríōn* (usually rendered in Latin as *De defectu oraculorum* [*Defect.*]), alludes to the much discussed "eclipse" or "evanescence" (cf. Gr. *ékleipsis* or *amaúrōsis*) of the oracles in the Roman-Hellenistic world (see below 8.1.3). Cicero had framed this topic in the form of rhetorical questions:

> Why are Delphic Oracles [—] not uttered at the present time and have not been for a long time? When pressed at this point their apologists affirm that 'the long flight of time has gradually *dissipated* (*evanuisse*) the virtue of the place whence came the subterranean exhalations which inspired the Pythian priestess to utter oracles.' [—] But what length of time could destroy a divine power? [—] When did the virtue disappear? Was it after men began to be less credulous?
> (2.117, trans. Falconer [s.v. Cic. *Div.*])

In the prelude to his treatise, Plutarch reframes Cicero's questions without making any literal references to the dissipation of subterranean exhalations:[119]

> [W]e see the *evanescence* (*amaúrōsin*) of the oracles here, or rather the total *disappearance* (*ékleipsin*) of all but one or two; but we should deliberate the reason why they have become so utterly weak. What need to speak of others, when in Boeotia, which in former times spoke with many tongues because of its oracles, the oracles have now failed completely, even as if they were streams of flowing water, and a great drought in prophecy has overspread the land?
> (411e, trans. Babbit [s.v. Plu. *Defect.*])

This opening question unfolds into a series of associated problems pursued along the meandering path of playful inquiry. Before examining a particular train of thought in this text more closely, however, it is essential to recall that we are dealing with an apology for an institution that had passed through a long period in decline.[120] Nevertheless, we are also dealing with an apology for notions considered philosophically untenable by Cicero, despite the latter's partial support for religious institutions (such as the augural college) owing to their political expediency. Besides earning a reputation as leading intellectuals in their time, Plutarch and Cicero had much in common. They had both studied philosophy in Athens under

119 Plutarch does indeed touch upon this phenomenon (cf. 437c–d) but prefers to include it among the various (both favorable and unfavorable) forces affecting the soul of the Pythia.
120 Plutarch's participation in restoring and defending the dignity of the oracular site has been the subject of several studies. For references to the relevant literature, see Lincoln 1999, 278.

teachers associated with Middle Platonism (Antiochus of Ascalon in the case of Cicero, and Ammonius of Athens in the case of Plutarch), they were involved in politics, and both occupied prominent religious offices in later life.[121] This being said, how did they differ in their philosophical approach to divination?

Cicero had quoted a Latinized verse from Euripides in order to emphasize the absurdity of the view that the conjectures of a diviner are superior to those of a specialist (say a pilot or a physician).[122] Plutarch responds by tackling what he considers to be the false assumption of the verse (*Defect.* 432c). Is "the best seer" (*mántis d'áristos*) really he who conjectures well? No, the best seer is he who has *noûs* (lit. "sense" or "mind"). Here, the term *noûs* is to be understood in its proper context of Middle Platonism as the ability to grasp the active principle of the universe by means of participating in that principle.

In order to clarify the relation between *noûs* and "presentiment" (*proaísthēsis*), Plutarch continues his line of argument with a simile: that which foretells the future cannot be rational in itself, but must be susceptible to impression *as a tablet without writing.* Just as the unwritten surface of the tablet lacks a sense of its own, the empty soul of the seer must remain "irrational and indeterminate" (*álogon kaì aóriston*). This pseudo-Aristotelean conception of the human soul[123] is fused into a previous treatment of the generation of numbers and the so-called "indeterminate dyad" (*aóristos dyás*), a theoretical anticipation of the algebraic concept of additive identity (e.g., the number zero) first propounded by Aristotle as an elaboration of Platonic metaphysics.[124]

Lamprias, the chief narrator in the dialogue, summarizes the theory as follows:[125]

> [O]f those numbers which come at the very first (I mean the number one and the indeterminate duality), the second, being the element underlying all formlessness and disarrangement, has been called *infinity* (*apeiría*); but the nature of the number one *limits* (*horízousa*) and *arrests* (*katalambánousa*) what is void and irrational and indeterminate in infinity, gives it shape, and renders it in some way *tolerant and receptive of definition* (*katagóreusin* [...] *hypoménon kaì dekhómenon*)

121 Cf. Ziegler 1964 and Plutarch's own biography of Cicero in *Lives* (20).

122 *Bene quí coniciet, vátem hunc perhibebo óptumum* (*Div.* 2.12). The place of the quote (no. 973 in Nauck's *Tragicorum graecorum fragmenta*) in the Euripidean corpus is uncertain.

123 Cf. *de An.*, 430a. Plutarch does not seem to share the Aristotelean notion of the immortality and immateriality of the soul. This denial is consistent with his "daimonological" assertion that even divine souls suffer death and dissolution (cf. *Defect.* 419e–420c). For a general discussion of this complex topic, see Brenk 1977, 112–144.

124 Cf. *Metaph.* 1081a, 1082a12, etc.

125 I chose to highlight a dominant theme in the passage (especially in regard to notions of limit and boundlessness) by italicizing a few terms and formulations.

> [—]. Now these first principles make their appearance at the beginning in connection with number; rather, however, larger amounts are not numbers at all unless the number one, created from the *illimitability of infinity* (*apeirías toû aorístou*), like all forms of matter, cuts off more on one side and less on the other. Then in fact, any of the larger amounts becomes number through being delimited by the number one. But if the number one be done away with, once more the indeterminate duality throws all into confusion, and makes it to be without rhythm, bounds, or measure [—] *For the indeterminate first principle is the creator of the even* (*ésti gàr hē mèn aóriustos arkhê toû artíou dēmiourgòs*), and the better one of the odd. (428 f–429b, trans. Babbit [s.v. Plu. *Defect.*])

So, what does all this have to do with divination? It appears from Lamprias' account that the quality of something indeterminate or undefinable – the strange quality of lacking a quality[126] – can only receive proper shape and expression through some arresting force of reason, design, purpose, and so forth. A similar phenomenon occurs when the horizon creates the sense of a seemingly regular visual boundary on a boundless surface.

In his attempt at redressing divination, Plutarch thus identifies this principle of limitation as a fundamental condition of creativity, exploration, and imagination. Just as when a painter mixes his pigments, causing them to lose their original color, the achievement of creating likeness cannot be reduced to material causes. Still, the generation of new things always proceeds from impure and unmixed matter in conjunction with reason.[127] The same principle applies to the so-called "imaginative and prophetic faculty" (*hē phantastikḕ kaì mantikḕ dýnamis* [438a]). It can be more or less attuned, like a musical instrument, to the divine agency of inspiration.[128] In other words, the prophetic expression is always going to be restricted and preconditioned by the indeterminate materiality of its medium.

In the light of these philosophical ponderings, Plutarch passes on a cautionary tale bringing his essay to a close.[129] Not so long ago, he recalls, one of the residing priestesses at Delphi lost her life. A foreign delegation had arrived to consult the oracle, but when the preparatory sacrificial procedures did not produce the signs of divine consent required to begin the consultation, the officiating priests simply

126 This figure of thought has had a significant impact on artistic and scientific discourse to this day, as exemplified by John Cage's notion of "purpose of purposelessness" (Cage 1961, 267) and John Archibald Wheeler's "law without law" (Wheeler 1983).

127 *Defect.* 436a-b.

128 *Defect.* 437e. Cf. also *De Pythiae oraculis* 404b-c.

129 *Defect.* 438a-c.

enforced these signs in their eagerness to please the delegates.[130] These actions turned out to have an injurious influence on the Pythia during the consultation. She went into the oracular seat unwillingly, behaved like a ship forced by the winds, and the roughness of her voice betrayed the shortcomings of her responses. Finally, she ran out of the temple in a state of agitation. A few days later she was dead.

This cautionary tale defines the critical nexus of the whole treatise. The protection of the well-being of the priestess (as well as the sanctity of the oracular institution) ultimately comes down to the formation of character. It is not by yielding to the excesses of scrutiny or superstition, but rather by developing a sense of care and restraint, that we commit ourselves to the open-mindedness from which imagination and creativity spring. Plutarch's apologetic concern with an institution allowing those "in a *proper state* (*oikeíōs*) to be *affected and undergo change* (*patheîn kaì metabaleîn*)"[131] can even be taken to represent the oracular site as a sort of counter-apparatus. As opposed to the modern clinic, where those in an improper state of affect are restored to a state of determinate sanity, the oracular institution rather promotes the careful staging and framing of unanticipated affects and changes.

It is illuminating to consider how two philosophically trained intellectuals in the Graeco-Roman world could end up expressing such dissentient views on divination. Cicero defended religious customs and institutions *despite their philosophical untenability*, considering them to be potential sources of virtuous behavior. Plutarch, on the other hand, saw religious equanimity as the very seedbed of philosophy and artistic creativity.[132] In his view, the cultivation of reason requires restraint precisely because it requires attention to the unexpected. By thus rethinking the philosophical practice of *epokhḗ* along the lines of a diviner's attention to indeterminate stimuli, he seems to imply that the act of putting oneself in this ecstatic state of mind requires momentary suspension. And yet, Plutarch's religiously reframed version of the philosopher's suspension of judgement should not be confused with the willing exposure to artificially devised wonders at religious sites. Hence, in order to appreciate this latter scenario as a typical instance of suspended disbelief, our final task will be to delve further into the framing and staging of such situations.

130 These procedures usually involved the sprinkling of a sacrificial goat, which was supposed to shiver from the hooves upward. Plutarch describes the priests as nearly drowning the animal before this reaction could be observed.

131 *Defect.* 438d.

132 *Defect.* 408d-e.

6.3

"[N]uminous experience and manipulation may overlap." With this cautious remark, Walter Burkert aims at the elaborate theatrical, and even mechanical, means of imparting oracles in Greek antiquity (Burkert 1985, 115). Although scholarly opinions differ as to the degree of elaboration, there is nothing to contradict Burkert's remark in principle. A case in point is the travelling author Pausanias' (*c.*110–*c.*180 AD) report on a so-called "descent" (*katábâsis*) to the oracle of Trophonius at Lebadeia in Boeotia.[133] Much to the same effect as Herodotus' account of Pisistratus' spectacular return to Athens, the fantastic description has led some scholars to assume that different kinds of machinery were used at the site to enhance the ritual experience.

After a series of preparatory rituals in the vicinity of the oracular site, the visitor is dressed in a linen tunic and has to climb up a hill beyond the grove in order to descend to the oracle. Having reached an artificially constructed chasm in the middle of the foundation, he is offered a narrow ladder on which to climb down into the dark. At the bottom of the chasm he finds a small opening in the structure, thrusts his feet into the hole, tries to get through with his knees, but is suddenly swept away, as if caught by a large and rapid river. After entering the shrine by these peculiar means, he learns about the future through some unspecified visual or auditory medium. He then returns through the same passage with his feet first, is brought by a priest to a place called the "chair of Memory," and is asked to reveal what was experienced in the shrine.

Recent attempts at determining the realism of the description have resulted in incompatible conclusions. Since Pausanias invokes personal experience to corroborate his report, he is either held to be the uninformed victim of mechanical contrivance, or to blend his report with elliptical references to incubated dreams. On the basis of other sources that seem to confirm the practice of dream incubations at the oracle of Trophonius, the things heard or said inside the shrine are even taken by one scholar to ensue exclusively from inner experience (Ogden 2001, 82f.). We are thus led to assume that Pausanias would never lay claim to veracity if he could infer that his marvelous encounter had to some extent been devised by human artifice.

Although dreams or dream incubations are nowhere referred to in the passage, they are still considered by modern scholars to be the more likely source

133 *Description of Greece* (see abbreviations under Paus.) IX xxxix. § 2–xl.

of such an extraordinary experience than any deducible sensory input.[134] As far as I can tell, however, such readings do not exhaust the full potential of Pausanias' testimony. Do we really *have* to presuppose that the author was unknowingly deceived inside the shrine unless he was simply having a dream there? We are never told that his experience was of an exclusively otherworldly nature, nor that it was attained at the cost of considerable risk-taking. The chasm is said *not to be natural* (*ouk autómaton*), but skillfully built in the shape of a baking-oven; the force that sweeps away the inquirer is figuratively said to be *like* (*hôsper*) a mighty river; no one has died in the chasm save for a person who descended in the hope of finding gold; the terrifying experience leaves the client in a state of temporary paralysis, but he is sure to recover with restored senses and the ability to laugh.

By thus ambiguously mixing strains of amazement with that of a safely staged performance, Pausanias' description inverts the logic of Plutarch's cautionary tale about the frenzied Pythia. Whereas the agitation of the Pythia is the result of a ritual failure to safely obey indeterminate processes, the descent to Trophonius may rather result in a safe yet agitating experience on condition that certain mechanical means of contrivance (the limits of the apparatus) are willingly and momentarily being overlooked by the participant.

So, what can be gathered from the conflicting views and reports discussed throughout this chapter?

6.4

In order to overcome a still dominant view that religious actions and dispositions are primarily informed by preconceived beliefs, it is crucial to appreciate the cross-cultural extent to which humans have been prepared to willingly suspend judgement and disbelief. Such cognitive processes do not only foster temporary astonishment and in-group sympathies, but they also induce attentiveness and creativity by holding certain preconceived notions in check. Instead of regarding indeterminacy and the apparatus as deceptive instances of instability and opacity by means of which social institutions can be effectively disclosed, we may productively reinterpret these concepts as focal concerns of social participation.

The pre-arranged processes with which we willingly engage in mental states of suspension cannot effectively deceive us, nor do they coercively expose us to the fortuitous aspects of nature. Rather, they allow us to enter into a state of affairs

134 References to dream incubations are likewise absent from a similar description of a descent to Trophonius in Philostratus' *The Life of Apollonius of Tyana* (9.19).

that has been overtly designed to serve as the temporary substitute for something else. It is a state of voluntary inhibition that can be overlooked and resolved, where indeterminate processes are intentionally triggered, and where the temporary inhabitants are expected to prevent certain assumptions about themselves and their world from being in force.

As I have sought to demonstrate in this chapter, a rhetorical jargon traceable at least back to Plato and Aristotle continues to associate the malfunctions of religion, ritual, and myth with an irrational blindness against which the hard-earned power of rational insight provides the only remedy. This tenacious critique creates a false dichotomy between two ways of being in the world – between the credulous submission to a spectacle, and the persistent practice of its rational disclosure – neither of which persuasively accounts for how religious behavior evolves and continues to thrive, nor for how it is critically overcome. As a counterpoise to this slanted view, I propose a more flexible model of co-existing religiosities in which there is room both for a devotional readiness to resist dogma and misinformed impulses of belief, as well as for an immersion in the marvels of make-believe spectacle. If the former attitude can be linked to a still dominant tradition of scientific inquiry, the latter pertains to the symbolic proclivities holding the very fabric of human culture together.

As we shall see in the following chapter, however, these attitudes sometimes tend to overlap and collapse into one another, leaving behind a detritus of distorted associations. The gradual Christianization of the ancient world is a prime example to that effect. Hence, it is to this towering challenge of historical inquiry that we must now turn.

7 Antinomies of the Cross

7.1

By the late 1st and early 2nd century CE, people in the Graeco-Roman world were beginning to perceive the growing presence of an unprecedented social phenomenon that suggested to some the urgency of an issue to be resolved in a court of law: the so-called "Christian issue" (*causa Christianorum*). Even if Christians would have appeared to an uninformed outsider as the members of a new group dealing in divine matters, they did not fit neatly into any preconceived category. They bore the "seal" (*signaculum*) of baptism like initiates into the mysteries, aspired like philosophers to the salvific gift of truth along the path of a self-chosen *bíos*, and identified elements of sacred revelation in the civic religion of the Jews. Still, they did not form a distinct ethnic group, did not enjoy the dispensational stature of philosophers, and dismissed everything reminiscently Christian in the doctrines and rites of the mysteries as a bland simulacrum.[135]

By whatever means this propensity to simultaneously blend in and defy classification can be considered a key to the eventual imperial success of Christianity, access to such understandings cannot be gained without first considering the anomalies of a related phenomenon: Hellenistic Judaism. As indicated by the very beginning of the Hellenistic period in Theophrastus' remarks on the Jews as a "people of philosophers" (see above, ch. 5) there was an enduring tendency among educated Greeks and Romans to hold Judaism in particularly high esteem. A prime feature of this tendency, the ancient ways of Jewish worship were being retrojected into the imaginary primordium of Greek philosophy.

Restrained ritualism, theology, and theoretical devotion to an inimitable divine being were not ideals based on a real historical prototype. Rather, they represented the symmetrical inverse of what public worship had long been held to be according to a familiar philosophical formula: excessively festive, idolatrous, and quotidian. Hellenized Jews had already begun to creatively instill this idea during the Second Temple period.[136] Yet, it was a notion befitted to develop a sense of urgency with Titus' destruction of the Temple in 70 CE.

135 My characterization of how Christians were identified and identified themselves (including the phrase *causa Christianorum*) is based on Tertullian's *Apologeticus* (*Apol.*) (esp. 1.1., 46.2 f., and 48.14) and *De spectaculis* (esp. 4).

136 A good example is Philo's treatment of the so-called *Therapeutai* in Alexandria in *De vita contemplativa.*

https://doi.org/10.1515/9783110460605-010

In consequence of its acute loss of a sacrificial epicenter, post-Second Temple Judaism sifted into an altered mode of religiosity reflected in the restyling and revaluation of its ancient rites and prayers (Stroumsa 2009, 64). Traits of what had previously distinguished a civic religion in praxis (such as daily blood sacrifices in the Temple) were now accommodated to the ideal of a decentralized spirituality without blood. Jewish religiosity underwent significant changes to compensate for what it *could no longer be*, but in so doing it also became what it was *already destined to become* according to a long-term interplay of mutual expectations (involving Jews and pagans alike) suggestive of a feedback system. Jan Assmann expresses the peculiarity of the situation as follows: "If Titus had not destroyed the Temple, one would have had to close it down" (Assmann 2003, 149 f.).

As a further indication of this gradual change, Second Temple Judaism had already begun to attract small groups of converts among philosophically inclined pagans (so-called "God-fearers") who anachronistically recognized its emergent mode of communitarian spirituality as the epitome of what they imagined to be the noble ways of an ancient priestly lineage (Sachot 1998, 88). By admitting converts (or "proselytes" [*prosḗlytoi*]) instead of adepts or initiates, Judaism did not conform to the regular pattern of a school or sect.[137] Rather, it was held to conceal in its sacred scriptures and behind a ritual form once elevated to the status of a proper *religio iudaica* – a licit form of civic worship under the authority of Rome – what some perceived as the medium of an ancient philosophy (cf. Tert. *Apol.* 21.1, Sachot 1998, 88).

Contrary to this deviant pattern, it was an otherwise characteristic feature of Roman-Hellenistic culture to receive the cult of deities once confined to the civic space of others (such as Egyptian Isis or Persian Mithras) in the converted form of co-existing mystery cults. Initiation into such cults was not the equivalent of a conversion, because it implied participation in a system that had already been (1) fully assimilated ("Hellenized" or "Romanized") and (2) depoliticized by being removed from the public space of licit worship into secret clubs of free association. Even if Judaism ended up likewise decentralized and depoliticized, it had followed an entirely different trajectory. The cult of Jahweh was still closely tied up with the identity of a people, whereas the worship of Isis or Mithras did not turn their devotees into Egyptians or Persians.[138]

It is easy to understand why early Christianity – especially in its new version of a movement separate from traditional Judaism – made the occasional impres-

137 The term "sect" should not be understood here in its modern, and often derogatory sense, but rather in the original sense of the Latin word *secta* (cf. Tertullian's own use of the term below 7.3.2).
138 In the case of the cult of Mithras, it is usually assumed that it transmitted very little (if anything) from its Iranian precedents.

sion of an oddity added to another. If Jewish prohibitions on idolatry could be tolerated as a dispensable affair by Roman authorities, the plain refusal to sacrifice *pro salute Augusti* without prerogative was rather treated as a forensic matter of civil disobedience (Noethlichs 2017, 62). In addition to such discrete expressions of nonconformity, Christians represented themselves on a par with a new "people" by referring to their *ekklēsía* ("congregation") as the all-inclusive organizational basis for a pious way of life complete with its own policies of sexual reproduction, education, and economic cooperation.[139] These traits of social behavior afforded little comparison with the individualized spirituality of the mystery cults (Burkert 1994, 53 f.). Christian responses to the condition of depoliticization did not just involve the practical consequences of being removed from political influence: it was a spiritual concern in itself, anticipated already in the writings of Paul as the preparation for a "citizenship in the heavens" (*políteuma en ouranoîs*) (Phil. 3:20). For those who live as enemies of the cross, Paul asserts:

> Their end is destruction, their god is the belly, and they glory in their shame, with minds set on earthly things.

His corollary resembles the declaration of a municipal charter:

> But our citizenship is in the heavens,[140] and from it we await a Savior, the Lord Jesus Christ, who will change our lowly body to be like his glorious body, by the power which enables him even to subject all things to himself. (Phil. 3:19 – 21)

Within this perception of superterrestrial polity, public space comes to define a hostile (pagan) territory polluted by the blood of animal victims, disfigured by statues of false gods, and jarring with the ungodly spectacles of others. Still, this precarious sense of being-in-the world did not suggest itself to the early servants of Christ out of thin air. The first champions of Greek philosophy had likewise sought perfection in a life at variance with prevailing norms of civic self-understanding. We need to recall, however, that the continuation and relative respectability of philosophy in the Graeco-Roman world depended largely on its gradual development into a private enterprise informed by the Aristotelean notion of contemplative life.

---

139 Another self-definition to account for in this connection is that of the "third race" (*trítos génos*), that is, of Christians as opposed to Jews and pagans (Lieu 2016, 72). It is first attested in the apocryphal *Kerygma Petri*, which probably dates back to the early 2nd century.

140 I follow the English translation of *Philippians* in Nestle-Aland's *Greek-English New Testament* (NT) with the exception of the expression *políteuma en ouranoîs* (Vulg. *municipatus in caelis*), which is rendered here in more accurate cosmological terms (pl. *ouranoí*) according to the suggested translation of *políteuma* in LSJ ("citizen rights, citizenship").

Philosophy had saved itself from the uneasiness in civilization by exchanging mundane concerns of autonomy and reform for individual matters of inner freedom and spiritual transformation (Aubenque 1979, 136–137). Hence, whereas the private pursuit of *theōría* remained a tolerable means of turning *away from the world*, the unchartered social program of Christianity suggested a call for action *against the world.*

As a consequence, Christians began to appear as enemies of Rome (or even of humankind as whole [Tac. *Ann.* 15.44]). Their unwillingness to join the sacrificial spectacle of public worship was at times even reciprocated in the most mischievously spectacular manner: Christians executed on public display in the theatres in an apparent attempt to mockingly expose them to the inversed sacrificial logic of their own teaching and liturgy, not just by having them thrown to the beasts, but also by representing them as wild beasts, or dressing them up as pagan priests and priestesses.[141]

7.1.1

I have sought to outline the essential features of an emergent social force that eventually was to shake the conceptual foundations of a whole world. In his lucid attempt to characterize the political culmination of this groundbreaking change, Guy Stroumsa observes how Christian emperors, from Constantine to Justinian:

> [S]ucceeded in giving Christianity the status and state role that had belonged to civic religion in pagan Rome, (but let us not forget) with the difference that Christianity, even as a state religion, remained a religion founded on personal decision, repentance, and faith – hence founded on the idea of a religious community (Stroumsa 2009, 92–93)

There are at least two important conclusions to be drawn from this general observation. First of all, while imperial Christianity shattered the foundations of the civic religion once seen to occupy its place, the communitarian ideals for which it sought to provide a political framework were likewise bound to a past. Secondly, in consequence of this radical transformation, concepts that had once marked out civic worship in contradistinction to a personal quest for truth and salvation were

---

141 Cf. the descriptions of the public mockery of Christians in Tac. 15.44 (*ut ferarum tergis contecti laniatu canum interirent*, "covered with the skins of beast, they were torn to pieces by dogs") and the dressing up of Christians in priestly clothing in the early 3rd century *Passio SS Perpetuae et Felicitatis.* An indispensable guide to this highly relevant document is Bremmer and Formisano 2012.

being subjected to alterations and dislocations (encryptions, inversions, substitutions, and subversions) so as to foster a wholly new model of religion.

Christianity's self-promotion as a *vera religio* ("true religion" or "religion of truth") implied that a pagan notion of *religio* defined by the "conscientious" (*religiosus*) execution of cultic practices and representations was being replaced by an altogether different notion defined by the faithful adherence to an objective property. Religion thus began to mean what it is often taken to mean today: the synonym of a *creed*, or a "conduct *indicating a belief in* (...) a divine ruling power" (OED). As a result, two domains of cultural practice that previously did not meet – such as proper civic worship on the one hand, and the philosophical acquisition of knowledge on the other – inevitably came to represent interdependent religious concerns.

In what follows, I shall present a set of minor case studies in order to delineate the new model of *vera religio* in its primary phases of development. What particularly interests me regarding this reorientation of piety is its tendency to appropriate and cross-correlate aspects of the pagan cultural heritage that it explicitly claimed to confront and reject. I begin by considering the first decisive step towards such a strategy in Paul's formulation of a uniquely Christian doctrine of faith. Additionally, a pagan testimony to Christian piety in the early 2nd century (Pliny the Younger's letter to Emperor Trajan) is reviewed as a means to demonstrate how the new doctrine of faith manifested itself in living practice.

Secondly, I proceed to consider how Tertullian, a particularly austere recipient of Paul's message in the late 2nd to early 3rd century, critically engages with two inherently distinct expressions of pagan cultural practice: the issue of theatrical entertainment on the one hand, and that of philosophical dress code on the other. Finally, I seek to demonstrate how repercussions of Tertullian's critical concerns can be perceived in the historiographical context of Christian/pagan controversies during the reigns of Constantine and Theodosius I.

7.2

Faith (Gr. *pístis, pisteúō*, Lat. *fides* and *credo*) is widely assumed to constitute a peculiarly Christian – and to an almost equal degree *Pauline* – category. No single term in Greek, Hebrew, or Latin parlance can be safely claimed to capture the Christian usage of *pístis* in its characteristic tendency to weigh out the term's legal connotations of obedience, trust, and fidelity against the propositional claims of philosophy.

Justice and truth are thus neither understood to ensue from law-abidingness (cf. Gal. 2:16, Phil. 3:9) nor from a stepwise progression of intellectual practice.

Rather, it is a term used almost unexceptionally by Paul to denote an act of *faith in Christ* (or the imitation of *Christ's faith* [*pístis Christoû*]), that is, a conversion to the proclamation of the death and resurrection of Jesus, through which everything to be hoped for irrevocably depends on the unmerited favor of God.

It should be noted that this understanding of *pístis* does not sit well with the always devalued senses of *pístis* (an approximate "belief" or "mode of persuasion") as opposed to superior forms of philosophical knowledge (*epistḗmē, lógos*, or *noḗsis*) in the dialectics of Plato and Aristotle. This circumstance presented a challenge to some of the early Christian apologists who sought to defend the superiority of their faith in epistemologically cogent terms.[142]

On closer consideration, however, the ambiguities of Paul's *pístis*-vocabulary do seem to reflect a general tendency in Roman-Hellenistic thought by this period to correlate the notion of faithfulness as an exemplary civic virtue with the philosophical (Platonic) ideal of godlike self-realization (*homoíōsis theôi* [see above, ch. 5]).[143] Another crucial factor to account for in the case of Paul's Jewish outlook is the underlying meaning of *pístis* (Hebrew' *ĕmet* [from the root *'mn* {"firm, reliable, trustworthy"}]) in the biblical context of the Mosaic covenant. Without this context, the renewed faith in a new covenant with God through the "faithfulness of Christ" (*pístis Christôu*) would simply lose its significance.

When Paul combines the three terms *alḗtheia, dikaiosýnē*, and *pístis* in formulations such as "by faith in the truth" (*pístei alētheías* [2Thess. 2:13]) and "righteousness through faith" (*dikaiosýnē* [...] *dià písteōs* [Rom. 3:22]), we need to recall that the Hebrew term*'ĕmet* (literally "steadfastness") is in fact translated by all these terms in the Septuagint. The quality of *'ĕmet* can mutually refer (1) to God's faithfulness, (2) to the truth of God in the spoken realization of his covenant, and (3) to the faithfulness of his people. For those who fail to trust in the faithfulness of God, God's truth becomes their judgement (Torrance 1957). What counts as truth and faith (= "steadfastness") in this connection should thus primarily be understood against the backdrop of a socially realized bond of trust, not so much in the epistemological sense of a propositional attitude.

The formal establishment of a bond of trust (such as swearing an oath) is undeniably true, because it implies the immediate realization of what it means. In other words, a person taking an oath is *de facto* bound by it. Unlike the linguistic realization of an oath, however, a propositional belief can always be disbelieved and eventually proven false. Hence, the ambiguous significance of Paul's *pístis* was apparently related to the means by which this concept could be variously per-

142 A useful overview is found in Lührmann (1992, 756–757).

143 For an in-depth discussion of the topic, see Sierksma-Agteres 2016.

ceived to exploit and conflate such distinct shades of meaning: a mutual bond of trust on the one hand, and an epistemic commitment on the other. While the Pauline concept of faith may resemble a propositional belief in its claim to indiscriminate universality, it remains a concept modelled after the local (civic, ancestral) allegiance to sacred law:

> But now the righteousness of God has been manifested apart from law, although the law and the prophets bear witness to it, the righteousness of God through *faith in Christ/Christ's faith* (*písteōs Iesoû Christoû*) *for all who believe* (*pántas toùs pisteúontas*). For there is no distinction. (Rom. 3:21–23)

Nevertheless, it is obvious that Paul took this peculiar sense of *faithfulness in faithfulness* (as implied by the *pístis Christoû* formulation) to be at odds with the self-chosen ways of wisdom that prevailed in his cultural surroundings. A frequently adduced example is the attack on eloquent wisdom in *First Corinthians* (1:18–31). After introducing his exposition with a quote from the prophet Isaiah ("I will destroy the *wisdom* [*sophía*] of the wise" [*Is.* 29:14]), Paul makes indubitably clear to the Christians in Corinth that his polemic concerns a specifically Greek way of wisdom ("For Jews demand signs and Greeks seek wisdom" [22]).

The fact that Paul avoids the word *philosophía* in this passage should not be taken to mean that his critique was thought to exclude philosophy. After all, the final message is quite univocal, namely that God cannot be known through wisdom (*ouk égnō* [...] *dià tês sophías* [21]), but that God will only share his wisdom with those who faithfully adhere to the apparent "folly" (*mōría*) of his testimony. What seems to be implied here is that the Greek sages and philosophers "seek wisdom" (*sophían zētoûsin*) by falsely assuming God to be an object of inquiry (*zētéō* → *sophía*), whereas the infinite grace and wisdom of God can only be considered imitable through a disposition of unconditional trust in a testimony that cannot be considered wise and graceful by any worldly standards, but rather must appear foolish, weak, and shameful (25–29) (*pisteúō* → *mōría* ← *sophía*).

In faith, God is not an object to be searched for, but a loving agent by whom to be found. God's gift of knowledge thus ensues from the faithful imitation of Christ in his obedience unto death. This line of thought finds its most pointed (possibly pre-Pauline) formulation in the so-called Christ Hymn (Phil. 2:611), according to which Christ is said to have given up his inimitable likeness to God in an act of self-emptying (*heautòn ekénosen*), being born in the likeness of a human being, and eventually short-circuiting the very logic of sacrificial economy by presenting himself as a sacrificial gift of atonement.

In direct conjunction to this passage, Paul asserts that he would rejoice with his fellow Christians at Philippi even if he were to be "poured as a libation upon the sacrificial offering of your faith" (Phil. 2:18). Towards the end of the same letter, he picks up the thread again by expounding on his own readiness to lose all in order to know Christ, in order that he may gain Christ and "be found in him" (*heurethô* [*heurískō*] *en autô*):

> [N]ot having a righteousness of my own [...], but that which depends on faith; that I may know (*gnônai*) him and the power of his resurrection, and may share his sufferings, becoming like him in his death, that if possible I may attain the resurrection from death.
> (Phil 3:9–10)

Paul's understanding of knowledge through faith brings the ancient ideal of imitation to its most extreme conclusion: devotion to a life in faith, on which supreme knowledge depends, ultimately implies the preparation for a sacrificial *becoming like* (*symmorphízomai*) Christ in his death and resurrection. In order to recognize the full implications of this ideal in living practice, it is illuminating to consider a familiar case of pagan intervention in Christian piety during the early 2nd century BC, some half century after the death of Paul.

7.2.1

Pliny the Younger's letter to Emperor Trajan (*Ep.* 10.96) was composed in the province of Bithynia-Pontus on the south coast of the Black Sea, where Pliny served as a governor between the years 111 and 113. It is widely recognized as being the earliest firsthand pagan testimony to organized Christianity in the Roman Empire.[144] Apart from the general pertinence of this document as a source of pagan reactions to early Christianity, however, it offers a particularly striking example of conflicting (forensic vs. spiritual) interests of knowledge. I am referring to the dialectical opposition between Pliny's action as a public official and the Christian practice of faith.

A chief concern throughout Pliny's letter is that of gaining knowledge. It is a concern implied, in a general sense, by the very fact that Pliny turns to the emperor for advice. He subserviently claims to have made it his habit to consult the em-

---

144 Two other pagan sources from the early 2nd century, namely Tacitus' *Annales* (1.44) and Suetonius' *De vita Caesarum*, confirm that some familiarity with Christian sectarianism already prevailed among Roman officials and intellectuals by this period. Unlike Pliny's firsthand testimony, however, Tacitus and Suetonius (*Nero* 16.2) only refer to Christians (*Christiani* [Suet.], *Chrestianos* [Tac.]) in retrospect to their persecution by Nero in the wake of Great Fire of Rome in the year 64. For further discussion, see Bremmer and Van der Lans 2017 and Bremmer 2021.

peror on all matters of incertitude, *for who is better suited to straighten out his doubts and inform his ignorance.* Pliny *does not know* what the usual penalties passed upon Christians might be, because he has never been present at a legal examination. His crucial question rather seems to be whether Christians should be examined *only* on the basis of the (unspoken) crimes – possibly abominations such as incest and ritual infanticide – of which they are accused, or if the mere fact of calling oneself a Christian should count as a crime in itself. If so, should the criminal pronunciation of this self-referential "mere name" (*nomen ipsum*) be considered irreversibly punishable, or can it be recanted?

Pliny then proceeds to outline the heuristic technique – his own preliminary "method" (*modus*) – that he has adopted so far. He asks the suspects brought before him if they are Christians. If they answer yes, he warns them of the penalties that this self-identification entails. Those who then willingly deny that they are Christians are asked to curse the name of Christ and perform an offering with incense and wine before the emperor's image. Upon doing this, they are immediately acquitted. If they should persist in answering yes to the same question three times, however, he sends them off to prison (or to Rome, in case they are Roman citizens).

Pliny draws a preliminary legal conclusion from this simple trial, namely that the pertinacity and inflexible obstinacy that the trial seeks to decide is its own cause for punishment. His additional assertion (or, if you will, *epistemic commitment*) as to the identification of "true Christians" (*veri Christiani*) is that the suspects who willingly curse the name of Christ cannot be Christians, whereas those who persist in refusing to do so in fact must be. They cannot be forced to curse Christ, because their self-identification as a group is held together by the commitment to an oath. Pliny finds support for this assertion in the testimonies of renegade Christians, who all confess to the previous minor error of having recited a hymn to Christ (as though he were a god) and then sworn an oath never to commit theft, robbery, adultery, or to "break faith" (*fidem fallerent*). Interestingly, this is the only occurrence of the term *fides* in the letter.

In summary, Pliny's main cause for worry in the face of *true* Christians is a dispositional quality (Pauline *pístis*) effectively reversing the epistemic concerns behind his own forensic means of establishing guilt. While he seeks to validate information in an evidential spirit of doubt and surmise, Christian piety is grounded in the fact of having sworn an oath that mutually mimics and invalidates his own allegiance to the emperor. Pliny no doubt understood what it meant to be bound by a sacred oath. As a subservient Roman citizen, he would have recognized a similar sense of commitment in the performance of ancestral rites. It is an attitude that finds explicit expression elsewhere in his letters to Trajan on the fixed date of the so-called *vota publica* (January 3, 112 and 113 CE [*Ep.* 10.35–36, 100–101]), in which the governor informs the emperor that he has summoned the troops and provincials in order to conduct the ritual renewal of vows. They have all, he asserts, prayed to the gods that they may preserve the State, and to the divine emperor in his obedience to Heaven; whereupon the emperor replies in an equally formulaic fashion that he has gladly received confirmation of these vows undertaken to the gods for his health and safety.

One cannot help noticing a strong resemblance between this system of public allegiance to the emperor's own obedience to Heaven, and the Christian system of faith implicit in the *pístis Christoû* formulation (see above). What Pliny and Trajan would have recognized in their mutual adherence to *religio romana*, however, was not something even remotely similar to a Pauline notion of truth and salvation. Roman religion was not grounded in some metaphysical postulate considered prior or superior to the political community in which it functioned (Ando 2008, 84). Hence, a sudden slip into the private domain of intellectual inquiry would have meant the temporary suspension of one's public authority.

Perhaps this is precisely the situation in which we are to imagine another public official at the moment when he, according to the Gospel of John (18:37–38), decides to interrupt his trial of Jesus. In his unanswered response to the man who has just claimed to have come into the world as a witness to the truth, Pontius Pilate seemingly slips into a state of philosophical brooding unbound by the formal strictures of a proper trial: "What is truth?" (*Tí estin alḗtheia?*). Pilate's subsequent declaration of the guiltlessness of Jesus ("I find no fault in him") can thus be taken to reflect an imperial policy that does not – at least not as of yet – seek to meddle in such open-ended queries.

7.3

"But Christians alone are prohibited from saying anything to clear their case, *to defend the truth* (*veritatem defendat*), in order to prevent making the judge appear unjust." A near century after the events in Bithynia-Pontus just touched upon, Tertullian begins his *Apology* (*Apologeticus* [*Apol.* {2.3–9}]) by picking up the thread of Pliny's letter to Trajan. The newly converted native of Carthage skillfully delivers his mocking critique of the Roman judicial system in the form of a forensic treatise. Here, Pliny's consultation with Trajan (*Ep.* 10.96–97) performs the function of a statement of the case to be treated (the so-called *narratio*) (Corke-Webster 2017). It suggests to Tertullian an inversion of the principles of truth and justice on which every good Roman citizen ought to rely. Christians are condemned without being hunted down, acquitted when made to deny, and falsely charged with the kinds of crimes and delusions – incest, the spilling of innocent blood, animal worship, etc., – that typically reflect the rites and mythological imagination of their pagan accusers.

Notorious for his misogyny and enthusiasm for martyrdom, Tertullian (*c.*155–after 220) is often viewed as an extremist. His fideistic approach to the truth of the Gospel stands out starkly against the Platonic predilections of his contemporaries Clement of Alexandria (*c.*150–*c.*215) and Origen (*c.*184–*c.*253). Another idiosyncrasy making Tertullian appear less representative as an ecclesiastical writer is his sympathy for the charismatic teachings of Montanus, which eventually turned him into an apostate of the orthodox Church, thus ineligible for the future recognition as a saint.

Nevertheless, Tertullian's response to the original message of Paul is equally indicative of a period in which no ecumenical councils had yet been called, no canon established, no ecumenical creeds adopted. He was also the first Christian writer to positively explore the pagan concept of *religio*, thus making him a key figure in preparing the entry of Christianity into the institutional category of *civitas romana.* More incisive for the purpose of the current discussion, however, Tertullian never hesitated to reframe his full-scale critique of pagan culture in a familiar philosophical idiom.

7.3.1

Above a world at once torn between the theatricality of civic life and the otherworldly aspirations of theoretical reason, Tertullian now seems to look down from the superior vantage point of faith. Hence, the story of the stargazer's plummet (see above, ch. 5) cannot afford being restored to the original purport of Aesop's fable, but rather has to be carried ahead of its purport in Plato's revisionist rendering:

> *Merito ergo Milesius Thales, dum totum caelum examinat et ambulat oculis, in puteum cecidit turpiter, multum inrisus Aegyptio illi: "in terra," inquit, "nihil perspiciens caelum tibi speculandum existimas?" Itaque casus eius per figuram philosophos notat, scilicet eos, qui stupidam exerceant curiositatem, in res naturae quam prius in artificem eius et praesidem, in uacuum dum habituros.* (Nat. 2.4.18–19)

> It consequently served Thales of Miletus well when he, having walked around examining the whole sky with his eyes, shamefully fell into a well. An Egyptian greatly mocked him: "Is it because you perceived nothing on earth that you now think you should explore the sky?" His fall can be used to figuratively describe the philosophers, that is, those who engage in stupid curiosity, vainly pondering the things of nature rather than the craftsman who preside over them.

In Tertullian's version, Thales is no longer being laughed at *from below* by an uneducated Thracian maid, but *from above* by an Egyptian, that is, by someone bound to an ancient tradition of wisdom in which Thales has only just begun to dabble (Blumenberg 1987, 49–51). It is thus not because of his failure to serve the common good that Thales becomes the object of scorn, but because of his trust in the arbitrary achievements of human reason. The Egyptian seems to know better. On account of his access to the deeper secrets of ancient lore, he understands that there is an intellectual limit to what the superintendent of nature is willing to reveal.

Tertullian's evocation of the philosopher's *stupida curiositas* creates a link in the tradition connecting Paul's notion of the philosopher's *inquiry* (*zḗtēsis*) (cf. 1Cor. 1:18–31 [see above]) and Augustine's notion of *curiositas.* It was not least through the latter's inclusion of this notion in his catalogue of vices (where it is also referred to as "lust of the eyes" [*concupiscentia ocolorum* {*Conf.* 10.35}]) that the intellectual leeway of Christian learning in the West would end up so restrained.

Additionally, since pagan philosophy essentially amounts to a form of ocular self-indulgence, it cannot be unaffected by the allurements of civic spectacle from which the theatrical metaphors of philosophy ultimately derive (*theōría, theṓrēma*, etc.). Tertullian is thus not willing to grant the speculating philosopher any moral or epistemological advantages over the crowd at a public spectacle. To those who seek pleasure instead of relying on faith and the simplicities of truth, God remains equally hidden. Still, the potentiality of theatrical metaphors is far from exhausted.

Ironically, Tertullian dedicated an entire treatise to pagan theatrical culture (*De spectaculis* [*Spect.*] [*c.*197–*c.*202]) in which his disdain for the artful means by which to agitate the mind and pervert the truth (*Spect.* 1; 15) conveys an unmistakable Platonic ring. The philosopher's original dissatisfaction with the mimetic arts is even echoed in what Tertullian takes to be the overarching fault of the spectacle: idolatry. Behind all its manifestations and legacies – whether it be athletic games, the circus, or tragic drama – he uncovers the same pomp of the devil, the same unworthy prototypes, the same lust of the eyes.

As far as idolatry goes, however, Tertullian's discourse is not designed to accurately represent the motivations behind pagan worship. One rather gets the impression that the only true idol involved in the anti-pagan rhetoric is the argumentative strawman. It seems to have taken an idolater's exaggerated folly to counterbalance the insistence on God's unity and inimitability. More specifically so, of course, against the biblical backdrop of God's making of man in the image (*kat' eikóna*) of God (Gen. 1:27, *Spect.* II) to which Christians are now able to add the crucial dictum that God has perfected this creative principle by being born in the likeness of man. What, then, could be more offensive to this humble act of divine intervention than the human forging of false gods in human form? Not only does this fraudulent act belie the unity and inimitability of God, but it also proudly attempts to reverse the principle of creation through which God has revealed himself to mankind.

Just as the sites of the spectacle are considered to form a continuity with pagan temples and *telestḗria*, so both the civic and private domains of the city in its entirety – the streets, the baths, the taverns, the residential buildings – can be taken to form a giant site of pagan worship ("the whole world is filled with Satan and his angels" [8]). Contrary to what certain God-fearers in his time may have argued, Tertullian is not even willing to derive temporary enjoyment from the spectacle *in its proper time and place* (*suo in tempore et suo in loco* [1]). A mindful commitment to *true religion* (*vera religio* [1]) does not square with any worldly pleasures, not even with the philosopher's tranquility of mind, because it relies solely on the promise of redemption in a world to come (28).[145]

Hence, the greatest pleasure is disdain for pleasure (29). This is the final, oxymoronic point in the line of argument at which the theatrical imagery is brought to its antithetical climax. In implicit response to the natural philosopher's metaphorical spectacle of truth, Tertullian's *spectaculum in proxime* (the "spectacle to come") conveys the hidden truth of the old metaphor in its apocalyptic sense of final revelation (30). He refers to the so-called Parousia, or the Second Coming of Jesus. What a wide-ranging spectacle on that eternal Day of Judgement, he exclaims, when the old world is devoured by fire! What a joy on that day when the kings and magistrates, sages and poets, actors and athletes – all those who raged against Christians, who excelled in erroneous doctrine, who brought shame on themselves in the theatres – will meet their torturous end in hell! No patron could ever provide funds for such sights. These are the unsponsored, unconceivable things realized (or "cashed in" [*repraesentata*]) only "through faith in the imagination of the spirit" (*per fidem spiritu imaginante*) [30]).[146]

---

145 Tertullian substantiates his claim with an explicit reference to Paul's desire "to depart and be with Christ" (Phil. 1:23): What else is our prayer *but to depart from life (in this world) and be brought back before the Lord* (*exire de saeculo et recipi apud dominum*) (XXVIII).

146 The obvious reference here is 1Cor. 2:9–10 ("What no eye has seen, what no ear has heard, and what no human mind has conceived – the things God has prepared for those who love him – these are the things God has revealed to us by his Spirit.").

7.3.2

Tertullian's engagement in a pagan legacy from which he simultaneously took his cue and dissociated himself – including civic institutions (*religio*), philosophical concepts (*substantia*[147] [Gr. *ousía, hypóstasis*]), reframed anecdotes (Thales' plummet), and extended metaphors (the universe as a "spectacle" free of charge) – was not limited to spoken discourse alone. He was also aware of how his visual appearance as an orator participated in this double-edged rhetoric. The theme is set out in an enigmatic treatise ("On the mantle" [*De pallio* {*Pall.*}]) occasioned by the fact that the author had begun to appear in the typical outfit of a philosopher (a wrapped rectangular mantle referred to as *pallium* [Gr. *himátion*]), and not in the clothes expected to be worn by a male Roman citizen at the time: the toga. If we assume that the text was composed for oral delivery (sometime by the end of the 2nd or beginning of the 3rd century), we must also assume that Tertullian sought to effectuate the gist of his speech by actually wearing a *pallium* as he spoke. Such a strategy probably involved a great deal of risk-taking in a milieu still dominated by pagan customs and policies.

Originally the quintessential token of a Greek philosopher, the *pallium* had gradually come to signify the cosmopolitan identity of intellectuals in general. It was not least through literary and artistic depictions of Socrates – his reported style of wearing a simple, rectangular mantle with worn-out edges (a so-called *tríbōn*), and without a tunic underneath – that this tenacious intellectual fashion had established itself throughout the Roman-Hellenistic world as the unifying token of virtue and austerity.[148] Now, Tertullian seems to base his revisionist argument *pro pallio* on three main qualities that positively characterize the practical and symbolic aspects of the philosopher's cloak: (1) it is a garment easy to wear, with or without shoes, and without procedure; (2) it grants freedom from the vices and restrictions of public life; (3) it symbolizes access to all realms of knowledge.[149]

---

147 The technical vocabulary employed in the Trinitarian expositions of the western Church is usually considered to have been coined by Tertullian. Although the doctrine never boils down to a single formulaic statement in his extant writings (e.g., along the line of *una substantia in tribus personis* [e.g., John Scotus Eriugena, *Periphyseon* 2.599 A]), it is clearly implied in formulations like *ubique teneo unam substantiam in tribus cohaerentibus* ("I always insist on one substance united in three (persons)" (*Adv. Prax.* 12).

148 For a summary treatment of philosophical fashion in Late Antiquity, see Arthur Urbano (2017). The broader topic of the visual appearance of intellectuals in Antiquity is treated at length in Paul Zanker's *The Mask of Socrates: The Image of the Intellectual in Antiquity* (Zanker 1996).

149 Cf. Marie Turcan's enumeration of the three symbolic qualities of the *palium* (as implied by Tertullian) in the introduction to *Pall.*, 39.

The first point makes a rather simple, practical argument. If the *pallium* is in fact more comfortable than the toga, then why insist on wearing the toga? The two following points are less clear-cut, for if the philosopher's cloak was already associated with pagan values, then why should a Christian insist on wearing it? Apparently because the most efficacious strategy of subverting pagan intellectual culture – its claims to knowledge, tradition, authority, and piety – was thought to consist in keeping its ancient signifiers intact while investing its signified foundational values with new meaning (Urbano 2017).

Tertullian's despise for pagan philosophy is ubiquitous. His negative reply to the famous rhetorical question "What has Athens to do with Jerusalem?" (*Quid ergo Athenis et Hierosolymis?* [*Praes. Haer.* 7]) is phrased in words that seem almost humorously to mimic those of a fanatic:

> *Nobis curiositate opus non est post Christum Iesum nec inquisitione post euangelicum. Cum credimus, nihil desideramus ultra credere. Hoc enim prius credimus non esse quod ultra credere debeamus.*
>
> We have no need for curiosity after Christ Jesus, nor for inquiry after the gospel. Now that we believe, we do not desire to believe anything else, for the primacy of our faith is that there is nothing else that we are bound to believe.

The rift between the two positions could hardly appear more definite. Still, we need to consider that the group to which Tertullian belonged was not always identified by his contemporaries in the terms that he would have preferred, that is, as a "divine sect" (*divina secta* [*Pall.* 6.2 {cf. *Apol.* 46.2}]), but rather as a "kind of philosophy" (*philosophiae genus*) (*Apol.* 46.2). He cannot accept this comparison as long as philosophers are granted privileges and dispensations for engaging in the things that bring Christians to trial: refusing to sacrifice or to take an oath, raging against the emperors, desecrating the gods. Some (the "Epicuruses and Zeno's") are even celebrated for their qualification of "wisdom" (*sapientia*) as a pleasurable end in itself (*Pall.* 5.4). It is thus rather in an attempt to appropriate the claims of pagan intellectuals, combining their pretensions to wisdom with an equestrian appeal to courageousness and duty, that Christian men are supposed to make themselves heard and seen in public. A new male identity was in the making, characterized by its capacity to unite, in one and the same appearance, a capable citizen and a teacher of true wisdom.

Towards the end of his speech, Tertullian introduces a forceful metaphor, the perplexing implications of which deserve to be examined in closer detail. Except for the final four sentences, the text marks the end of a discourse (beginning at V. 4) designed to render the *pallium* a voice of its own (hence the closing quotation marks):

> *Viderit nunc philosophia quid prosit; nec enim sola mecum est. Habeo et alias artes in publico utiles. De meo uestiuntur et primus informator litterarum et primus enodatur uocis et primus numerorum harenarius et Grammaticus et rhetor et sophista et medicus et poeta et qui musicam pulsat et qui stellarum coniecat et qui uolaticam spectat. Omnis liberalitas studiorum quator meis angulis tegitur. Plane post Romanos equites. Verum et eccendones et omnis gladiatorum ignominia togata producitur. Haec nimirum indignatis erit 'a toga ad pallium'!"*
> *Sed ista pallium loquitur. At ego iam illi etiam diuinae sectae ac disciplinae commercium confer. Gaude, pallium, et exulta: melior iam te philosophia dignata est, ex quo Christianum uestire coepisti.*

> Now let philosophy see of what use it is. For with me she is not the only one; I have other arts that are of public benefit! I dress the first teacher of letters, the first unraveller of the voice, the first sandman of numbers, the grammarian, the rhetor, the sophist, the medic, the poet, the maker of music, the observer of what is starred, the watcher of what is winged. All liberality of arts *is covered by my four tips.* These stand below the Roman knights certainly. But take all ignominy of the master of fighting and the gladiators: they perform in toga! This then, surely, will be the outrage in the maxim 'from toga to pallium'!"
> But these are the words of the pallium. I will go further and also grant it communication with that divine sect and discipline! Rejoice, pallium, end exult! A better philosophy has deigned you worthy, from the moment that it is the Christian whom you started to dress.
> (VI. 1–2, mod. trans. Vincent Hunink [s.v. Tert. *Pall.*], my italics)

Tertullian has just asserted that the many faults of pagan philosophy – conceived allegorically here as a female personification – were at least not aggravated by her choice of modest clothing. Rather, it has been a great benefit of the *pallium* to make "bad morals blush with shame" (*improbi mores* [...] *erubescunt*) at the very thought of wearing it. Furthermore, this simple piece of clothing does not just cover philosophy proper. All the techniques of artistic performance and scientific interpretation to which philosophy extends its influence are said to be "covered" (*tegitur*) within its four corners: from oratory, poetry, and music to medicine, astronomy, and augury. Hence, the new version of the *pallium* provides a covert pretext for what it no longer overtly signifies.

One may speculate that this seemingly unimportant detail in an obscure speech by Tertullian was in fact the very prototype of a metaphor that would only develop its full scholarly potential a millennium later. I am referring to the conceptual device of *integumentum* ("covering" or "wrapping" ([*in* + *tego*]) with which an otherwise rejected part of the pagan heritage was continuously exploited in learned discourse throughout the Middle Ages. The tendency is particularly notable in the works of scholars associated with the twelfth-century Renaissance, such as William of Conches (1080–1145) and Bernard Silvestris (*c.*1085–*c.*1178). It was not least through the influence of Macrobius' fifth-century CE commentary on Cicero's *Dream of Scipio* that these scholars sought to advance a positive evaluation of pagan myth as the tool by means of which to decipher the secrets of nature (cf. Hadot 2004, 113–115). Both the ancient myths themselves and the secrets supposed to be concealed beneath the surface of fabled narrative were referred to as *integumenta* (Dronke 1974, 25). Since a similar tendency can be discerned already behind Augustine's positive appropriation of similar rhetorical concepts (e.g., that of *involucrum*), it would not be entirely far-fetched to associate Tertullian with this tradition as well. Perhaps he was even its initiator.

The symbolic act of donning the pagan philosopher's mantle thus comes to involve more than just a means of challenging pagan authority. Rather, it is an early example of what will eventually turn out as a dominant strategy among Christian authorities in dealing with pagan culture, namely that of exploiting it as a potential resource of power and knowledge through acts of encryption. Philosophy and its auxiliaries should perhaps not so much be considered the targets of eradication that the fierce Christian rhetoric may seem to imply. Instead, the pagan heritage is transformed and disguised under a familiar "covering" that simultaneously represents and disqualifies what it once stood for. It should thus not come as a surprise that Tertullian's strategic choice of clothing by the turn of the 2nd century anticipates a tendency to represent Jesus of Nazareth in the clothes of a philosopher.

A good example is the early fourth-century depiction of Jesus healing a bleeding woman (one of the miracles described in the synoptic Gospels [Matt. 9:20–22, Mark 5:25–34, Luke 8:43–48]) found among the frescoes in the Catacombs of Marcellinus and Peter in Rome (fig. 3). Contrary to the iconographic standard that was to develop in the Byzantine Empire during the 6th century, Jesus is depicted here barefoot, clean-shaven, and short-haired. He stretches his right hand with fingers splayed towards a kneeling woman, who reciprocates his wonder-working gesture by touching a piece of his clothing with her right hand. He carries a tunic underneath and a *pallium*, simply wrapped around his body and held fixed with his left hand. This is not the clothing of a working man, nor that of a public dignitary: it is the easily recognizable attire of a philosopher.

7.4

It might seem unjustly disproportionate to attach such weight to an idiosyncratic figure like Tertullian in an attempt to encompass three centuries of nascent Christianity. His extreme views on pagan learning and morality cannot be held to represent a mainstream in his own time, nor were they single-handedly selected to define the program of imperial Christianity in the 4th century. Nevertheless, he did play a decisive role in preparing for the semantic reversal and substitution that facilitated the founding of a new state religion – the true religion of the true God – on the doctrinal content of faith (Sachot 1998, 188). Behind Tertullian's

Figure 3: Jesus in philosopher's attire healing a bleeding woman. Early fourth-century fresco from the Catacombs of Marcellinus and Peter, Rome (from Grabar 1967).

full-scale critique of pagan thought and practice one perceives a general (and perhaps generalizable) discontent with a cultural environment in which things divine

– those rendered civic or cultic on the one hand, and epistemic or salvific on the other – were subsumed under different categories, appreciated and approached through the assumption of two largely complementary dispositions of mind.

At the risk of appearing grossly anachronistic, one way of imagining the harmonious coexistence of such mental dispositions would be to consider the shifts between two distinct domains of contemporary cultural practice – say, just to make sure the examples are already a bit outdated, an IMAX 3D screening and an experiment in quantum interference – respectively held in sway by the willing suspension disbelief and the suspension of judgement. As suggested by the examples discussed in the previous chapter, we have no reason to assume that people in the ancient world were unable to adopt such shifting attitudes depending on the changing circumstances. Whatever visual or narrative representations of gods and heroes that participants at a public festival encountered in an effervescent state of suspended disbelief, they are likely to have held these distinct from the divine reality encountered by a sceptic philosopher in an ataraxic state of suspended judgement (*epokhḗ*).

Even to the extent that ancestral cults and the traditional topics of myth had stimulated advanced artistic and intellectual elaborations, they had not primarily served such ends in their capacity as tenets of faith or philosophical persuasion. With the gradual influx of Christian thought and practice into public affairs from the 4th century onwards, however, a new attitude to divine affairs was brought into the bargain: that of faithfully inviting God into one's life. This new attitude is brought to bear upon virtually all aspects of pagan culture without resulting in their complete cancellation. It can be understood (to borrow Stroumsa's biological metaphor [Stroumsa 2009, xv]) as a sort of mutation, resulting in an alteration of the program controlling the structure of that culture.

It is with this process of transformation in mind that we are best equipped to appreciate the two anecdotal examples bringing this chapter to a close. The first concerns popular responses to the disputes of Christian prelates during the reign of Constantine, and the second a passing remark in an account of the events that unfolded in Alexandria shortly before the destruction of the Serapeum in 391 CE.

7.4.1

The first ecumenical council of Nicea (convened in the year 325) is commonly recognized as the first attempt to officially encode and rectify the heretofore dissentient doctrines of Christianity under the auspices of a Roman emperor. Its prime triggering factor was an encyclical issued by Alexander, the patriarch of Alexandria, in which the non-trinitarian teachings of Arius were denounced as heretical. Before his excommunication, Arius was a presbyter under Alexander's jurisdiction who had begun to attract a following by expounding on the scriptural characterization of Christ as the "only begotten" (*monogenê* [John 3:16]) son of God. If Christ was indeed *begotten*, Arius opined, he could not have existed forever, and hence could not be consubstantial with God. Rather, he must have been created out of nothing *by* and *subsequent* to God.

According to Socrates Scholasticus' (Soc.) account of the controversy, it was Alexander himself who had accidentally prompted Arius to develop this heretical doctrine. As Alexander had once addressed the presbytery in an attempt to explain the mystery of the Holy Trinity – with *excessive philosophical zealousness* (*philotimóteron* [...] *philosophôn* [*HE* 1.5.1]) – Arius had demonstrated considerable logical acumen in presenting the views of the patriarch as similar to the reputed Monarchian teachings of the third-century theologian Sabellius. Although we cannot reconstruct the details of the argument, it must be assumed that Alexander knew full well that there was no such thing as a systematic exposition of the Holy Trinity in the earliest Christian writings, let alone in the letters of Paul. Hence, we may speculate that Arius' clever response to Alexander's untenable exposition of that doctrine aroused the latter's fear of having invited too much philosophical nitpicking into the sacred confines of faith.

While Alexander's encyclical contains a great deal of scripturally grounded reasoning to prove Arius wrong, the letter also cautions against attacking heretical teachings in public so as to propagate them and attract undue attention to their delusiveness. These fears were in fact fully justified, for as it turns out some of the bishops and other prelates did not side with Alexander at all, but rather began to quarrel with those who did (Eus. *VC* 2.61.4; Soc. *HE* 1.6.35). What began as a disagreement about doctrinal minutiae in Alexandria became the spark that ignited a fire that was soon to spread erratically all over Egypt and Libya. The affair finally reached such a level of absurdity that Christianity was being subjected to *shameful mockery even in the theatres of the unbelievers* (*en autoîs* [...] *toîs apístōn theáthtrois* [...] *aiskhístēn khléuēn*) (*VC* 2.61.5; cf. also Soc. *HE* 1.6.35). A few additional notes on Constantine's reactions to the controversy are in order before we can return to this fascinating datum.

Upon learning that the doctrinal quarrels of ecclesiastical leaders had reached such a level of gravity, Constantine must have felt an urge to intervene in the dispute. It was, after all, due to his benefactions that the Christian congregations were now flourishing as never before. Even if the emperor himself could hardly have had strong opinions about the theological peculiarities of the debate, there is an unintentional irony in the fact that it was a quarrel about the divine properties of distinctness and unity – namely, of Christ remaining forever *consubstantial with* the Father in spite of being *begotten* – that was to cause such a disunity among the bishops. As apparent from his letter to Alexander and Arius (first quoted in Eusebius' [Eus.] [ca. 263–339] unfinished bibliography of Constantine [*VC* 2.64–72]), the emperor's primary concern was not to make the two parties reach full agreement on all matters of exegesis, but to avoid disputes over minor issues that might grow out of proportion, resulting in schism or public blasphemy (2.69.3). It is conceivable that the last remark was in fact occasioned by the mockery in the theatres. Although the emperor chooses to be discrete about the details, the information supplied by Eusebius and later chroniclers give us reason to assume that Constantine was worried that the universal religion now prospering under his tutelage had begun to appear a bit ridiculous:

> On the subject of divine Providence therefore let there be one faith among you, one understanding, one agreement about the Supreme; the precise details about these *minimal disputes* (*elakhíston zētḗseōn*) among yourselves, even if you cannot bring yourselves to a single point of view, ought to remain in the mind, *guarded in the hidden recesses of thought* (*tô tês dianoías aporrḗtō tērýmena*
> (*VC* 2.71.7)

The emperor's epistolary pleadings were not enough to solve the case. It took the far more ambitious effort of a large-scale ecumenical council to do so, resulting in the so-called Nicene Creed and the official banishment of Arius.

The history of dogmatic controversy certainly did not end here, yet the story of its occasional mockery in pagan theatres has remained largely untold. What preliminary conclusions can be drawn from this apparent source of embarrassment? We can only guess at the various angles of comedy, satire, or burlesque by which pagan actors and playwrights explored the no longer hidden recesses of theological thought and quarrel. To be sure, it was not the first time that the studious exercises of detached intellectuals had been ridiculed in the theatres. An early example already touched upon is Aristophanes' depiction of the young Socrates in *Clouds* (cf. ch. 5.3 above). Nevertheless, the case of Socrates occurred in an altogether different context of civic power play. If we are to trust Plato's and Xenophon's more sympathetic portrayals of Socrates (not least in their respective versions of the *Apology*), a characteristic feature of the discerning philosopher was an ironic stance on professional artists and intellectuals who drew on the funds of resourceful citizens. If Socrates had appeared as a queer and irritating figure in his time, this was largely because of his willful disrespect for the political and intellectual establishment of Athens. Contrary to him, the fourth-century prelates did not afford such a comparison once they had come to depend on the worldly power for which they had previously displayed such contempt.

Whereas the public cultic affairs of the pagans – such as the cult of the emperor's *genius* – would rarely have been conceived as matters of intellectual devotion, the otherworldliness of Christian theology had suddenly become a public concern of unexpected political impact. If the antinomian behavior of sages, philosophers, and even Christian preachers had long been recognized as somewhat *out-of-place* (*átopos*), it was now rather the internal disputes of officially recognized ecclesiastical leaders that had begun to appear *spectacularly out-of-place* (*atopías* [...] *théa* [2.61.5]).

A good century had passed since Tertullian raged against the pagan spectacle. Yet, whereas in his days Christians were still being martyred in the circuses as the innocent victims of religious intolerance, Christian prelates in the days of Constantine had come to represent a new religious elite. We need to consider the curious dialectic of theatrical representation that was now approaching its grand finale: (1) Jesus of Nazareth as a figure of mockery in the Gospels; (2) Christians turned into theatrical props in the imperial circuses; (3) the Christians' mockery of pagan theatrical concupiscence; and finally (4) the pagans' theatrical ridicule of quarrelling Christian theologians supported by a Roman emperor representing the same office under whose authority Jesus had once been interrogated, mocked, and sentenced to death.[150] It is a fascinating thought that the last days of pagan theater resounded with laughter at the new spiritual order which eventually was to cancel the performances. The comic effect consisted not just in theologians arguing loudly and dedicatedly over spiritual matters long considered submitted to the quietist parlors of philosophy, but in their doing so under the auspices of a Roman emperor.

7.4.2

Theatrical entertainment is not the only matter of Tertullian's critical concern by the end of the 2nd century to which the forthcoming Christian/pagan controversies during the 4th century add depth and contour. A likewise significant case involves, once again, the visual rhetoric of the philosopher's mantle. The example adduced here to highlight this final point is gathered from the account of an event that likewise occurred in Alexandria nearly seven decades after the ill-fated quarrel between Alexander and Arius. This time, however, the focus of attention is not the

150 Unsurprisingly, Constantine did not seem in the least prepared to put any blame on Roman authorities for the death of Jesus. In his letter to the churches transmitted as a record of the council of Nicea, the Jewish practice of Easter is being denounced as incompatible with the Christian celebration since the Jews are said to have sullied their own hands with a heinous crime, as being bloodstained, and mentally blind (*VC* 3.18.2).

pagan ridicule of debating Christians under the emperor's auspices, but the diametrically opposed case of a disadvantaged pagan community in its exposure to public ridicule by Christians. I am referring to the destruction of the Serapeum in the year 391.

Despite a strong tendency in recent scholarship to downplay the consistency and efficacy of anti-pagan religious policies during the 4th century, there is no denying that the moralizing language of the late antique laws would have played a significant role as pretexts for action. Furthermore, the category of (right vs. wrong) *belief* in legal discourse marks a decisive change of attitude by the end of the 4th century, which must have limited the leeway of pagan communities now officially denounced as being engaged in organized crime under Roman law (Kahlos 2019, 29). My task in this connection is not, however, to reconstruct the details of the skirmished in Alexandria, but rather to focus on a few significant features in the triumphalist Christian representation of Christian/pagan polemics.

Let me begin by briefly outlining the course of events according to one of the testimonies, Sozomen's fifth-century *Historia Ecclesiastica* (*HE*, VII, 15, 2–10): The bishop of Alexandria is said to have been granted permission by the emperor (Theodosius I) to convert a temple of Dionysus into a church. All statues were removed, and the secret objects hidden in the innermost sanctuaries (the so-called *adýta*) *were being exposed* (*anakalyptoménōn*). In order to dispose of the pagan mysteries, the bishop arranged a procession for the public display of the sacred objects, among which were several phalluses. All that was, or appeared to be, *ridiculous* (*katagélastos*) the bishop decided to exhibit for all to see. The pagans were so outraged by this purposefully offensive act that they began to attack the Christians, killing and wounding many of them, and finally taking shelter in the Serapeum (2–3). This vast and beautiful temple complex, constructed during the reign of Ptolemy III Euregetes (*c.*280–*c.*222 BC), also functioned as a site of learning with its own library, incubation sanctuaries, and dormitories for priests. – With the Serapeum as their temporary citadel, the pagans now held Christians hostage, torturing them, forcing them to sacrifice, and crucifying those who refused. Since the local rulers of the prefecture of Alexandria did not succeed in making the pagans give up the Serapeum, they decided to seek advice from the emperor (4–5). – In the meantime, a man among the pagans named Olympius is said to have addressed his co-religionists, in the *appearance of a philosopher* (*en philosóphou skhḗmati*), with an aim to fuel their spirit of resistance. He told them that they ought to die rather than to neglect their ancestral customs. Nevertheless, no matter how discouraged they may have been in seeing their statues purged away, they should not take counsel to renounce their religion on account of that. Whereas the "carved images" (*xoánoi*) *are mere appearances made of perishable matter* (*hýlēn phthartḕn kaì indálmata*), the powers that once dwelt inside them have flown to heaven (6). When the emperor was informed about the events, he decided that all Christians who had been massacred should be given the honor of martyrdom. As a sign of clemency, and in the hope of winning over the pagans to the Christian faith, he also decided to acquit them from all criminal charges. He finally ordered the destruction of the temples considered to have caused the conflict. This last exhortation is said to have made the Christians rejoice, since they took it to imply that the emperor put the major blame for the disturbances on the pagans (7–8). On the night before this public announcement, Olympius is said to have heard someone chanting "hallelujah" inside the Serapeum, which he immediately took as a miraculous sign. He secretly left the sanctuary to embark on a ship for Italy. Finally, when the Christians took possession of the Serapeum and began to demolish the temple, certain stones were found, on which hieroglyphic characters in the form of a cross had been inscribed. These were interpreted by learned men at the site as signifying "life to come" (*zōèn eperkhoménēn*) (9–10).[151] Sozomen closes his report by asserting that many pagans decided to convert upon learning these things, as if suddenly presented with a previously misapprehended piece of evidence, and by stating that the Serapeum was soon converted into a church.

Two details in Sozomen's account stand out as significant markers of a pertinent rhetorical tactic: the dismissal of Olympius as a fake philosopher, and the decoding of the hieroglyphic handle-shaped cross as a latent sign of the true cross. These discrete notices are mutually employed to convey the same underlying message, namely, that the things once falsely claimed by the pagans are now the things reclaimed by the Christians in full assurance of what they truly are. There is an irony in the fact that Olympius is reported to have consoled his fellow pagans by diverting their attention (in good philosophical manner) from the mere "appearances" (*indálmata*) of their carved images, while he is himself claimed to have addressed them "in the appearance" (*en skhḗmati*) of a philosopher. Although the term *skhḗma* could potentially have referred to the simple fact of Olympius appearing in the characteristic "dress" (i.e., a *pallium*) of a philosopher (LSJ, s.v. 4b), there is good evidence in other versions of the same incident to confirm that Sozomen is here reproducing an ironic formula frequently used by Christian writers in their characterizations of pagans.[152] The only "true" philosophers, then, would

151 The hieroglyphic symbol referred to here is apparently the ankh, which could mean "life" in ancient Egyptian, and which was most likely still acknowledged by the priests in the Serapeum as a symbol for the revival of human souls in the afterlife. It is now commonly referred to, not least due to its prevalent use among Coptic Christians, as the *crux ansata*.

152 Cf. Rufinus' *Historia Ecclesiastica* II, 22, according to which Olympius is claimed to have been "a philosopher by mere habit" (*habitu solo filosofum*). For further comments on the matter, see footnote 2 on page 138 f. in the edition by Bidez et al. (see references under Soz.).

have been Christian ascetics. They were the only ones to deserve the signs of not just seeming to be wise.

As can be inferred from a notice in the tenth-century Byzantine encyclopedia commonly referred to as the *Suda* (or *Souda*), Olympius was likely a native of Cilicia who settled in Alexandria to serve as a priest in the cult of Serapis (*O.* 218). A probable member of the Neoplatonic community in Alexandria, he fits well into the image of a pagan intellectual who perceives the religious policies of the Christian empire as a growing threat to his unworldly lifestyle. He was certainly not just pretending to be a philosopher, but the wisdom for which he had declared his love was no longer deemed worthy of love. In Sozomen's retrospect, a pagan's wisdom had to seem just as little worthy of love or attention as those idolatrous games of pretense beyond which a Thales, a Socrates, or an Olympius aspired to discover the uncreated manifestations of truth. What Tertullian had once hoped to achieve by his audacious investment almost two centuries earlier had eventually come to pass.

7.5

Public religion in the ancient pagan world depended largely on a culture of affirmative pretense and participation, whereas the spiritual quest for truth and salvation was typically conceived as a private matter of choice. The ideal lifestyle of Christian piety, on the other hand, can be characterized by its eschewal of a pagan culture premised on the tendency to inconsistently switch between such situational dispositions of mind.[153] From this new perspective of faith, disinclined pagans could be considered equally lead astray in their propensity to (1) participate in the make-believe spectacle of civic religion, and to (2) seek self-fulfillment in an endlessly unfolding spectacle of truth. Neither of these motivations could be fully endorsed by a theology grounded in the unambiguous commitment to the proclamation of the Gospel. It was no doubt in this resolute spirit of faith that Augustine encouraged his fellow Christians to keep their *minds* rather than their *bodies* separate (*separatio mentis*) from those of the pagans.[154]

It would of course be wrong to assume that the authorities of the Church somehow managed to switch off such shifting dispositions of mind. They surely did not. And yet, it is safe to say that the official stance on theatrical participation

---

153 Kahlos (2016, 14) evokes a similar sense of "situational identities" in her discussion of Christian polemics against the participation in pagan festivals.

154 *Sermo* 198.1–2. Cf. Kahlos (2016, 21) for further references.

and autotelic intellectual exploration – at least to judge from the reactions of ecclesiastical leaders – took a different turn in the wake of imperial Christianity (Kahlos 2016). Such ecclesiastical interferences in both private and public affairs were to have a deep and lasting impact on intellectual culture, and they continue to do so by all sorts of implicit and vestigial means in modern secular society.

In order to catch the gist of this process, it is essential to proceed from the basic assumption that a multitude of religious activities, expressions, and motivations in the ancient world belonged respectively in either of the following (vaguely distinguishable and at least partially incommutable) spheres of interest: (1) the social cohesiveness of civic *religio*, and (2) the spiritual transformation of a self-chosen *bíos*. As I have sought to demonstrate throughout the last two chapters, these spheres of interest correlate in their turn with a participatory spirit of suspended disbelief on the one hand, and a disciplined practice of suspended judgement on the other. Hence, it stands to reason that the definite establishment of Nicene Christianity as the official state religion of the Roman Empire in the late 4th century could only be accomplished at the cost of extensive conceptual confusion.

First of all, it implied a crossbreeding of two independent species of religiosity (one of which did not even conform to the pagan category of *religio*) into an unprecedented mode of piety premised on the Pauline notion of faith. Secondly, state-sponsored Christianity creates a unifying structure – a kind of superorganism – into which virtually everything old is retained by being assigned a secondary value and function. Pagan forms of thought and practice are thus overtly suppressed by being covertly resuscitated.

It is easy to make a long list of those pagan anomalies that were to subsist in their old places, in their old forms, or under their old rubrics through an official alteration of their initial value: pagan temples cleansed by the sign of the cross; profane public places (e.g., the pagan basilica) lending their design to Christian churches; the ancient periodization of sacred time (Lat. *saeculum*) reinvented as a new measurement of things transient and mundane; pagan myths turned into integumental tools while an equally fabulous biblical narrative received canonical status; the pagan sacrificial apparatus (its priestly offices [e.g., *pontifex*], victims, and implements [e.g., *hostia, altaria*]) transferred to the context of bloodless communion; philosophical categories in the service of biblical exegesis, dogmatics, and liturgical theology; pagan idolatry disenfranchised by Christian iconolatry; and so on and so forth.

We notice how the introduction of new vocabularies, rites, and visual displays did not always result in the eradication of previous equivalents, but often in an adjustment of their previous purport. There are even examples of Christian emperors decreeing that pagan statues should be preserved due to their lasting artistic value (Kahlos 2016, 25; CTh, 16.10.8). All in all, no matter what historical event one selects to mark the critical turning point in Europe's past beyond which it no longer makes any sense to speak of its *ancient* past – whether it be the fall of the western Roman Empire or the rise of Islam – it is hardly possible to do so without acknowledging the crucial part played by state-funded religions of salvation in that process. This process implied more than just religious change. In the end, it implied a change of the conceptual matrix within which religion no longer accorded with what the ancients had once held it to be.

III Nascent Modernity (Reflux)

Preamble

According to a still widespread opinion, the last branch of Neoplatonism to resist the official Christianization of the Roman Empire was finally broken in the first half of the 6th century. Emperor Justinian, who had used different legislative means to suppress both paganism and heterodox Christianity in the Byzantine Empire, issued a decree in the year 529 to instigate the closing of the last Neoplatonic school in Athens. Justinian's religious policy is usually considered a catalyst for the last pagan philosophers – Damascius, Simplicius, and a few of their companions – to take refuge in the Sasanian court, from which they were permitted to return three years later. Due to the incertitude as to the group's continuous fate and whereabouts, the closing of the Academy is often considered the death blow to paganism in the Byzantine Empire. Since a chain of transmission appears to be broken at this point, we are left with a gap in the transmission of Greek philosophy to the Arabs a few centuries later.

Before resuming the question of this enigmatic gap, I shall bring attention to a set of intertwined themes that rather seem to point ahead of Christianity in the era commonly referred to as the European Renaissance. As we shall see, these themes are not just conceptually intertwined, but also function as intermediaries, as points of return and departure, connecting a less familiar past with a future in which they are sometimes held to be unprecedented symptoms of modernity and secularity.

https://doi.org/10.1515/9783110460605-011

8 The Return of the Pagans

8.1

The complete thematic set occurs in a particularly evocative passage from Shakespeare's comedy *All's Well That Ends Well*, a play probably composed sometime between 1602 and 1605. In the third scene of the second act, Lafeu, an old lord at the court of France, begins a conversation with Bertram, another lord of France, and Bertram's companion Parolles, about the orphaned daughter (Helen) of a great physician (Gerard de Narbon) who has just cured the aging French King of a fistula by means of her father's prescriptions (AS 2.3.1 ff[155]):

> LAF. They say that miracles are past; and we have our philosophical persons to make modern and familiar, things supernatural and causeless. Hence is it that we make trifles of terrors, ensconcing ourselves into seeming knowledge when we should submit ourselves to an unknown fear
>
> PAR. Why, 'tis the rarest argument of wonder that hath shot out in our latter times.
>
> BER. And so 'tis.
>
> LAF. To be relinquish'd of the artists –
>
> PAR. So I say – both of Galen and Paracelsus.
>
> LAF. Of all the learned and authentic Fellows –
>
> PAR. Right; so I say.
>
> LAF. That gave him out incurable –

Apart from merely doing service to the play's unfolding by evoking an atmosphere of astonishment, the piece of dialogue shows a remarkable concurrence of terms and topics suggestive of a time to come: (1) the theme of disenchantment, or, more precisely, the cessation of miracles; (2) the autonomous philosopher or scientist (a Galen or a Paracelsus) who partakes in unveiling the mysteries, making them modern and familiar; and (3) the conception of a supernatural world that, in its very capacity of being so labelled, can only exist by default. The dialogue's affirmation of the miraculous nature of the cure creates an ambiguity suggestive of a miraculous science. We know, after all, that Helen has used the prescriptions of a renowned physician to cure the King. At the same time, however, there is

155 The reference is to the 1998 edition of *The Arden Shakespeare Complete Works*. See the bibliography (s.v. AS) for further information.

https://doi.org/10.1515/9783110460605-012

something more to the medicine ("There's something in't / More than my father's skill") [AS 1.3.228–232]), and Helen's prediction of the cure's duration is buried in pagan imagery (cf. AS 2.1.160–167).[156] What might an audience living in this era – the final phase of what later scholarship labels the Golden Age of the English Renaissance – have pondered as to who these philosophical persons were, whence they had arrived, and in what respect they had deprived the world of its alleged supernatural causes? Were the London playgoers really pioneers in mastering the "imaginary puissance" that Shakespearean dramaturgy would seem to require of a disenchanted world?[157]

Such questions give us reason to reconsider certain tacit presumptions about modernity. The impossible sense of unprecedented disenchantment is one, because it implies a sense of original enchantment already inscribed with the sensibilities of a world in which "miracles are past." The concept of arriving moderns is another, because it deprives a present state of unprecedented affairs of its novelty. One might suspect a trope of defamiliarization to be at work here, and indeed in all conjurations of enchanted pasts, rather than an accurate characterization of changing mentalities. The enchanted world is a world that will only appear as such ahead of, or outside of, itself. Similarly, the terms "sorcery" or "witchcraft," when deployed as labels of malevolent ritual practice, usually appear in the language of the accuser as a third-person attribution; almost never in the language of the actor as a first-person self-designation (Smith, 2004, 219). Disenchantment may thus tentatively concern us as a manifest emotional state, but one that typically distorts the prolonged historicity of such experienced states of detachment from a likewise distorted memory of enchantment.

In order to work out how the Renaissance figure of the philosopher, or proto-scientist, was considered to herald the modern age of disenchantment, it might avail to scrutinize one of the first texts to subject this experience to sociological theorizing.

8.1.2

Despite its miraculously deep past, the theme of disenchantment owes much of its current pertinence in academic discourse to Max Weber's essay *Wissenschaft als*

156 The play's pagan-spiritual underpinnings are examined in the article "Where hope is coldest" by Kiernan Ryan (Fernie 2005, 28–49).

157 Cf. the prologue to *King Henry V* (AS 431): "Piece out our imperfections with your thoughts. Into a thousand parts divide one man. And make imaginary puissance. Think, when we talk of horses, that you see them. Printing their proud hoofs i' th' receiving earth."

Beruf ("Science as a Vocation") from 1919. Originating from a talk held at the University of Munich in 1918 on the initiative of the progressive student association *Freistudentischer Bund*, it is a text clearly marked by the devastations of war in its aim to offer young university students guidance in their choice of a future vocation.[158] While avoiding programmatic political jargon, Weber's talk resounds with worries that the devotion to a scientific career, including the implied sense of an intellectual "vocation" (*Beruf*) to combine strife for clarity with a willingness to serve society, was coming under threat.

A cause of concern behind the League's initiative to sponsor the talk was a recently published article *Beruf und Jugend* (1917) by the young socialist intellectual Alexander Schwab, in which the bourgeois cult of professionalism was denounced as an obstacle to the attainment of true humanity (Poggi 2014, 147). Weber is keen to rehearse his assumption that modernity's leaning towards an immanent world, including an escapist longing for "experiences" (*Erlebnisse*) and antiquarian religious paraphernalia, has replaced a pre-modern inclination towards wonder and revelation (Weber 1951, 587, 596.). A modern predicament no doubt, but not one easily compensated for. If moderns fail to understand the world, he submits, it is not because they consider it unfathomable, but because they consider themselves unready to grasp the details. The important point is that the world is perceived to be inherently intelligible; nothing is mysterious about it, nothing lies hidden beneath or beyond it; and since the world is the sum-total of what we progressively learn about it, it has to lack an end in itself, that is, an end outside of our being within it. Weber considers this uncanny condition of modern civilization to form a stark contrast against a pre-modern pursuit of pure being, which he illustrates with an idiosyncratic adaptation of Plato's parable of the cave (Weber 1950, 579).[159]

From its heroic beginnings in fifth-century Athens, via Renaissance quests for the rediscovery of nature through a synthesis of art and science, conceptual truth no longer belongs to a solar sphere of ideal purpose, but rather inversely to an endlessly growing mine shaft devoid of ultimacy. The modern intellectual spirit, Weber complains, seems only to regain a sense of divinity, experience, and community by

158 The pagination of Weber's essay (first printed as a pamphlet in 1919) refers to Johannes Winckelmann's revised edition of *Gesammelte Aufsätze zur Wissenschaftslehre* (Weber 1951, 566–597).

159 In Weber's version, one of the captives breaks free by his own power, ascends to the outside, and finally succeeds in leading the other captives up the same path. Weber's simplification of the allegory's original purport, his crass characterization of modern science, as well as the stark contrast between modernity and antiquity that he thereby sought to illustrate, soon became a critical concern of figures such as the theologian Ernst Troeltsch and the philosopher Heinrich Rickert (cf. Blumenberg 1989, 722 f.).

romanticizing irrationality. In a time when sublime values have lost both their scientific grounding and monumental public exposure, the fatal consequence is the experience of a disenchanted world for which compensation can either, at best, be attained through the retention of intellectual honesty in a world of conflicting values, or, at worst, by submitting to a fanatic faith in false community embraced by the so-called *Kathederprophetie* ("prophecy from the lectern") (Weber 1951, 596 f.).

Weber's characterization of the contemporary intellectual conveys the impression of stark contrasts – historical as well as sociological – between an irreversible premodern rationality and a regime of unconditional faith. Lacking from his account, however, is a distinction between the intellectual's past and modernity's flawed perceptions of it. An apparent cause for the flaw is that disenchantment narratives, alongside the premonition of an emergent rationality, have multiple, both Christian and pagan pasts. They mark an end to the work of the prophets in an ensuing age of complete Christian revelation on the one hand, and an end to naive credulity in a pagan tradition of philosophical scrutiny on the other.

Incompatible as they may seem at the outset, the storylines conflate and eventually develop synergies of apparent consent. Regardless of the remedy prescribed, whether it authorizes faith in a new revelation or distrust in an old one, it implies a perceived dissolution of an old world order which, from the perspective of the disenchanted, typically appears excessively monolithic. For Weber's part, the urgent task does not so much concern the dissolution of such perceptions, but rather the making of proper choices. If today's religiously inclined youths consider a life in divine communion to require a sacrifice of the intellect ("Erlösung von dem Rationalismus und Intellektualismus der Wissenschaft ist die Grundvoraussetzung des Lebens in der Gemeinschaft mit dem Göttlichen."), they are not necessarily entertaining false notions about religion's current status, but rather risk making a bad choice in the latter's favor (Weber 1951, 582).

The consideration that the intellect cannot enter into divine communion – a doctrine that Weber falsely attributes to Augustine by misquoting Tertullian (Weber 1951, 595)[160] – could not have been more alien to Plato's understanding of divinity. Plato's "intellect" (*noûs*) must be considered divine by its very nature, save at the cost of serious conceptual distortions, because it is naturally disposed to discover uncreated truths. Modern secularist precepts of the intellectual's task are thus by no means conceptually aligned with ancient philosophical ones in terms of

160 The "Augustinian" sentence quoted by Weber (*credo non quod, sed quia absurdum est*) finds its closest match in Tertullian's *De Carne Christi* (5.4) ("On the Flesh of Christ") *prorsus credibile est, quia ineptum est* ("it is to be believed precisely because it is senseless").

what the intellect might be. What the precepts do seem to share, however, is a discontent with institutions of unwarranted divine authority whose evanescence they gladly predict, and whose past pertinence to defy intellection they typically exaggerate.

As we shall see, the growing presence of autonomous intellectuals in western Europe during the 15th and 16th centuries – the "philosophical persons" of which Lord Lafeu seems to be speaking in the excerpt from *All's Well* – can be linked to a tradition of a no less ancient spiritual pedigree than the Christian establishment which deems it modern and irreligious. Modernity in its self-proclaimed newness may in fact signify a precedent phenomenon; a point of return falsely conceived as an unprecedented point of departure. It marks the encrypted reappearance of a pagan religiosity that once thrived beyond the confines of civic religion, and which, once again, was to pose a threat to the religious establishment.

8.1.3

Often read as an apologetic testimony to paganism on the wane in the Graeco-Roman world, the so-called last oracle at Delphi is framed by an account – found in works by medieval Byzantine historians, who probably culled it from a fifth-century ecclesiastical history – of how the last non-Christian emperor Julian (AD 331–363) sends the physician and State treasurer Oribasius to rebuild Apollo's temple at Delphi. Upon arrival, the delegate receives the following oracle:

> εἴπατε τῷ βασιλεῖ· χασμαὶ πέσε Δαίδαλος αὐλά
> οὐκέτι Φοῖβος ἔχει καλύβαν, οὐ μάντιδα δάφνην,
> οὐ παγὰν λαλέουσαν, ἀπέσβετο καὶ λάλον ὕδωρ
>
> Tell the emperor that the Daidalic hall has fallen.
> No longer does Phoebus have his chamber, nor mantic laurel,
> nor prophetic spring; and the speaking water has been silenced.[161]

Opinions diverge as to the oracle's invention by Christian writers, or its quotation out of context to mask an original plea for revived paganism. More importantly, however, the notion of the oracle's dissipation was clearly not a Christian invention, for it had been a topic of conversation among pagan philosophers centuries before Christianity's entrance into imperial policies. A case in point is Cicero's already discussed dialogue *De divinatione* (44 BC) (see ch. 6) in which the pro-divinatory views of the Stoa (represented by Cicero's brother Quintus) are confronted by

161 Cf. Gregory 1983 for further references.

those of the Academy (represented by Cicero himself). Despite their conflicting views on divine foresight, the debaters clearly share the view that the oracle at Delphi no longer delivers trustworthy prophesies. Whereas Quintus tackles the failure of a once glorious institution in mechanistic terms – what once was, as attested by the abundant proof of oracular collections from the past, will have to cease as the rivers of divine inspiration now seem to dry up or change their course (1.37) – Cicero cannot accept that the divine virtue of a place simply evaporates (2.118). Could it perhaps rather be, he continues, that men have become less credulous (cf. Yelle 2012, 34).[162]

These are typical attitudes of a cosmopolitan intellectual in a world where local priesthoods and time-honored sites of worship have little to offer the urbane in search of truth and solace. The old customs, while still observed in a mixed spirit of civility and antiquarian curiosity, meet with occasional scorn. Worthy models of the divine were no longer supposed to be derived from local customs, nor from the standard plots of drama and poetry, but from schools of philosophy. Even if Cicero worshiped like a Roman citizen, nothing had prevented him from remaining an academic sceptic in matters of truth and spirituality.

The last example should make clear that the concept of disenchantment, besides often being falsely assumed to mark the advent of modernity, is neither exclusively based on a Christian notion (= the cessation of charismata) nor is it exclusively tied to an Enlightenment discourse according to modernity's distorted recollections of its own past. Rather, it is a concept defined by a more fundamental area of tension between civic forms of public religiosity and unofficial forms of spirituality that eventually were to inform new patterns of tension between representatives of the Roman Catholic Church and privately sponsored intellectuals in western Europe during the 15th century.

8.2

Before seeking to disentangle this curious case of resurgent paganism in a nascent age of disenchantment, it is necessary to begin by sketching out a plausible genealogy. This will have to be a somewhat hasty sketch that cannot appeal to everyone in its vague outline, yet it will hopefully facilitate the reconstruction of a narrative that would otherwise have lost all sense of cohesion and continuity.

---

162 The theme is discussed at length above (ch. 6.2), where we also notice that Plutarch (*c.*46 AD–*c.*120 AD) picked it up in a dialogue composed one and a half century later, most likely in the last period of his life, while serving as a priest in Delphi. It bears the significant title *The failure* (or *cessation* [= Gr. *ekleloipótōn*]) *of oracles.*

In what follows, I shall proceed from two independent contributions to the postclassical fate of pagan philosophy by Michel Tardieu (1986 and 1987a).[163] Although the proposition is never explicitly stated by the author himself, it remains a fascinating intellectual exercise to conceive Tardieu's studies as the united parts of a diptych – beginning, as it were, at the end (of antiquity), and ending at the beginning (of modernity) – devoted to the secret lives of pagan philosophers in the long period of their apparent absence.[164] We need to ask: is it conceivable that there was a continuous transmission of Greek philosophy – bridging the gap between sixth-century Byzantium and Renaissance Europe – besides those milieus in which scholarly approaches to the pagan heritage required a prior intellectual commitment to the truth revealed by the Bible, Christ, or the Qur'ān?[165] Into what kind of secluded space, then, may we suppose that the pagan philosophers of Athens disappeared by the 6th century, and whence did their distant heirs return, almost a millennium later, in fifteenth-century Florence?

Tardieu's solution to this conundrum is almost certainly not entirely accurate in all its details. Still, the proposal deserves praise for its imaginative grasp, and for the audacity with which it seeks to fill in the blanks in a fragmented narrative that the otherwise unexplained revival of pagan philosophy in Arabic translation would seem to require.[166]

---

163 Cf. also the contributions by Tardieu and Ilsetraut Hadot to the edited volume *Simplicius: sa vie, son oeuvre, sa survie* (Hadot, 1987).

164 This is precisely what Pierre Chuvin seems to suggest in his epilogue to *A Chronicle of the Last Pagans* (Chuvin 1990, 149–150).

165 The ancillary function of philosophy in relation to the superior practice of theology is expressed in a maxim that was still frequently used by scholastic theologians in the Middle Ages: *philosophica theologiae ancilla*. Whereas the maxim's particular bearing on revealed scripture can be traced back to Philo's allegorical interpretations of the Bible in the 1st century CE, the Stoics' allegorical attempts to reconcile the poetry of Orpheus, Musaeus, Hesiod, and Homer with their philosophical teachings predated Philo by at least three centuries (Henrichs 1968, 437–438).

166 Van Bladel (2009, 71 [footnote 30]) provides a good bibliographical overview of the discussion (up to 2007), involving both the initial arguments laid out by Tardieu and his followers (not least Ilsetraut Hadot) as well as scholarly works presenting counterarguments and alternative hypotheses. Prominent points of disagreement concern (1) whether Simplicius ever settled in the city of Ḥarrān; (2) whether there ever was a Platonic school in Ḥarrān; (3) to what extent the Ḥarrānians transmitted genuine parts of the Greek *Hermetica* into Arabic; and (4) to what extent the Ḥarrānian pagan community consisted of two distinct groups, that is, a group of common worshipers vs. a group of elite sages (Van Bladel 2009, 74). Ilsetraut Hadot has persistently defended Tardieu's hypothesis, most recently in the critical overview published in 2014 (see Hadot 2014).

8.2.1

By way of a preamble, the following statements seem to be speaking their own clear language: the scholar Ṯābit ibn Qurra, who transferred to Baghdad from his native town of Ḥarrān (Lat. Carhae) in the 9th century, supposedly claimed that his birthplace had "never been sullied by the error of Nazareth" (cf. Chuvin 1990, 140 and Pingree 2002, 34); in a seeming response to that statement, the thirteenth-fourteenth century Ḥanbalī theologian Ibn Taymiyyah, another native from Ḥarrān, claimed that the philosophers (*falāsifa*) and Mu'tazilites "had drunk from the same polluted springs, notably the doctrines of the Ṣābians of Ḥarrān." (Green 1992, 133). Here, we first have a ninth-century witness claiming descent from some sort of pagan community in Upper Mesopotamia, then a fourteenth-century witness describing the doctrines of the Ṣābians of Ḥarrān as the polluted wellspring of Islamic heresy.[167] Is there any historical support for these claims? And if so, what was the particular status of the city of Ḥarrān and the community that seem to have flourished in its midst well into the 11th century?

As intimated above, the various entry points of Greek philosophy into Islam is a matter of much controversy, not least in regard to the continued teaching of pagan philosophy between the official closing of the school in Athens in 529 and the beginning of the so-called Islamic Golden Age by the mid-8th century.[168]Even if Jews and Christians certainly did play a prominent role as mediators of classical learning in the intellectual centers of the Abbasid caliphate, they were hardly the only ones to do so. Some of the doctrines and living ritual practices (such as polytheism, belief in metempsychosis, and the occasional practice of blood sacrifice) for which we find evidence in works such as al-Nadīm's *Fihrist*, the *Epistles of the Brethren of Purity* (*Rasā'il Ikhwān al-Ṣafā'*), and al-Šahrastānī's *Book of Religions and Sects* (*Kitāb al-Milal wa'l-niḥal*) would easily have been disqualified as either pagan or outrageously heretic by rabbinic leaders and ecclesiastical officials alike. And yet, these doctrines and practices were apparently maintained by individuals who likewise felt strongly attached to the philosophical legacy of Pythago-

167 Unsurprsingly, Ibn Taymiyya's writings are frequently being employed today as sources of inspiration for Islamist hardliners. One example is the pseudonymous Abu Bakr Naji, author of the caliphist strategic document *Idārat at-Tawaḥḥuš* (*Management of Savagery*). The e-book, first published in Arabic in 2004, was made publicly accessible in an English translation by William McCant through the John M. Olin Institute for Strategic Studies at Harvard University in 2006.

168 The appointment of the Neoplatonist philosopher Stephanus of Alexandria as a teacher in Constantinople under the Emperor Heraclius in the year 610 suggests that Neoplatonism was in fact continuously taught in Alexandria (and occasionally in Constantinople as well), possibly at least until the time of the Muslim conquest of Egypt between 639 and 646 (Blumenthal 1993, 323f.)

ras, Plato, and Aristotle. Prominent among the groups repeatedly placed into this slot were the Ṣābians (sg. *ṣābi'*, pl. *ṣābi'ūn*) of Ḥarrān. Ṯābit's above mentioned transfer from Ḥarrān to Baghdad in the 9th century can thus be taken to mark a *terminus post quem* for a specific variety of classical intellectual impact on Islamic scholarship that did not ensue from a distinctively Judeo-Christian environment.

Ḥarrān is usually held to have been one of the last outposts of Hellenistic paganism. Nevertheless, the name of the community with which the city had become associated by the 9th century suggests a conscious tactic of religious self-designation in a world dominated by the Abrahamic religious legacy. Ḥarrān is mentioned already in the Hebrew Bible as the city where Abraham lived with his family before being instructed by God to settle in the land of Canaan (e.g., Gen. 11:31–12:5). Furthermore, a religious group referred to in the Qur'ān as "Ṣābians" (*ṣābi'ūn*) is the only one besides Muslims, Jews, and Christians to be granted special recognition as true believers "in God and the Last Day" (2:62; 5:69).[169]

While the Qur'ānic Ṣābians are never explicitly associated with the city of Ḥarrān, the fact that Islamic authorities recognized them as believers in a revealed book apparently prompted members of the Ḥarrānian community to adopt this effectively vague self-designation in order to avoid persecution.[170] The Ḥarrānians feature prominently in postclassical literature as accomplished astronomers and students of the *Hermetica*.[171] They could thus have claimed license to the practice of a respectable sacred science (astronomy) under the authority of a figure (Idrīs = Hermes) who by elaborate exegetical means had been inserted into a quasi-Biblical lineage of pre-Abrahamic prophets (Pingree 2002, 25). Against the background of late antiquity religious polemics, the name Hermes Trismegistus would still – at least from the early 5th century CE (cf. Augustine's *De civ.* 8.23) – have functioned as a summary reference for all sorts of doctrines and practices defined by the error of pagan idolatry. By the time of Ṯābit's transfer to Baghdad, however, the

169 The two Qur'ānic passages form the basis of the somewhat flexible Islamic usage of the label People of the Book (*ahl al kitāb*), i.e., believers in a revealed book.

170 This tactical choice of self-designation is confirmed by an anecdote recorded in the *Fihrist* (ch. 9, section 1) concerning the last campaign of the Caliph al-Ma'mūn in the year 218 AH/833 CE. The Caliph is supposed to have asked the Ḥarrānians about their religious identity, threatening to slay them if they did not convert to a licit religion, whereupon some eventually decided to call themselves Ṣābians in order to escape extermination (cf. Pingree 2002, 23).

171 There are a few notices in Arabic sources to indicate the Ḥarrānians' familiarity with a discourse of Hermes to his son, and between Hermes and Tat, which clearly point to some of the texts in the Greek *Corpus Hermeticum*. Nevertheless, Van Bladel is sceptical to the idea that such texts would have been widely known, nor does he find any traces of them in Arabic works (Van Bladel 2009, 114).

name seems to have lost some of its previous stigma without the Ḥarrānian Ṣābians ever having ceased to self-identify as pagans.

In his attempt to retrace the pre-Abbasid past of the intellectual community in Ḥarrān, Tardieu takes great care to show that this city was most likely the only place where the exiles of the defunct school in Athens would have found the proper sociocultural conditions to continue their work. A peace treaty between Justinian and the Sasanian king Khosrow I in 532 stipulates the philosophers' safe return to Byzantine territory, yet there is nothing to indicate that they ever returned to Athens. Although Ḥarrān lay close to the Iranian border, its inhabitants were exempt from paying tributes to Khosrow because they remained true to the ancient religion (Tardieu 1986, 23). There is even a conspicuous notice in Simplicius' commentary on Aristotle's *Physics* (book V) to suggest that Simplicius addresses a community of readers accustomed to the syncretistic usage of pagan calendars. Once again, the city of Ḥarrān would be just the right place in the Byzantine empire to address such a community (Tardieu 1987b).

Apart from such vague indications, Tardieu's most decisive piece of evidence comes from a relatively late description of what could suggest a still operational Neoplatonic school in Ḥarrān by the mid-10th century. In the only surviving first-hand eyewitness account of the city and its pagan inhabitants from a visit in 332 AH/943 CE, the travelling historian al-Masʿūdī describes a religious milieu that one would have expected to be but a distant memory in the Levant by this period. He divides the Ḥarrānians into two categories: the "philosophers" (*ḥašwiyya*); namely, vulgar adherents of the city's ancient religion, and the "sages" (*ḥukamāʾ*) in the strict sense of the term; that is, the true heirs of the Greek philosophers.[172] The vulgar pagans practice divination, sacrifice animals to local divinities (the foremost among which is Šamāl), and celebrate cultic meals inside their temple. The sages categorically reject such sacrificial and divinatory practices in favor of their own secret ceremonies. A door knocker on the gate to the their "gathering place" (*maǧmaʿ*) carries an inscription in Aramaic. It is explained to al-Masʿūdī

172 Van Bladel is convinced that Tardieu has misunderstood a crucial sentence in al-Masʿūdī's account by falsely taking it to make a distinction between the Ḥarrānians in general, and the Ṣābians as the true heirs of the Greek philosophers in particular. The correct translation, according to Van Bladel, should run: "This community, known as the Ḥarrānians and Ṣābians, has philosophers [*consists of philosophers]; however, they are some of the common riffraff of the philosophers, differing from their élite sages [scil. the élite sages of the philosophers] in their doctrines. I consider them philosophers only by way of lineage, not by way of wisdom, because they are Hellenes (*Yūnānīya*); not all of the Hellenes are philosophers; only their [scil. the Hellenes'] sages are philosophers." According to Tardieu's interpretation of this sentence, the possessive pronoun in *ḫawāṣṣ ḥukamāʾihim* (lit. "[differing from] *their* elite sages") refers back to *Ḥarrānians*, and not to *the philosophers*, which Van Bladel takes to be the more natural referent.

by a certain Mālik ibn ʿUqbūn and other members of his sect as a quote from Plato: "He who knows himself in truth becomes God." Tardieu identifies a close (if not verbatim) match for this maxim in Plato's *First Alcibades* (133c), which he proposes to be read as a kind of invitation to the philosophical life (Tardieu 1986, 14 f.):

> τῷ θεῷ ἄρα τοῦτ' ἔοικεν αὐτῆς, καί τις εἰς τοῦτο βλέπων καὶ πᾶν τὸ θεῖον γνούς, θεόν τε καὶ φρόνησιν, οὕτω καὶ ἑαυτὸν ἂν γνοίη μάλιστα.
>
> Then this part of her resembles God, and whoever looks at this, and comes to know all that is divine, will gain thereby the best knowledge of himself.
> (Trans. Lamb [s.v. Pl. *I Alc.*])

Tardieu makes the striking additional observation that the inscription of the "Delphic" maxim from *First Alcibades* on the door knocker of the *maǧmaʿ* corresponds axiomatically to a well established principle of Platonic teaching in the Hellenistic world. Among others Olympiodorus, one of the colleagues of Simplicius in Athens before the official closing of the school in 529, characteristically compares *Alcibades* to a "gateway" (*propýlaios*), whereas the more profound message of the dialogue *Parmenides* is referred to as the "innermost sanctuary" (*ádyton*) (*In Alcibadem,* page 10 [= 11, 3–6], quoted from Westerink's edition in Tardieu 1986, 27). It was perhaps not by chance that the fact of perceiving Platonic teaching in such specific architectural terms by the 6th century was retained as a perfectly legible embellishment on the gate to the school of the Ḥarrānian sages. Rather, it is a circumstance to which a contemporary scholar like Tardieu (with a more complete sense of the picture than al-Masʿūdī himself) can now refer in order to authenticate Mālik ibn ʿUqbūn and his as fellow students as the heirs of a still living pagan tradition.

If there ever was such a thing as a distinguished group of pagan intellectuals in Ḥarrān, then al-Masʿūdī's testimony can be characterized as the perfect instantiation of three parallel religious orientations, the two first (and obsolete) of which as if they had been captured and refracted through the optics of a future observer, and the third of which (that of the observer himself) as if it had been able to recapture its own formative past. In their still disentangled state, as it were, two once distinct modes of pagan religiosity exist side by side in Ḥarrān: public temple worship with its emphases on periodicity and festive communion, and the secret ceremonialism of sectarians with its emphases on permanent self-discipline, study, and spiritual transformation. In the eyes of the temporary third-party passerby, the divided pagan community of Ḥarrān must have appeared acutely out of place in the midst of a world so long dominated by competing empires and their competing monotheistic creeds. At the same time, however, there is something strangely prophetic about this panoptic situation, with its Muslim observer unknowingly catching a sudden glimpse into a secular world to come: a world in which academies and universities are once more claiming their own intellectual authority as distinct from the authority of traditional religious institutions. The Platonic revival of the Florentine Renaissance still lay centuries ahead, but it no longer seems as distantly detached from its classical model of revival.

If Ḥarrān was indeed the place where Simplicius decided to settle sometime after 532 CE, it is conceivable that the city's still thriving community of pagan intellectuals in the 10th century were committed to the same ideals that had once turned Simplicius and his peers into *personae non gratae* in the Byzantine empire.

8.3

With the destruction of Ḥarrān by Seljuk Turks in the 11th century, the last enclave of its kind in the eastern Mediterranean to preserve pagan civic worship alongside the spiritual exercises of a philosophical sect is likely to have met its definite end. An equally complex coexistence of civic and non-civic cults is unlikely to have survived among those few indigenous groups to resist Christianization in the Peleponnesse, such as the Maniots of western Laconia, who only converted to Christianity during the reign of Basil I in the 9th century.[173] In so far as ancient philosophy is concerned, it would thus seem that its legacy was now being exclusively passed on by scribes and teachers associated with universities, *scholae monasticae*, yeshivas, and madrasas under the supervision of religious authorities, all of which took pains in distinguishing classical learning from the inalterability of sacred scripture. Hence, one would no longer expect any remaining free spaces to have been left for those genuinely pagan scholars who insisted on regarding intellectual exploration as a spiritual end in itself.

On closer inspection, however, this way of imagining the intellectual landscape of Europe and the Near East during the last centuries prior to the Renaissance period does not appear altogether accurate. It could of course be argued that those eccentric fourteenth-and-fifteenth century intellectuals who incurred the accusation of paganism were either being falsely accused, or that they simply reinvented themselves as such out of nostalgia. A third, controversial, yet still not entirely implausible option is that pagan coteries, insisting on the perpetuation of certain moribund spiritual ideals, were in fact never properly reinvented, because they had never been completely extinguished. If we can establish a continuous presence

173 Cf. the brief notice in the work *De administrando imperio* (ch. 50) by the emperor Constantine VII Porphyrogenitus.

of influential intellectuals in Judeo-Christian as well as Muslim scholarly milieus who self-identified as pagans right up to the 11th century, and the presence of those who were at least identified as such by others in the 14th century, then it does not seem entirely far-fetched to assume that they had been around all the time.

It may, at least, be of anecdotal interest to recall that the fifteenth-century Italian humanist and founder of the *Accedemia Romana*, Julius Pomponius Laetus, was imprisoned and tortured by order of Pope Paul II in 1468 on charges of apostasy, worship of false gods, and conspiracy against the authority and life of the pope. Although Pomponius was set free for lack of positive evidence and through the intervention of an influential cardinal, discoveries made in the catacombs of S. Calixtus as late as 1852 revealed evidence that would have been enough to get Pomponius and his peers executed. On the white plaster ceiling of a remote crypt in the catacombs, the archaeologist Giovanni Battista de Rossi found an inscription written with the smoke of a tallow candle: "January 16, 1457. Pantagathus, Mammeius, Papyrius, Minicinus, Æmilius, Minucius, all of them admirers and investigators of antiquities, and delight of the Roman dissolute women, [have met here] under the reign of Pomponius, supreme pontiff."[174] During their secret gatherings in the catacombs, the members of the *Accademia Romana* had apparently indulged in promiscuous sex, conceived of themselves as members of a pagan priesthood, using titles such as *sacerdos* and *pontifex*, and with their Christian names exchanged for those of pagan heroes (Lanciani 1891, 358–361). Although we cannot determine exactly what these pagan tendencies entailed, their adherents were apparently taking extreme precautions in keeping them secret.[175]

---

174 For further details, see Lanciani 1891, 358–361. A plausible reason for gathering on this particular date may have been to commemorate the Roman senate's official appointment of Octavian as *Augustus* and *Princeps* on that same date in the year 27 BCE.

175 A detailed if strongly biased account of the affair is found in Ludwig Pastor's *The History of the Popes, from the Close of the Middle Ages*, vol. IV (London: Kegan Paul, Trench, Tübner & co., Paternoster House, 1894), 41 ff. E. g., 51: "Paul II had much more to tell of the evil deeds of these Epicureans, who seem, indeed, to have adopted the doctrines promulgated by Valla in his book 'on pleasure.' They despised the commands of the Church, he said, ate meat on fast-days, and reviled the Pope and the Clergy. They said that the priests were the enemies of the laity, that they had invented fasting and forbidden men to have more than one wife. Moses, they taught, deceived the Jews, his law was a forgery, Christ was a deceiver, Mahomet a great intellect, but also an impostor. They were ashamed of their Christian names and preferred those which were heathen, and they practiced some of the most shameful vices of antiquity. Some of these freethinkers are said to have contemplated an alliance with the Turks."

8.3.1

A more decisive datum in this connection is the fact that one of the figures considered absolutely seminal to the Platonic revival in the West, the Byzantine scholar Georgios Gemistos Plaethon († *c.*1452/1454), was much less discrete in hiding his pagan predilections. Born in Constantinople sometime between 1355 and 1360, Plethon had established himself as a lay teacher of philosophy in the Byzantine capitol when he (sometime before 1410) was commissioned by the emperor Manuel II Palaeologus to resettle in the city of Mystras in the southern Peloponnese as a politician, judge, and advisor to the rulers of the Despotate of the Morea. Plethon's reputation as an exceptionally erudite and politically skilled man even made the new emperor John VIII Palaeologus request his advice and eventual participation at the ecumenical Council of Ferrara-Florence (1431–1449).

It is, however, not so much for Plethon's role in an ultimately failed attempt to solve the schisms between the Greek and Latin churches that his two years in Florence (between 1438 and 1439) are remembered today, but for his off-duty lectures on the "Platonic mysteries" that were to leave such a lasting impact on the Florentine intelligentsia and its patrons. When in 1462 Cosimo de' Medici, who may himself have attended Plethon's lectures in Florence, decided to donate a codex containing the complete works of Plato to the young philosopher Marsilio Ficino, it was a gesture anticipating Cosimo's sponsorship of a Platonic Academy (or the Neoplatonic Florentine Academy) under Ficino's leadership (Stausberg 1998, 98).[176]

The codex which had been given to Ficino – still preserved in the collections of the Laurentian Library as Codex Laurentianus LXXXV 9 – was in all likelihood a copy of a Byzantine original once in Plethon's possession as he had visited Florence more than 20 years earlier. It was a rarity to say the least, for nowhere in the West by the 15th century (not even in the Vatican Library!) was there such a thing as a book containing a complete Platonic corpus (Hankins 1990, 157 f.). This sense of completeness can be considered to capture the very idea behind Cosimo's (re-) opening of a Platonic Academy in Florence, since the primary aim of this initiative was to instigate a complete translation of Plato's works into Latin.[177]

---

176 The only fifteenth-century source to explicitly state that Cosimo de' Medici actually met Plethon, attended his lectures ("on the Platonic mysteries"), and was inspired to found a Florentine Academy is an otherwise largely legendary account in Ficino's preface to the Latin translation of Plotinus' *Enneads* from 1492 (see below).

177 As argued by James Hankins, there was a strong tendency among the scholars around Ficino to use the label "Academy" reference to the works of Plato, so that the "opening of the Academy" could be likewise understood as a metonymic reference to Cosimo's plans on commissioning a complete Latin translation of the Platonic corpus (Hankins 1990, 14–156).

On coming back to the issue of Plethon's pagan predilections, it will not suffice to recognize that he was instrumental in bringing about a reopening of the files of a long-lost ancient philosophical heritage in the West. This competence alone would not have made him unique as a scholar coming from the East, nor would it make him a pagan. The crucial point in this regard is that Plethon in fact quite explicitly tried to bolster a pagan self-image in his own writings. This is particularly evident from his last major work, the *Nómōn syngraphḗ* ("Book of Laws"), of which only parts survive today since the first patriarch of Constantinople under Ottoman rule, Gennadios Scholarios, made a good attempt to have all circulating copies of it destroyed a few years after Plethon's death.

In the second chapter of this infamous treatise, Plethon adopts a familiar strategy in pagan philosophy to establish hierarchies and genealogies of sages, or masters of wisdom (he calls them "lawgivers" [*nomothétai*]), through whose mediation a once uncorrupted divine message has been passed on. The first and most distinguished of them all was, according to Plethon, Zoroaster.[178] Not a singular figure belonging in the Judeo-Christian tradition is mentioned by name. As a primary lawgiver, even Moses is erased from the system, just as was (unsurprisingly) Aristotle due to his fundamental impact on Christian and Islamic theology. Plethon even left behind a kind of pagan creed, devised and divided in articles after the model of an ecclesiastical decree.[179] All references to divine powers in this creed are labelled as "gods" (*theoí*) in the plural, he acknowledges no creator, but conceives of the universe as an uncreated and eternal compound of singular entities without a beginning or an end.

It is remarkable that Plethon could persist in expressing such anti-Christian views without any legal consequences, especially as he did not even seem to bother about sharing his ideas with his opponents. According to the indignant testimony of the Catholic convert and humanist George of Trebizond, who engaged in a conversation with Plethon during the Council of Florence, the latter is claimed to have said that he believed the whole world to soon accept one and the same religion. When asked if this religion would be Christianity or Islam, Plethon is reported to have replied: "Neither, but it will not differ much from paganism" (*Neutrum inquit, sed non a gentilitate differentem*).[180] How are we supposed to unravel and backtrack Plethon's incentive for this pagan obstinacy? Was his eccentric religious

178 Cf. Stausberg (1998, 71) with reference to Alexandre's 1858 edition and translation of the *Nómōn syngraphḗ* (28).
179 For further references, see Stausberg (1998, 77–79).
180 *Comparatio Platonis et Aristotelis*, fol. V63.

identity merely an idiosyncrasy composed of arbitrarily concocted pagan ingredients, or was it grounded in some living tradition.[181]

The only available clue in this regard is a controversial biographical datum concerning the young Plethon's apprenticeship with a certain Elissaeus, a man identified as an influential figure at the "court of the barbarians" (most likely a reference to the court of Murad I [† 1389] in the Ottoman capitol Adrianople), a Jew in appearance, but in reality a "pagan" (*hellēnistḗs*[182]) and a polytheist. The sources of this datum are the two letters (one addressed to the princess of the Peloponnese, Theodora Asanina, and the other to the exarch Joseph) written by Gennadios Scholarios apropos of the burning of Plethon's treatise. Despite the polemical character of the two letters, with their additional anti-Semitic overtones in portraying Elissaeus as an equally corrupted and corrupting phony Jew, they still reveal details about Ellisaeus' philosophical/spiritual leanings (e.g., Averroes and Zoroaster, and other Persian and Arabic commentators on the Aristotelian corpus) that conform well to two dominant intellectual trends in the Islamic world by this period. The first of these can be linked to an Aristotelian influx from the Muslim West through the school of Averroes (= Ibn Rušd), and the second to a syncretistic influx from the Muslim (Persian) East through the school of al-Suhrawardī (often labelled Illuminationism [Ar. *al-falsafa al-išrāqīya*]). Both of these trends are likely to have conglomerated among Jewish scholars by the Black Sea in the 14th century: to Averroes they would have been introduced via Jewish exiles from Spain who had studied him in Hebrew and Latin translations, and to Illuminationist philosophy through its increasing popularity in the Muslim world after the Mongol conquest in the 13th century (cf. Tardieu 1987, 145–146).

Suhrawardī (1155–1191), the founder of Illuminationism, was a native from the hamlet Sohravard in northeastern Iran who ended his days in Aleppo, where he was executed as a heretic by order of Saladin the Ayyubid. In the historiography of Islamic philosophy, Suhrawardī is commonly acknowledged as the author of a self-consistent system distinct both from Avicenna's (= Ibn Sīnā) previously dominant Peripatetic system, and from the theologically informed philosophy known as *kalām al-falāsifa*. Hence, Suhrawardī's system should neither be understood as a preamble to Islamic theology, nor to be based on the unprecedented theoretical authority of Aristotle. Rather, it is a style of reasoning placing more emphasis on Plato and the lineage of ancient sages in which the last pagan philosophers of late antiquity were inclined to inscribe figures such as Hermes, Zoroaster, Pytha-

181 For a positive evaluation of the latter option, see Hanegraaff 2012.

182 Contrary to a recent assumption (Mariev 2019, 58, 67), the label *hellēnistḗs* is clearly used here to characterize Elissaeus as a heathen or gentile (much in the way the label was used by emperor Julian [*Ep.* 84a]), and not in the sense of a Greek-speaking Jew.

goras, and Empedocles. Due to his use of pre-Islamic Persian names and symbols, Suhrawardī is also assumed to have been more directly influenced by Zoroastrianism, although details and channels of this influence are difficult to charter (Ziai 2004 and Marcotte 2019).

Scholarios' claim that Elissaeus "accustomed" (*exethízomai*) Plethon to Zoroaster may seem odd in view of the fact that the Hellenized version of the Iranian sage would have been familiar to any Byzantine student of the classics (not least of Plutarch's *Moralia*). The likeliest circumstance behind this distorted notice is that Elissaeius introduced Plethon to texts in the Hermetic and Neoplatonic tradition claiming descent from Zoroaster and the Magi (Ar. *majūs*), or variously evoking them as spiritual (pre-Platonic) authorities. One body of texts which Elissaeus may have reintroduced to Plethon within this alternative interpretative framework were the third-to-sixth century CE so-called *Chaldean Oracles* (Tardieu 1987, 146–147).

Plethon's critical edition of the *Chaldean Oracles* is accompanied by two extant treatises that can be regarded as commentaries (a proper exegesis and a set of minor notes). These texts probably date back to Plethon's earlier days and may have originated as lecture notes (Woodhouse 1986, 55). Throughout his systematic comparison of Plethon's exegetical approach to the *Oracles* with that of another Byzantine scholar active in the 11th century, Michael Psellos, Tardieu is able to demonstrate Plethon's advantages in restoring the original character and purport of these texts. Whereas Psellos' commentaries are often anachronistic and apologetic in character, those of Plethon are sober and precise, restoring to some of the oracles what seems to have been their original theurgical sense. Nonetheless, Plethon's superior conjectures were long ignored (or mistakenly attributed to Psellos) by modern editors. It now seems more accurate to conceive of Plethon not just as the last Byzantine scholar to comment on the *Chaldean Oracles*, but also as the first scholar to produce an edition and commentary of the corpus according to acceptable modern standards (Tardieu 1987, 151–164). In what respect this approach was really *modern* is another question, for what Plethon had aimed to accomplish was perhaps rather an interpretation of the oracles within a continuous pagan tradition.

When we consider Plethon's astuteness in steering his way through the *Chaldean Oracles* by such well-informed means, it seems plausible that there was at least a quantum of (living) influence on his original approach to ancient philosophy that did not ensue exclusively from the mainstream of Byzantine classical scholarship. Elissaeus is a plausible candidate for such an early influence. To be sure, a figure of whom we know virtually nothing, and who left no apparent traces in recorded history except for in two polemical letters premised on the condemnation of Plethon's book to an auto-da-fé, can be used as an empty screen onto which contemporary historians might project all sorts of wishful thinking. On the other hand, the reduction of Elissaeus to a piece of pure fiction would be something of a conversation-stopper.[183] For a historiography to open up new paths to the past, and not just leave us embarrassed with a reminder of how little we know, it has to afford a certain amount of qualified guesswork.

Even if Plethon's whereabouts and intellectual influences during his formative years remain largely obscure, we can assume with a reasonable amount of certainty that his (even by Byzantine standards) unusual approach to ancient philosophy had a long-lasting impact on the Florentine intellectual milieu in which Ficino sought to set a new standard among his younger associates. One of these, born in the auspicious year of 1463 when Ficino claimed to have begun his Latin translation of Plato, was Giovanni Pico della Mirandola. It is to his famous *Oration* (*De hominis dignitatae*) that we shall soon turn.

8.3.2

Before turning to Pico, however, I am closing this section with a highly tentative biographical genealogy of postclassical pagan philosophy which – provided that there ever was such a thing – should not be considered more than a jeu d'esprit (fig. 4). My point in using the label "pagan" is merely to indicate a trajectory of ideals and ideas followed by a group of intermediaries, interlocutors, and obstinate key players in a process of transmission that does not fit neatly into the mainstream of Islamic and/or Judeo-Christian learning. Many of these figures will remain unknown to us, others only show up in passing (e.g., Mālik ibn 'Uqbūn and Elissaeus), and others yet were surely not self-identifying as pagans at all, but rather participated in the process of transmission by cherry-picking parts of a discourse that they would have rejected as a whole. [184]

---

183 I take this to be a characteristic tendency in Sergei Mariev's recent treatment of Elissaeus' historicity (Mariev 2019).

184 Coda: Since some of the figures included in the flow chart are not even mentioned in this chapter, a few remarks on who they were, where they travelled, and with whom they exchanged ideas are in order. Al-Kindī was an associate of the caliphs al-Ma'mūn and al-Mu'taṣim during the early flourishing phase of the "House of Wisdom" (*Bayt al-Ḥikmah*). His works show a familiarity with the late pagan teaching practices in Alexandria during the 6th century, and he was at least partially familiar with those in Ḥarrān through his acquaintance with Ṯābit ibn Qurra (Jolivet and Rashed 2022). An important early source to the latter's background among the Ḥarrānian Ṣābians survives as a quote from al-Kindī transmitted to al-Nadīm, the author of the *Fihrist* (see above), by the 11th scholar al-Saraḫsī (cf. Tardieu 1986, 12). –'Abd al-Laṭīf al Baghdādī was a well-travelled polymath who studied and interacted with numerous influential scholars in places

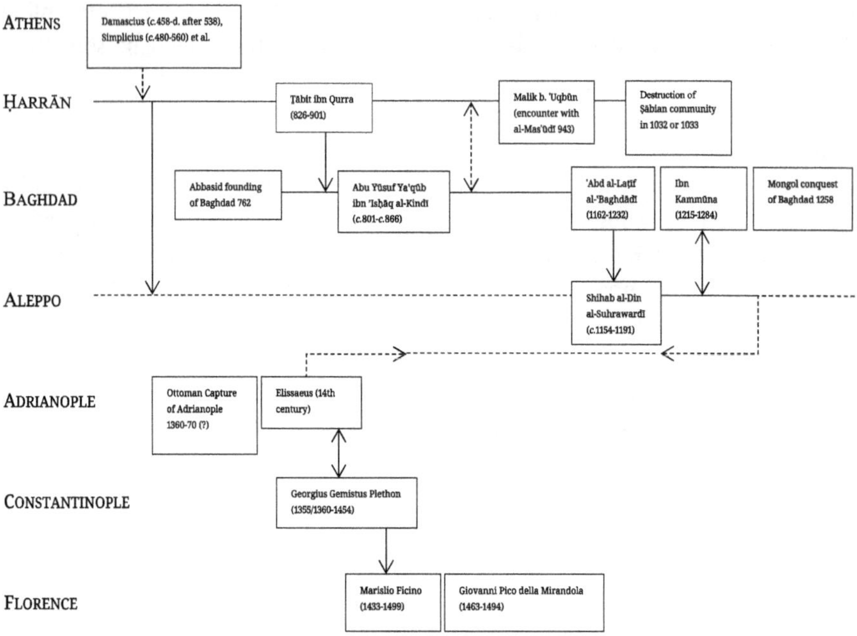

Figure 4: Tentative flow of post-classical pagan philosophy from Athens to Florence (529 CE-1487)

---

such as Mosul, Damascus, Cairo, and Aleppo. Through his studies of the works of Suhrawardī in Mosul, and repeated visits to Aleppo in the early 13th century (just a few decades after the latter's execution), he is likely to have moved in the same intellectual circles as the founder of Illuminationism. During his visit to Cairo, 'Abd al-Laṭīf was introduced to the works of the Hellenistic philosphers Alexander of Aphrodisias and Themistus through the otherwise unknown scholar Abu 'l-Qasim al-Šāri'ī. This new acquaintance is supposed to have turned 'Abd al-Laṭīf away from the philosophy of Ibn Sīnā (Stern 2022). A break with the prescribed peripateticism of Islamic theology by this period can perhaps be considered analogous to the equally provocative break with Thomistic scholasticism among European Humanists during the 15th century. — Ibn Kammūna was a Jewish occultist and philosopher living in Baghdad during the 13th century. He wrote commentaries on Suhrawardī and a comparative treatise of interreligious polemics. Due to the latter book's disinterested dissection of the three monotheistic faiths, it caused al-Kammūna to be attacked by an infuriated mob in 1280 a few years before his death in 1284. As a Jewish scholar active in Baghdad after the Mongol conquest, he belongs in a period and cultural environment that was perhaps not entirely different from that of Elissaeus in the Ottoman capitol of Adrianople (Perlmann 2022).

8.3.3

When Giovanni Pico della Mirandola (1463–1494) came to Florence in 1484, he had already completed a highly ambitious course of study at the Universities of Bologna, Ferrara, and Padua. Beginning already at the age of fourteen as a student of Canon Law in Bologna, he eventually shifted his attention to texts and languages far-off the beaten track of Christian learning in the West by this period. He learned Greek, Hebrew, Aramaic, and Arabic; studied Averroist Aristotelianism with the Jew Elia del Medigo in Padua; and is likely to have been the first Christian in the West to seriously immerse himself in Kabbalist writings.[185] Although Pico and Ficino had already met shortly in 1479, it was only from this moment that they were to become more deeply acquainted and involved in each other's work.

In his 1492 preface to Plotinus' *Enneads*, Ficino recalls his meeting with Pico in 1484 as a spiritual revelation, alerting the reader to the mysterious impregnation of minds through which he immediately felt akin to the young Pico. He ponders the strange coincidence that Pico should be born in the year when Plato was being reborn (i. e., when Ficino was beginning his Latin translation), come to Florence on the very day when the complete translation was published (in 1484), and inspire Ficino to finally begin his translation of Plotinus (just as Cosimo had once urged Ficino to do back in 1462). A divine cause brought it to pass ([*d*]*ivinitus profecto videtur effectum*)! According to Ficino's interpretation, Cosimo would himself once have felt so "ensouled" (*animatus*) by Plethon's lectures in Florence as to conceive the Academy in his mind, and then selecting Ficino while still only a boy to undertake the labor more than 20 years later (cf. Hankins 1990, 151).

After a short period of theological studies in Paris between 1485 and 1486, Pico returned to Florence with an ambitious plan to organize an international council in Rome at which he proposed to publicly defend a collection of nine hundred theological and philosophical theses with any scholar inclined to oppose him. Most of the theses (labelled *doctrinae*) had been excerpted from a variety of Christian and non-Christian sources (Latin, Arabic, and Greek; Platonic, Pythagorean, Chaldean, Hermetic, Kabbalistic, etc.), whereas others had been devised "according to his own opinion" (*secundum opinionem propriam*).[186] The *Conclusiones CM* were published by the printer Eucharius Silber in Rome on 7 December, 1486. The date

185 Among the works with which he familiarized himself through learned Jews in his surroundings were those of the thirteenth-century Italian rabbi Menahem Recanati and his Spanish contemporary Abraham Abulafia.

186 A useful electronic version both of the *Conclusiones CM* and the *Oration* is made accessible through Brown University's Pico Project at https://cds.library.brown.edu/projects/pico/ (last accessed on March 2, 2023). It is to these editions that I shall refer in the following.

proposed by Pico for the beginning of the debate – 6 January, 1487 – was most likely purposely chosen to coincide with the feast of Epiphany ("the feast of the Magi") as a means to symbolically evoke the restored legacy of the pagan sages (see below apropos of Gozzoli's fresco under 8.4).[187]

Contrary to Pico's rather unrealistic expectations, the debate never took place. Instead, Pope Innocent VIII appointed a commission of theologians and experts on Roman and Canon Law to examine the theses. After first imposing censorship of thirteen particularly inappropriate ones (found by the commission to be either "heretical or of dubious orthodoxy" [Edelheit 2008, 279]), the Pope eventually decided to play it safe and condemned the whole printed edition of the *Conclusiones CM* in 1487. Most of the copies were burned. This papal intervention did not prevent Pico from continuing his struggle (he had his *Apologia* of the thirteen theses published in the same year). What shall concern us in the following, however, is rather Pico's deployment of these heterodox ideas in the tradition of pagan teaching from which previous key players (such as Ficino, Plethon, and Elissaeus) would have likewise profited. His attempt at bringing such resources into effective action is best demonstrated in the preamble to the 900 theses, now usually referred to as *De hominis dignitatae.* It is a text that, in spite of its long history of relative neglect, has come to represent one of the most programmatic and widely read statements (its "manifesto" as it were) of the fifteenth-century Humanist movement.

8.3.3.1

The *Oration* is remarkably foreseeing in its espousal of intellectual ideals that did not begin to inform educational policies in the West – not least through the so-called *Humboldtian model of higher education* – until the early 19th century. When Pico describes the human condition as a matter of choice and ambition, allowing us to become what we chose to be by *bending our intellectual efforts to the attainment of the highest things* (§19 [50]), or when the cultivation of mind and knowledge is understood as an end and reward in itself (§25 [158–159]), it is easy to find contemporary grounding for such isolated ideals in a secular environment.[188] If these characterizations of intellectual self-realization are to be appreciated in the context of Pico's own spiritual program, however, they also need to be linked up to the ancient texts and traditions in which they first took shape. Partic-

---

187 Cf. the conclusive discussion of the matter (with references to previous scholarship) in Hanegraaff 2012, 57.

188 E. g., articles 26 and 27 in UN's *Universal Declaration of Human Rights* with their emphases on an education directed to the full development of the human personality, the right to freely share in scientific advancements, etc.

ularly prominent among these are the ones still maintained by the last adherents of pagan philosophy in the Levant. Interestingly, the famous "Delphic" epigraph from Plato's *First Alcibades* (133c) is referred to here – just as once on the gate to the *maǧmaʿ* in Ḥarrān – as a veritable invitation to the philosophical life: from knowledge of the self comes knowledge of the whole in one's self (§21 [124]).

According to Pico's anthropocentric vision of the cosmos, human beings are particularly fortunate in that they may voluntarily transform into all sorts of sentient beings (man is a "work of an indistinguishable image" [*indiscretae opus imaginis*] [§5 {18}]). Those who lead a vegetative life will become plants; if they lead a sensual life they will become brutes; celestial beings if they lead a rational life; angels and sons of God if they lead a life of the intellect (§6 [30]).

Gods, angels, and demigods have been restored to what Pierre Hadot calls a "hierarchic monotheism" (*monothéisme hiérarchique* [Hadot 2004, 114 f.]). These are no longer the mere metaphors of material reality to which mythological beings had been reduced in the medieval poetics of nature. Still, these divine creatures are neither the anthropomorphic agents of epic narrative nor the models of marble statues with their temples and bloodstained altars, but the gods of the Middle- and Neoplatonic philosophers.

In Plutarch's writings (e.g., *Defect.* [see below, 6.2]), for instance, gods and demigods (so-called *daímones*) are downsized to a hierarchy of finite and durable beings (superior to, but still in contiguity with humans and animals) ascending towards the same infinite and unchanging source of light. This unifying core of being is also the divine source from which information can either flow vertically (synchronically) through a more or less noisy channel – from higher to lower mediating divinities –, or horizontally (diachronically) through a more or less uncorrupted chain of mediating sages.[189]

Pico brings this Hellenistic model to bear on a variety of seemingly unconnected traditions so that they eventually begin to appear perfectly concordant: he finds it in the Biblical story of Jacob's dream of the ladder (with "angels of God ascending and descending on it" (Gen. 28:12–15 [e.g., §15 {86}]), in Origen's assertion that Jesus Christ revealed secrets to his disciples that were never committed to writing (§41 [265]), and in the ancient Greek mysteries producing *epopteía* (= immediate vision of divine things) as the end result of expiatory phases of initiation (§ 20 [112]). This glorious experience of divine revelation is described in Mosaic terms as the moment of being finally permitted, through the merit of sublime theology, into God's tabernacle "with no interceding veil of an image" (*nullo imaginis intercedente velo* (§19b [107]).

189 For a comprehensive treatment of Plutarch's religious cosmology, see Brenk 1977.

Towards the end of the *Oration* (§41 [267 ff.]), Pico begins to dwell more extensively upon his presumed rediscovery of Christian doctrine (the Trinity, the Incarnation of the Word, and the divinity of the Messiah §43 [278]) in the ancient lore of Jewish mysticism (Lat. *cabala*). He must have considered it an advantage to have had firsthand access to sources so far largely unknown in the Christian West, because these now seemed to overflow with evidence of a hitherto ignored agreement between the Mosaic and Christian revelations. Yet, we need to recall that the Jewish tradition in which he had just begun to dabble was of course ultimately linked to the same Hellenistic world in which Greek philosophy had once functioned as an intellectual lingua franca, simultaneously interconnecting and transforming discrete religious traditions so as to make them seem far less unique and incommutable than they had once been.

What Pico took as a successful means to uncover a uniform spiritual message behind the mysteries of the ancient world would thus have been nothing but an oblique attempt to decipher a philosophical language that had once functioned as an interface between Hellenistic intellectuals (a Babylonian priest like Berossus, a Jew like Philo, an Egyptian priest like Anebo) in spite of their different ethnic backgrounds; a "language" that had eventually begun to dissolve into the (once more) less compatible idioms of exclusive creeds, denominations, and traditions (of Rabbinic Judaism, of Christianity, and of Islam). One of the keys to this largely forgotten language may well have been accessible all along. It consisted in the transmitted practices of reading and commenting on ancient texts according to standards endorsed by scholars who never felt fully committed to these new creeds. Thẹ Ṣābians of Ḥarrān need not have been the last ones to do so, nor the intellectuals of Adrianople with whom the young Plethon studied, nor Ficino, nor his young adept Pico della Mirandola.

8.4

One can hardly imagine a more evocative visual response to the long-lasting cultural impact of the Council of Florence, with its cavalcade of dignitaries arriving from the dwindling Byzantine empire, than Benozzo Gozzoli's spectacular fresco in the Palazzo Medici-Riccardi's Chapel of the Magi. Closely followed during its three years of completion by Cosimo's son Piero ("the Gouty"), the fresco (usually referred to as the *Cavalcade of the Magi*) was completed by 1462, possibly in the very same year as Cosimo handed over his codex to the twenty-nine-year old Ficino. Prominently seated on horseback in a procession reaching Bethlehem, the three Magi are usually assumed to have received their features from the aged Joseph,

Patriarch of Constantinople (= Melchior); the middle-aged emperor John VIII Palaeologus (= Balthasar); and possibly Cosimo's grandchild and future patron of Ficino's circle, the young Lorenzo de' Medici (= Caspar) (Cardini 2001, 33). The entourage of each Magus is most likely rich in portraits of persons that a fifteenth-century Florentine onlooker would have easily identified as contemporary associates of the Medici clan, such as the scholars attending the Academy, and, according to some, perhaps even Gemistos Plethon himself (Cardini 2001, 43; Seitter 2007). Besides its many references to persons and events with a more direct relation to the Florentine present, however, the visual program of the fresco must have been variously informed by the ancient theme of the three Magi.

The figures of the Magi were certainly already inscribed with a multiplicity of symbolic meanings (the Trinity, the three ages of man, various dimensions of cosmic time etc.), not least due to the fact that they were being annually present in the Florentine commemoration of Epiphany on January the 6th ("the feast of the Magi"). Still, it seems plausible that the commission of Gozzoli's fresco was also prompted by a more idiosyncratic reading of the popular legend against the immediately relevant background of Cosimo's efforts to instigate a Platonic revival in the West. According to this reading – which effectively inverts what seems to have been the original purport of the legend according to the Gospel of Matthew (see ch. 5.3) – the Magi would also have come to represent the unexpected arrival of an obsolete pagan tradition that was not simply perceived as a worthy precursor of Christianity, but rather as its primordial realization in the so-called *prisca religio* ("ancient religion").[190] This divinely inspired, first, or natural religion was conceived by Ficino and his Academic peers as the theological grounding of Christianity preferable to that of Aristotelean metaphysics (Edelheit 2008, 206–229).

Since the Magi were not just understood as any gentiles or pagans arriving from afar, but rather as the harbingers of an ancient wisdom, how else could they have been considered fit to confirm the arrival of Christ? Why else would their story occasionally reveal such apparent links to another (and much earlier) auspicious visitation, had it not been to confirm the return of a lost past that was simultaneously envisioned as the coming of a new era? In another famous painting executed in Antwerp only two decades later (1485–1500), Hieronymus Bosch's *Triptych of the Adoration of the Magi*, the second Magus (Caspar?) is represented with a prefigurative depiction of the visit of Queen Sheba to Solomon on his cloak

190 A similar understanding may lie behind Ficino's eulogization of the Magi as "the first fruits of the Gentiles" in a work written between 1480 and 1489, *De vita libri tres* ("Three Books on Life"), and apparently also in the preface to his translation of Plotinus from 1490 (for further thoughts on the matter, see Hankins 1990, 150 f.).

(fig. 5).[191] The visual evocation of such "sequential arrivals" is an interesting reminder of how the ancient theme of the eccentric sage may have been given a new meaning by the beginning of the early modern period.

Figure 5: Second Magus (Caspar) with a decorated metal cloak showing depictions of Queen Sheba's visit to Solomon. Hieronymus Bosch, *Triptych of the Adoration of the Magi*, executed ca 1494. Grisaille, Oil on oak panel. Madrid, Museo Nacional del Prado. (Detail) ©Photographic Archive Museo Nacional del Prado.

191 Cf. André Chastel's conclusive treatment of the Biblical legend and its continuous transmutations in Christian art and literature, including the links established between Sheba and the Magi (Chastel 1938, 163).

8.4.1

Admittedly, the prevalence of paganism among Renaissance intellectuals should not be exaggerated. There are considerable Christian tendencies in the writings of figures such as Valla, Ficino, and Pico, some of which may even have anticipated elements peculiar to the reformation and counter-reformation (Edelheit 2008, 24f). A telling example to that effect is the spiritual influence of the reformist preacher Savonarola on Pico towards the end of the latter's life. Nevertheless, when the idea of a "pagan Renaissance" is downplayed to such an extent that it is reduced to "a historical cliché whose classical formulation we owe to the nineteenth century, but whose roots extend as far back as the seventeenth," one may wonder how far back in time the roots of that cliché must extend before its sense of being a cliché gets lost (cf. Monfasani 1995, 24)? If it was a cliché already in such proximity to the presumed original, then why not rather assume some rudimentary sense of continuity? Although it would be going too far to describe the secular impact of the Humanist movement as a pagan revival, it certainly did pave the way for a thoroughgoing rehabilitation of a pagan intellectual heritage that had been largely defunct in the West for almost a millennium. One way of strategically justifying this rehabilitation was to present it as a form of Christianization, and more specifically, as a historically and philosophically informed attempt to recuperate a purer Christianity beyond the empty ceremonies and scholastic opinions of the Catholic Church (Edelheit 2008, 24f.). The consequences were nonetheless pervasive, for when this process reaches its culmination, assuming that it also did play a part in the intermediary reformation and counter-reformation of Christianity itself, we end up with a secularized Christianity so permeable and flexible in relation to what it once rejected as pagan or heretic that it largely survives – through the concepts, institutions, and habits of which it no longer holds any copyright – as a kind of cultural background radiation.

If Christian scholars in the Middle Ages had effectively managed to encrypt a pagan heritage by adding various auxiliary pretexts to it, the new academics of Renaissance Europe – not to forget, of course, Shakespeare's "philosophical persons" – became instrumental in decrypting a pagan intellectual heritage that rather was to provide a rationalizing pretext for Christianity, demystifying its supernatural claims, making the obsolete things of its premodern past appear modern and familiar.

9 Postscript: Survivals of Religion in the Western Imaginary

9.1

Before coming to a close, the extensive chronological outline of this study requires at least a few provisional remarks on more recent manifestations of the topics at issue. Whereas the technique referred to as *suspension of judgement* (a.k.a. *attention*) was conceptualized already by the Pyrrhonian sceptics, Coleridge's formula *willing suspension of disbelief* (a.k.a. *pretense*) has been mostly associated with the spirit of secular modernity in which it was coined.[192] Still, I hesitate to associate these complementary dispositions of mind – in spite of the occasional habitus to think otherwise – with different epochs or phases of cognitive evolution. As I have sought to show throughout this book, the propensity to alternately suspend judgement and disbelief is only modern in so far as *we have always been modern*, that is, modern in the anthropological sense of accommodating perceptions of the world not just as it appears, but *as if* it were to appear.[193] This intuition has led me to identify two equally pertinent attitudes that may replace those of rational judgement and irrational belief, namely (1) the attitude of attentively perceiving things *as if* lacking any preconceived notions about them (suspension of judgement), and (2) the attitude of pretending things to be *as if* they are thus conceived to be (i. e., *as if* not being artificially designed, exaggerated, etc.) (suspension of disbelief).

It was not least due to the introduction of a uniquely Christian form of piety, alongside similar devotional attitudes that were to follow in its wake, that the do-

---

192 Although there are certainly earlier references to similar techniques (e. g., Shakespeare's *imaginary puissance* [King Henry V {AS 431}], see above, ch. 8), Jacob Brucker's often adduced reference to Carneades' *assensus suspensione* cannot be kept conceptually distinct from that of *epokhḗ* (*id est adsensionis retentio* [Cicero] ≈ suspension of judgement). Even Coleridge himself was not entirely clear on this point. The closest conceptual candidate is probably Carneades' *probabilis phantasia*, which is kept distinct from that of *assensus suspensione* as a necessary criterion for a happy life (cf. Chandler [1996] for a short and elucidating discussion of these matters). Since from the skeptic's perspective, however, this attitude would have to include all aspects of life that are not placed under philosophical scrutiny, Coleridge was clearly seeking to capture a more specific attitude vis-à-vis art and literature than the condition of everyday habituation.

193 The more familiar formula *we have never been modern*, which serves as the dictum of Bruno Latour's influential book from 1991, should not necessarily be taken to represent the opposite view. Whether the claim is made that we have either *always* or *never* been modern, the crucial move in both cases is to downplay the exaggerated sense of being cut-off from a past in which human perceptions were fundamentally different.

https://doi.org/10.1515/9783110460605-013

mains of attention and pretense became so conceptually entangled as to represent one and the same thing. At the risk of oversimplifying the matter: Faith makes no distinction. You put trust in the things that your intellect defies, but you believe in doing so by adopting the techniques of genuine intellectual exploration.[194] Naturally, this strangely self-cancelling attitude cannot keep the ghosts of the past from re-entering the stage. And so they did – they are among us right now.

In the triumphalist parlance of liberal democracy, secular modernity is sometimes defended as a viable condition of life by turning religion into an antithetical thing of the past. According to this rash sense of juxtaposition, religion comes to stand for all sorts of residual malfunctions of society, such as naïve credulity, pathological self-deception, backward ressentiment, and so on. As long as the ill-fated term itself is carefully avoided, however, it is always possible to cherry-pick aspects of religion by renaming them *existential concerns*, *spirituality*, or *tradition*, and yet some of the prime motivations of attention and pretense with which the assumed properties of premodern religious life were associated are no longer conceived as religious at all. Now, they rather belong in secular domains such as art, entertainment, jurisprudence, and science. We must therefore ask if our *perceptions* have really fundamentally changed, or if it is not rather our way of *conceptualizing* these perceptions that changes with the dwindling influence of religious institutions?

These are questions to which I shall come back, but before doing so let me begin by picking out a few telling examples of how such previously unseen venues of artful science were being imagined by prominent exponents of the early modern period. They are telling examples precisely because of their evocation of wonder and spectacle in the near absence of explicit references to religious notions and institutions.

9.2

During the period of his formative years in Paris on a diplomatic mission, the young Gottfried Wilhelm Leibniz composed a brief text entitled *Drôle de Pensée, touchant une nouvelle sorte de REPRESENTATIONS* (September, 1675) in which he

194 The notion of faith as an act of the intellect is a prominent feature of scholastic theology, as exemplified by Thomas Aquinas' assertion "[c]redere autem est immediate actus intellectus: quia obiectum huius actus est verum, quod proprie pertinet ad intellectum" ("[b]ut to believe is an immediate act of the intellect, because the object of this act is true, which properly belongs to the intellect") (*Summa theologiae*, 2a2ae, q. 4, a. 2.).

outlines a fanciful plan (or "thought-quip" as suggested by the title) for a public enterprise designed to cross-fertilize serious scientific innovation with delightful spectacle (Bredekamp 2005). He claims to have received the idea for the draft while watching a demonstration by the Seine of a machine with which to walk on water. Leibniz imagines a kind of utopian play-palace where assemblies of artisans, showmen, and scientists (sculptors, musicians, poets, carpenters, watchmakers, jugglers, charlatans, engineers, and mathematicians) join forces to increase public knowledge and curiosity. Besides allowing the artificial workings of magic lanterns, fountains, and fireworks to create attention-grabbing effects of immediate sensuous appeal, demonstrations and explanations of mechanics and the natural sciences would tickle the intellect.

By combining artistic performances, lectures, and colloquia on the most varied topics with elements of playful participation and gambling, the play-palace becomes a hub of creativity and amazement – a kind of epistemic machine – defined by its function to alchemically transform the simplest satisfactions of public desire and crazy frolic into higher forms of wisdom. It accommodates a process of social engineering so as to result in the awakening of mankind and inventions of a hitherto unimaginable beauty and importance to be admired by future generations.[195] To be sure, such noble goals could never be achieved without some subtle means of superintendence. The interconnected compartments of the play-palace will all be equipped with a surveillance system allowing its master to secretly audit and monitor the things said and done inside the structure through an inbuilt arrangement of pipes and mirrors. This is the only detail in Leibniz' witty proposition to explicitly (if only figuratively) evoke the function of a traditional religious institution. He considers the surveillance system to greatly benefit the state by functioning as a kind of "space of political confessional" (*une espece de confessional politiqve* [173]). Less than a matter of sacramental absolution, however, curiosity is regarded here as a source of creative energy under the management and surveillance of the secular state.

Modern readers of the *Drôle de Pensée* have not failed to notice its allusions to – once again – Plato's parable (or allegory) of the cave. An especially striking case is the detailed description of shadow theatres in the last supplementary paragraph (218 ff.). While similar instances of projection technology are described in an etching by the Dutch artist Samuel van Hoogstraten published just a few years later, in 1678, it has

195 *Enfin tout le monde en seroit allarmé et comme éveillé, et l'entreprise pourroit avoir des svites aussi belles et aussi importantes qve l'on se sçauroit imaginer, qvi peut estre seront un jour admirée de la posterité* (135–137). Here, and in what follows, I am relying on Horst Bredekamp's edition of the text in *Fenster der Monade: Gottfried Wilhelm Leibniz' Theater der Natur und Kunst* (Bredekamp 2004).

been suggested that both Leibniz and Hoogstraten made independent allusions to Plato's parable through the common influence of previous artistic renderings in the style of Jan Saenredam's early seventeenth-century engraving *Plato's Cave Allegory* (fig. 6) (Bredekamp 2005, 272). Nevertheless, one needs to bear in mind that the optimistic setting of Leibniz' play-palace utopia differs fundamentally from Plato's dystopian machinery of distraction and manipulation. Plato's cave is not a place in which to gradually ascend towards the light of reason, there is no reduced inhibition threshold, no educational disclosure of the artifice. Visitors to the play-palace, on the other hand, enter and exit the structure willingly. Save for the fact of being secretly monitored, they are not being deceived at all, but participate joyfully in the rational celebration of scientific progress and demystification.

Figure 6: Plato's allegory of the cave. Engraving by Jan Sanraedam (1604).

A similar tendency to indulge in the exploration of optical allurements on the pretext of demystification can be noticed in the work *Ars Magna Lucis et Umbrae* ("The Great Art of Light and Shadow" [1st ed. 1646 {3rd ed. 1671}]) by the Jesuit scholar Athanasius Kircher, with whom Leibniz had corresponded about combinatorics shortly before his Paris years. There is even a passing reference to the latter's Roman cabinet of curiosities in the *Drôle de Pensée*. A prominent theme running through Kircher's description of recent optical techniques – all those cunning means by which to artificially represent the world through the manipulation of mirrors and lenses – is the demystification of the occult. It is a rhetoric worthy of a Jesuit, for if the ghosts are not properly revealed in terms of their artificial causes, they will remain the secret weapons of necromancers (Kircher 1671, 734, 780).[196]

Still, Kircher's scientific curiosity went further than such pious motivations might suggest. He rather proudly admits to the excitement among visitors to his museum at the display of a device producing the illusion of solid objects floating in midair. They admire it, he asserts, without trying to hide their rational disposition in regard to the mechanism behind the optical thaumaturgy (Kircher 1671, 782).[197] One could hardly wish for a more accurate characterization of what it means to *willingly suspend disbelief.* Kircher was apparently aware of this centuries before Coleridge saw the need for a formula. Yet it is an altogether different task to determine in what sense Kircher's philosophically informed religious beliefs differed from his scientifically informed beliefs in the rational emancipation of consciousness. The influx of Neoplatonism and alternative trends of biblical hermeneutics was already massive enough in the West to make Kircher withstand the occasional critique and censorship of his Jesuit peers. He concludes his *Ars Magna* with a verse that could just as well have been quoted directly from Julian's *Hymn to king Helios:*

> [—] *Disperge has radiis animae fulgentibus umbras, ut tua sit mea lux, lux mea sit tua lux.*
>
> [—] Disperse the shadows of the soul with shining rays, so that your light be mine, and my light be your light.[198]

Despite his equally controversial stance on theological matters, Leibniz was to remain in the Lutheran confession throughout his life. His choice not to convert to the Catholic faith, in spite of the advantages that such a step would have brought

196 The artificial projection of dazzling apparitions onto a wall by means of transparent conductors and other optical instruments is already described in some detail by Iamblichus as a focal element in the ritual practice of theurgy (*De myst.* 3.8). Such techniques would thus not have been understood as deceitful, but rather as being "worthy of the gods." I am grateful to Wouter Hanegraaff for bringing this fascinating datum to my attention.

197 *Hujusmodi machinamentum ego in Musaeo meo exhibere soleo: quod omnes mirantur quidem, nemine tamen occultam dispositionis rationem percipiente: de quo plura in Mechanico nostro Thaumaturgo.*

198 Kircher 1671, 810. Despite the apparent allusion to James 1:17 (cf. the quote in the epilogue [Kircher 1671, 797]), the message of the final epigraph conveys a more straightforward Platonic sense of intellectual apotheosis.

to his academic career, suggests that his religious persuasions were not just an esoteric outgrowth of his philosophical system. At the same time, however, he was strongly committed to the ecumenical cause. Unsurprisingly, perhaps, in view of the religious conflicts that had troubled large parts of Europe during the first half of the 17th century, yet more surprisingly so in consideration of his philosophical preoccupation with the minutiae of Christian doctrine. Some would probably find it awkward that the inventor of the calculus and the modern binary system was also eager to show that the bread of the Eucharist likewise afforded the real bodily presence of Christ (in accordance with the confession of Augsburg) and a change of its whole substance without affecting its species (in accordance with the council of Trent).[199] More importantly, however, Leibniz partook in laying the modern foundation of what is usually referred to as natural theology. Besides outlining a general argument for the objective provability of divine creation in the unfolding of a "divine science" (the so-called *mathesis divina*), he also insisted in more particular terms on the possibility of the Christian mysteries without claiming rational access to their actual origin (Goldenbaum 1998, 187).

The important conclusion to be drawn from this circumstance is that once the experimental sciences were beginning to merge into a unified project during the early modern period, it was a reified religion that granted the project proper grounding, not some atheist tendencies to demonstrate the dispensability of religion. Contrary to a nowadays somewhat carelessly accepted popular assumption, modern science did not emerge as an independent contrast case for religion (Harrison 2015, 187).

Leibniz' and Kircher's original rhetoric of demystification in regard to the magic lantern continued to hold sway well into the late modern period. Even by the turn of the 19th century, Etienne-Gaspard Robertson – a French master in the art of optical showmanship usually taken to represent the closest precursor of modern cinema (the so-called phantasmagoria) – could open his shows with the following words:

> That which will occur shortly before your eyes, Gentlemen, is not a frivolous spectacle; it is created for the thinking man, for the philosopher who likes to lose himself for a moment, with Sterne, among the tombs.[200]

199 Cf. letter to Antoine Arnauld [A II, 1: 175] quoted in Goldenbaum 1998, 179.
200 Robertson's *Mémoires* (Vol. I, 278) quoted in Mannoni 2000, 160 f.

9.3

If pagan residuals had long been maintained in the Christian West through learned as well as vernacular strategies of displacement and encryption, a significant change can be perceived in how secular versions of a once religiously coded pagan spectacle (in the form of festivals, theatrical performances, and oracular consultations) are being rehabilitated at the height of the early modern period. Against a predominantly scholastic model of Christian learning, a new intellectual culture of curiosity and experimentation was gaining ground during the 16th and 17th centuries. One may even perceive a correlation between experimental natural philosophy and experimental religion, as exemplified by the emphasis in Puritanism on the first-person encounter with God. An experimental attitude towards God, much like an experimental involvement with the natural world, implies the replacement of a reliance on previous authorities and written traditions with that of individual experience (cf. Harrison 2007, 193).

This new attitude of self-cultivation can be paradoxically seen to reaffirm a pagan philosophical model of *epokhḗ* as opposed to a scholastic model based on the achievement of virtues and spiritual ends through repeated practice (Harrison 2015, 85). Without hesitating to emphasize the limitations and corruptibility of human knowledge, "[e]xperimental philosophy [...] sought the slow recovery of Adamic knowledge, but with an acute awareness that human investigators no longer possessed the perfect faculties of their first father" (Harrison 2007, 138). In spite of such superficially sound rejections of traditional religious authorities and paraphernalia, however, the uncompromising attitude of conservative Puritans is also a necessary factor to account for in order to make historical sense of events such as the Salem witch trials (1692–1693). How is this possible?

It is a fascinating and somewhat unsettling thought that the early modern witch hunts belong in an age that we begin to vaguely recognize as our own, not necessarily in spite of certain lingering elements of popular superstition, but perhaps rather by force of the fact that the popular beliefs of the early modern period are being accommodated to a discourse of antiquarianism and scientific exploration with its own ideals of amusement, its own explication of sacred scripture, its own principles of naked terror unbound by the theoretical authority of the old ecclesiastical institutions. Grandiose efforts to rejuvenate and purify the world have a familiar tendency to spill over into a superstitious aversion to the filth and darkness of the past. As shown by Peter Burke apropos of the early modern perceptions of witchcraft, there is but a thin line distinguishing the abjuration of things efficacious but wicked from those merely foolish but harmless (Burke 1994, 241). Whereas the fear of witchcraft can of course be considered a serious social concern in itself, there seems to be a definite change in attitude towards the purported object of that fear characteristic of the transition from an initial and second phase of the so-called "reform of popular culture" around 1650.

This change in attitude can be illustrated with two characteristically ambiguous examples from Swedish seventeenth-and-eighteenth century learned discourse. The first example (Bureus) serves to show how an antiquarian attitude towards pagan conceptions confirms itself as a continuous part of pagan culture, whereas the second (Linnaeus) illustrates how a scientistic rhetoric of abjuration is used in regard to the pre-scientific past.

9.3.1

Johannes Bureus (1568–1652) was a polymathic antiquarian, linguist, mystic, and poet who served for a long time as a national archaeologist and head of the National Library. As an assistant teacher of prince Gustavus Adolphus, Bureus exercised a strong influence on the nationalistically informed antiquarian yearnings that were burgeoning in the wake of Sweden's rise to European power during the Thirty Year's war. Among the books and manuscripts that Bureus donated to the National Library in 1651, a particularly bulky specimen is referred to as *Sumlen* ("Collection"). It originally consisted of circa 900 pages (some of which are now lost) interspersed with unordered notes and drawings, so-called *collectanea*, which the donator believed could be of benefit to the future cultivation of antiquities (Klemming 1886, intr.). The content is extremely diverse. Some of the notes are of an almost impenetrable private character; others contain descriptions of local folk practices, omens, anecdotes, artifacts, and strange (often culturally encoded) natural formations; and others yet consist of firsthand reports in regard to which Bureus' role of an antiquarian observer is impossible to tell apart from that of an indigenous participant.

Among the dispersed biographical notes related to those in *Sumlen*, there are two rather striking references to trolls being struck by lightning.[201] Whereas the first reference merely builds on hearsay, it remains significant in that it attests to the vernacular survival of a pagan mythological topos.[202] In the year 1598, a cer-

201 *Sumlen* proper contains at least one such reference (concerning "a troll hit by lightning on the island of Visingsö" [*ett trol som Asökian slogh på Wisingzö*]) (Klemming 1886, 79).

202 Thor, the Scandinavian god of thunder, is characterized in the Icelandic thirteenth-century *Edda* by Snorri Sturluson as "having fared eastward to slay trolls" ([*Þórr*] *var farinn í Austrvega at beria trǫll*) (*Edda*, [*Skáldskaparmál* 3]). Since Snorri's mythological compendium remained fairly unknown outside Iceland before its first publication in 1665, it is unlikely to have had any influence on Swedish popular beliefs by the late 16th century.

tain Nils Masson from Övernäs (17 km southeast of Västerås) is reported to having "seen the troll which was struck by the thunderbolt (lit. Thor's bolt) on the ridge of Balung (today's Badelunda) by Västerås."[203] Bureus continues the paragraph with a detailed description of the troll's clothing and bodily characteristics, how it communicated with visitors to the ridge, and suddenly disappeared out of sight after having been turned around by someone (Klemming 1886, 84).

In another reference to trolls and lightning, Bureus describes a small scientific expedition to the village of Danmarksby outside Uppsala. Two trolls are said to have been burned during a thunderstorm on the night of the 10th of July 1623. Ten days later, on the 20th of July:

> [C]ame I and the gentlemen Jon and Joh. to the village of Danmark and saw the bones of the two trolls which were burned by lightning (lit. Thor's fire), a 6 ells (= 3,56 meters) long skeleton on display in the lodges, the other in the cellar, bones and blood I took home.[204]

The curious report testifies to the extreme imaginative force with which the observation of a natural phenomenon, its cultural encoding, and follow-up documentation can attract the notion of a thunderstruck troll so as to make it appear perfectly tangible and real. Whatever the character and origin of the physical remains that Bureus observed in the lodges of Danmark on that summer day in 1623, they apparently made sense to him.[205] The fact that they did so suggests that his antiquarian curiosity was by no means cut-off from the symbolic universe in which he lived and labored. He was not conducting his investigations with an aim to gather revealing counterevidence, but in a hermeneutical spirit of affirmative participation. The question with which Bureus appears to have grappled was not whether trolls existed, but rather how to interpret them, how to incorporate them into an increasingly complex patchwork of continental learning, how to keep them informed.

---

203 [*S*]*eet det Trullet som Torwiggen slogh på Balungz ås vid Westerås* (Klemming 1886, 84).

204 [*V*]*ar jagh och her Jon och Joh. til Danmarks byn och sågom benen efter de tu trollen som af Torelden brende voro, 6 alner lång ben radh, som i stugu benken syntes, det andra i kellaren, ben och blodh togh iagh hem.* (Klemming 1886, 86)

205 The incident is discussed perceptively by Mathew Norris in a doctoral thesis about Bureus and the early days of Swedish antiquarian scholarship (Norris 2016, 177–176). He believes that Bureus was simply deceived with a hoax, since he was already reputed to be a "muddle-headed dreamer" in many intellectual and clerical circles. Although I see no reason to dispute this claim, Bureus' idiosyncratic personality would not make him less of an exponent to a living vernacular tradition involving trolls.

9.3.2

Unlike the lesser-known Bureus, Carl Linnaeus (1707–1778) is an internationally acknowledged scholar due to his groundbreaking contributions to systematic botany and zoology. Although largely superseded today, his attempt at a complete cladistic classification of nature (the so-called "empire of nature" [*imperium naturae*]) has fundamentally influenced the modern biological nomenclature. Linnaeus was a co-founder of the Swedish Royal Academy of the Sciences in 1739, a professor of medicine and botany at Uppsala University between 1741 and 1778, and three times its rector. There is an irony in the fact that Linnaeus owned a summer residence in the same parish of Danmark where Bureus had once collected the blood and bones of the two thunderstruck trolls. The former's attitude to the local cosmology of past generations could hardly contrast more starkly with the latter's.

In the second period of his rectorate at Uppsala University in 1759, Linnaeus made a famous speech in the presence of King Adolf Fredrik, Queen Lovisa Ulrika, and Crown Prince Gustav. It is a discourse expressive of the culture of the Enlightenment, and not least of its devotion to the refinement of human civilization through the cultivation of science. Still, the rhetoric of refinement is premised on an awkward sense of contrast. Without the sciences, he asserts, we would:

> [P]rescribe priests from Rome, physicians from Montpellier, architects from Venice, musicians from Naples [...] yeah, forest nymphs would hide in all bushes, ghosts would haunt all dark corners, gnomes, goblins, nixies, and other followers of Lucifer would live among us as grey cats and superstition, witchery, and invocations would swarm among us like mosquitoes.[206]

The remarkable fact about Linnaeus' antagonistic imagery is not the equation of Catholic aberrancies with the rural superstitions of a once Catholic country, but the lack of distinction between modes of existence. Goblins, nixies, and other followers of Lucifer seem to inhabit the same unscientific world as priests from Rome and physicians from Montpellier. They would all still live among us, alongside the swarming presence of their conjurers and devotees, if it was not for the sciences. Although Linnaeus certainly perceived a difference between goblins and Catholic priests, his rhetoric would have lost its persuasive force if it was not for this sense of indistinctiveness. The emphasis is not placed on the ontological status

206 [F]öreskriva *Präster* från Rom. / *Läkare* från Monspelier. / *Architecter* från Venedig. / *Musicanter* från Neapel. [—] / Ja, *Skogssnuvor* skulle gömma sig i alla buskar. / *Gastar* spöka i alla mörka vrår. / *Tomtgubbar, Vettar, Næckar* och andra Lucifers anhang / leva med oss som gråkattor. / samt *Vidskeppelse, Hexerie, Signerie* svärma omkring oss som Mygg (Uggla 1939, 94).

of various abhorrent things, but on their being actively denied an existence, on their being scientifically forced (or exorcized) out of existence.

The discrete cases of Bureus and Linnaeus can be characterized as representing two very different responses to the early modern paradigm of scientific exploration. Whereas Bureus was a relatively early exponent to reformed Christianity and a latecomer to the eclectic ideals of the Renaissance, Linnaeus belongs in a period of coordinated scientific progress and systematic challenges to the philosophical foundations of religion (David Hume's *Natural History of Religion* had appeared in print just two years before Linnaeus' rectorial address).[207] The question remains, then, how two such fundamentally different approaches to the natural world – with Bureus and his scientifically accommodated trolls representing one side, and Linnaeus' and his scientifically exorcised entities the other – can shed further light on the oxymoronic conjunction of religion and modernity? How are we supposed to make historical sense of the life and survival of religion in an age so obsessed with redefining the legacy of its own premodern past?[208]

9.4

Many of the now classical definitions of religion are premised on two factors, that is, (1) a variety of truth claims and some (2) metaphysical quantity in regard to which these truth claims are being constructed alongside certain forms of organized behavior, sacred scriptures, institutions, etc.[209] Such definitions have a familiar tendency to induce ethnocentric and anachronistic distortions of what some scholars rashly identify as religion in a long-term historical and cross-cultural perspective.

If there is anything about the familiar features of religious discourse and practice that can be identified without access to a set of truth claims, it might avail to begin with these features before trying to establish their raison d'être. What seems

207 Although Linnaeus' himself was far from an irreligious man, he did not hesitate to advance symbolic interpretations of Biblical narrative in so far as it seemed to contradict scientific knowledge.

208 One of the most emblematic expressions of this obsession is the image of the ruin. Its continuous artistic exploration and reinvention throughout the modern period (from the ruins of ancient Rome in Patrarch's letter to Giovanni Colonna, via Caspar David Friedrich's Eldena Abbey, to Albeert Speer's pre-programmed ruins) is reminder of an age struggling to define itself in terms of an absent witness.

209 A now equally classical summary of such definitions, most of which are divided into the categories of intellectualistic and voluntaristic definitions, is found in the appendix to James H. Leuba's *A Psychological Study of Religion: Its Origin, Function, and Future* (Leuba 1912, 339–363).

to remain, then, could perhaps best be characterized as a set of collectively sustained representations and perceptions of the world distinct from how it is provisionally conceived to be. Hence, it is not chiefly by proceeding from preconceived beliefs or well-grounded judgements that such representations become perceptually accessible, but to a larger degree through the suspension of judgement and belief.

The modern concept of religion is in itself a kind of chimera, since its origins in the first encounters with the previously unknown civilizations of Meso-America during the early modern period (with its new conceptual encompassment of any "*belief system* to result in *ceremonial behavior*" [my italics] [Smith 1998, 270]) is premised on a combination of the pre-Christian (Ciceronian) sense of religion (with its primary focus on the proper observance of civic worship, excluding superstitions, and sectarian tendencies), and its Christian (Lactantian-Augustinian) sense (with its focus on truth, piety, and faith).

9.4.1

Few would probably insist on reducing religious behavior to the kind of practical knowledge that had already established itself in various human populations hundreds of millennia ago out of pure necessity (how to exploit food sources, manufacture tools, make fire, etc.). Instead, it is a form of behavior linked to the culturally specific means by which humans persistently elaborate, encode, obfuscate, and deviate from precisely those practicalities of life that would otherwise have appeared indispensable or universally comprehensible in themselves. Religion belongs in a universally recognizable repository of cultural artifacts that becomes partially recognizable to us because of the costly, locally distinctive, contingent, and arbitrary characteristics of its contents. In the interest of constructively applying the category of religion as a generic term for some of the species contained within this massive reservoir, therefore, it seems advisable – leaving behind the nitpicking involved in such an exercise – to at least avoid doing so by specifying in too narrow terms the epistemic and emotional commitments on which they thrive.

In order for such an exercise to improve our historical perception, however, it will also have to reflect back on our ways of understanding the contemporary status of religion. A tentative precept might be to begin by specifying whether we are interested in the contemporary status of religious residuals or in residual religion, that is, in the purportedly demystified legacies of once overtly religious aspects of culture, or in the overt survivals of religion? Whereas the first category would not even qualify as religious in everyday parlance, the latter is still acknowledged as such because it remains bound to certain officially recognized religious organizations, holidays, institutions, and ethnic communities.

To be more precise, religious residuals are not necessarily considered irreligious because people have lost faith in them, but rather because they were never considered to involve faith in the first place. Since modalities of belief (creeds, confessions, faiths, etc.) to such an overwhelming extent have come to define religion, an inevitable side effect of this moderately prescriptive definition is that all sorts of culturally significant comportments in a contemporary setting will appear as the disenchanted, secularized, and vacuous properties of unbelief. They remain attractive and affordable only in so far as they do not put any reality-testing abilities at stake.

Another consequence of this definition is that it fosters certain unwarranted notions about premodern religiosity.[210] Religiosities of the premodern past – or at least some of the factors that contributed to their motivational force – will thus necessarily begin to appear more alien to a rashly conceptualized modern mindset than they actually were. In short, premodern equivalents to the shallow distractions of secular modernity have a tendency to become religiously coded in retrospect, but idiosyncratically (and anachronistically) so on the Christian premise of faith and revelation.

9.4.2

Another prominent category of religious residuals belongs in a domain where they are possibly even less expected to belong, namely in the world of academia. There are of course numerous branches of academia (such as economy, education, business administration, and the applied sciences) in reference to which it would make little sense to sketch out such a genealogy. If, on the other hand, we were to take a general vote for the disciplines that are currently enjoying the greatest respect as autotelic intellectual pursuits, it should probably not come as a surprise if they were also the ones in which the cult of the genius is still best preserved: astronomy, mathematics, theoretical physics, and at least some branches of philosophy. These geniuses almost invariably conform to the exaggerated, still pertinent stereotype of a male intellectual: a socially unconventional, distracted, anomalous, and antinomian updated version of the ancient sage.

---

210 Needless to say, whatever form of religious credulity understood to have been pertinent *back then* will also characterize cultures *over there.* As long as distance is understood as a qualifier of cultural difference, it matters less if the approach is historiographic or ethnographic (for further thoughts on this topic, see ch. 2).

In 1995, the artists Jake and Dinos Chapman caused an outrage of critical disdain with their twelve foot tall fiberglass sculpture *Übermensch.* It represented the physicist Stephen Hawking perched on the edge of a rock in his wheelchair, as if gazing into the ineffable abyss of cosmic beginnings. Without seeking to meddle in the critical discussion of the work's artistic and moral dimensions – the *The Guardian's* Jonathan Jones referred to it as the "most repellent work of modern art" – I cannot disregard the cultural significance of the provocation precisely for the reason that it was understood by so many as an iconoclastic gesture.[211] To be sure, the Chapman brothers' sculpture did not cause public annoyance because it seemed to mock a poor man in a wheelchair, ironically referring to him as an *Übermensch,* but because it mocked the popular image of Hawking according to which he was indeed already being conceived as a heroic figure with superhuman intellectual powers.

In the popular imagery, Hawking had come to represent more than just a brilliant scientist who contributed decisively to modern cosmology in spite of his severe physical disabilities caused by a motor neuron disease. It was as if his lifework could be meaningfully linked to his precarious physical condition in response to some archaic logic of self-sacrifice. There was simply something too suggestive about the negative correlation between Hawking's intellectual capacities and his physical incapacities to be considered accidental. As if to emphasize the fact of having transcended the limits of his vocal and bodily presence, his synthesized speech and seated position in a hi-tech wheelchair suggestively resonated with the western iconology of the prophet or genius. The figure that Hawking involuntarily seemed to "quote" by his mere broadcasted appearance can be effectively traced, via its more recent conceptualizations in eighteenth-century literary theory, all the way back to the notion of the philosopher's godlike "strangeness" or "being-out-of-the-way-ness" (Gr. *atopía*) in the works of Plato (cf. ch. 5).

In long-term retrospect (just to emphasize a point already made in previous chapters), the figure of the eccentric sage can be identified as the paragon of self-examination and spiritual transformation on which the lives of the early Christian saints were modelled. Unrecognized among the licit varieties of public worship, the self-chosen lifestyle of the sectarians and teachers of wisdom required its own rites of initiation and purification, its own communal meals, its own founding figures, oral instructions, texts, and commentaries. Their adherents

211 Jones' text in *The Guardian* is in fact clear testimony to this effect: "They [the Chapman brothers] got it bizarrely, horribly wrong. Hawking's story really is an epic triumph of the human mind. His defiance of illness is profoundly moving, his ability to mentally explore the universe in spite of it an inspiration for our time and times to come. How many lives are so poetic?" ("Thin line between art and hate: is this the most repellent work of modern art?" [Thu 12 Jan 2012]).

may have differed decisively in their epistemic commitments, but they all sought justification for their ritualized way of life in such commitments. Among them were also those who called themselves academics, the philosophers, the last pagans. They did not merely try to live as they learned, but practiced a form of devoted learning by means of living.

What eventually came to make a crucial difference between these spiritualities of the *biós* was not so much the preferences of thought and practice, but rather the massive influence on public discourse and practice that eventually was to become an exclusively Christian concern. Once a uniquely Pauline understanding of repentance, truth, and faith had come to define the only acceptable, codified form of *religio* in the Christian West, all those spiritual practices of the *biós* that either predated or otherwise obfuscated the doctrinal framework of Christian piety were not just beginning to appear suspect, but necessarily becoming conceptually vague. The new conceptual category of *religio falsa* would thus not just imply the fact of being religiously committed to false beliefs and the worship of false gods, but in a certain sense also the likewise impious fact of not being religious at all.

9.4.4

If, today, wonders and fantasies continue to tickle the escapist cravings of secular society, these are typically redescribed as consumerist concerns of entertainment and recreation. At the same time, however, a new kind of mind-boggling reality is continuously being theorized, calculated, and experimentally demonstrated in the arcane recesses of scientific exploration. Even if the properties of a Calabi-Yau manifold or a decaying Higgs particle can only be adequately encoded in a recondite hieratic idiom, they keep resurfacing as superficial items of popular awe and amusement in flashy visualizations of popular science magazines and science docs. These conflicting concerns of scientific attention and popular pretense are not just analogous to, but to some necessary degree genealogically akin to the discretely sacred (alchemical, ataraxic, epistemological, spectacular, thaumaturgic, etc.) concerns of a premodern world.

Without implying that residual religion and religious residuals can always be neatly unpacked according to some clearly distinguishable, coexisting characteristics – their contemporary merger is not least evident in the "grey zones" of New Age spirituality and various forms of fandom subculture[212] – it does make sense

212 A characteristic trait of such intermediary phenomena, so-called hyper-real religions are currently attracting increasing interest among students of religion. See, for instance, the edited vol-

to acknowledge those aspects of secular culture that owe their religious significance not so much to their appearance of being substitutes for religion, but rather in terms of their religious genealogies.

As evidenced by the intellectual spirit of the early modern period (see above 9.2), religious residuals owe their equal share to an experimental science once seeking its original justification in natural theology, and a modern entertainment industry devoted to the charitable cause of social recovery and the cultivation of popular curiosity. As it seems, the contemporary characteristics of autotelic science and popular entertainment correspond by a fairly large measure of matches to what is retrospectively recognized as pagan religiosity (= religious residuals). What remains religiously coded (= residual religion) outside of these domains can be largely understood to result from a confluence of these once independent fields of practice (i. e., the make-believe pageantry of civic worship, and the philosopher's or mystagogue's quest for truth and salvation) as conceptualized, on the one hand, in the early writings of Christian theologians, and as realized, on the other hand, in the religious policies of the first Christian emperors.

Institutionalized religion, then, as it is nowadays typically conceived in the West to ensue from some sort of soteriological creed, retains much of what comes to represent the end result of an experimental attempt in late antiquity to coordinate aspects of cultural practice that in their present manifestations are no longer perceived as having any obvious religious significance. Religion no longer seems to be what it once was, and what it once was no longer seems to be religion.

9.5

I should like to close this discussion by referring once more to another closing statement, namely, that of Claude Lévi-Strauss' programmatic preamble to the structural study of myth: "[M]an has always been thinking equally well; the improvement lies, not in an alleged progress of man's mind, but in the discovery of new areas to which it may apply its unchanged and unchanging powers." (see above 2.5) (Lévi-Strauss 1955, 444). My point in rehearsing this quote is not to rehabilitate Lévi-Strauss' now largely defunct program of structural anthropology. On the contrary, I take it to be a statement about precisely those timeless aspects of

---

ume *Fiction, Invention and Hyper-reality* (Cusack and Kosnac 2018) and the *Handbook of Hyper-real Religions* (Possamai 2012).

thought that all too easily get confused with certain contingent areas of application (including those of structural anthropology).

While there is little explicit disagreement today about the always equally *bad* notion of the so-called primitive mind, the concomitant notion that the recent progress of science should not have qualitatively altered the intellectual process may still cause occasional discomfort. Furthermore, it may seem equally unsettling to some that the unchanging conditions of being, the good, beauty, and language to which the human mind continuously struggles to apply its unchanged and unchanging powers should remain as enigmatic and contested today as they were 2500 years ago. When privileged individuals in the ancient world were first given the opportunity to devote themselves full-time to such intellectual exercises, we should not be surprised to discover that their preliminary results would soon reach such a high level of accomplishment as to appear fully compatible with those of the modern era. It should also be kept in mind that these early exercises of the mind were also spiritual exercises, that they were ritually and mythically informed, not in the sense of an encumbrance, but as a necessary condition of affordance and efficacy. There is consequently nothing intellectually naïve about Parmenides' sixth-century BCE ontology, nor about Pāṇini's sixth-to-fourth century BCE theory of grammar, just as there is nothing artistically naïve about the cave paintings of Chauvet and Lascaux. When it comes down to the real fundamentals, the theorists of ancient Greece and India are apparently still conversant with modern figures such as John Archibald Wheeler and Noam Chomsky (Wheeler 1990, 7; Chomsky/Halle 1968, 435).

What has changed in the meantime is not so much the quality of the intellectual process, but the gradual depreciation of that process in its soteriological decipherment of itself.

And as for the masks, did we ever believe in them?[213] All those games of pretense, were they ever somehow taken to be more of the real deal? Probably not. There was most likely never a first mask mistaken for a face, never a first cave

---

213 I am referring here to the psychoanalyst Octave Mannoni's (1969) discussion of the ambiguities of belief with its repeated quotes from Don Chuka Talayesva's *Sun Chief: The Autobiography of a Hopi Indian* (1942). In seeking to make sense of the masks used in ritual dances to represent the Hopi spirits known as *kachina*, Talayesva asserts that *he knows full well* that the masks are not the spirits, they are his relatives masquerading as such, *yet all the same* they are there. Mannoni takes the statement "I know well, but all the same" (*Je sais bien, mais quand même*) to be a particularly significant qualifier of religious belief alongside the notion that the disambiguation of belief ("In former times, we used to believe in the masks" [*Autrefois, on croyait aux masques*]) somehow defines the naïveté of an irrevocably lost, unqualified past (Mannoni 1969, 16).

mistaken for a world – there can be no truly human face without a temporary mask to hide behind, no truly human world without a temporary cave to hide in.

Bibliography

Primary Sources

Abbreviations (ancient works and authors), editions, and translations

Arist. = Aristotle

de An. = *De Anima*. Edited and translated by W. S. Hett. *On the Soul. Parva Naturalia. On Breath.* Cambridge, Mass.: Harvard University Press, 2000 (revised ed.).

Mech. = *Mechanica*. Edited and translated by W. S. Hett. *Minor Works*. Cambridge, Mass.: Harvard University Press, 1936.

Metaph. = *Metaphysics*. Edited and translated by Hugh Treddenick. Cambridge, Mass.: Harvard University Press, 1989.

NM = *Ethica Nicomachea*. Edited and translated by H. Rackham. *The Nicomachean Ethics*. Cambridge, Mass.: Harvard University Press, 1982.

Protrepticus = *Der Protreptikos des Aristoteles*. Edited and translated by Ingemar Düring. Frankfurt am Main: Vittorio Klostermann, 1969.

Beowulf = Edited by Eliot Van Kirk Dobbie. *Beowulf and Judith*. The Anglo-Saxon Poetic Records IV. New York: Columbia University Press, 1953.

Cic. = M. Tullius Cicero

Div. = *De divinatione ad M. Brutum*.

Edited by R. Giomini, *De Divinatione, De Fato, Timaeus*. Leipzig: Teubner, 1975.

Edited and translated by W. A. Falconer. *On Old Age, On Friendship, On Divination*. Cambridge, Mass.: Harvard University Press, 1923.

CFA = *Corpus Fabularum Aesopicarum*. Edited by August Hausrath and Herbert Hunger. Leipzig: Teubner, 1959–1970.

DK = *Die Fragmente der Vorsokratiker.* Edited and translated by Herman Diels and Walther Kranz. Zurich: Weidmann, 1996 [repr. of the sixth edition from 1951–1952].

D. L. = Diogenes Laertius. Edited and translated by R. D. Hicks. *Lives of Emminent Philosophers*. Cambridge, Mass.: Harvard University Press, 1972.

Epicur. = Epicurus

Ep. = *Epistulae*. Edited and translated by Cyril Bailey. *Epicurus. The Extant Remains*. Oxford: Clarendon Press, 1926.

Eur. = Euripides. Edited by J. Diggle. *Euripidis Fabulae*. Oxford: Clarendon Press, 1984.

Alc. = *Alcestis*

Bacch. = *Bacchae*

Eus. = Eusebius

VC = *Vita Constantini*. Translated by Averil Cameron and Stuart G. Hall. *Eusebius. Life of Constantine*. Oxford: Clarendon Press, 1999.

Hes. = Hesiod

Th. = *Theogonia*. Edited and translated by Glenn W. Most. Theogony. Works and Days. Testimonia. Cambridge, Mass.: Harvard University Press, 2006.

Fr. = *Fragmenta Hesiodea*. Edited by Reinhold Merkelbach and Martin L. West. Oxford: Clarendon Press, 1967.

https://doi.org/10.1515/9783110460605-014

Hdt. = Herodotus. Edited by Haiim B. Rosén. Herodoti Historiae. Vol. I, Libros I–IV. Leipzig: Teubner, 1987.
h. Hom. = *Hymni Homerici.* Edited and translated by Martin L. West. *Homeric Hymns. Homeric Apocrypha. Lives of Homer.* Cambridge, Mass.: Harvard University Press, 2003.
Hom. = Homer
Od. = *Odyssea.* Edited by Arthur Ludwich. Vol. I. Leipzig: Teubner, 1889.
Translated by Barry B. Powell. *The Odyssey.* Oxford: Oxford University Press, 2014.
LG = *Lyra Graeca.* Edited and translated by J. M. Edmonds. Vol. I–III. Cambridge, Mass.: Harvard University Press, 1924–1927.
Liv. = Livy (T. Liuius)
A.U.C. = *Ab Urbe Condita/The History of Rome*
Ov. = Ovid (Ouidius Naso)
Met. = *Metamorphoses.*
OF = *Poetae Epici Graeci II. Orphicorum et Orphicis similium testimonia et fragmenta.*
Fasc. 1/2. Edited by Alberto Bernabé. Munich and Leipzig: Sauer, 2004–2005.
Paus. = Pausanias. Edited and translated by W. H. S. Jones. *Description of Greece.* Vol. I–V. Harvard, Mass.: Harvard University Press, 1918–1935.
Pi. = Pindar
Edited by Herwig Maehler. *Pindari Carmina cum fragmentis.* Pars 1, *Epinicia.* Leipzig: Teubner, 1987.
Pars 2, *Fragmenta; Indices.* Leipzig: Teubner, 1975.
Edited and translated by William H. Race. *Olympian Odes. Pythian Odes.* Volume 1. Cambridge, Mass.: Harvard University Press, 1997.
Edited and translated by William H. Race. *Nemean Odes. Isthmian Odes. Fragments.* Volume 2. Cambridge, Mass.: Harvard University Press, 1997.
O. = *Olympian Odes*
P. = *Pythian Odes*
N. = *Nemean Odes*
I. = *Isthmian Odes*
Fr. = *Fragments*
Pl. = Plato
I Alc. = *Alcibades I.* Edited and translated by W. R. M. Lamb. *Charmides. Alcibades I and II. Hipparchus. The Lovers. Theages. Minos. Epinomis.* Cambridge, Mass.: Harvard University Press, 1979.
Ap. = *Apology.* Edited and translated by Harold North Fowler. *Euthyphro. Apology. Crito. Phaedo. Phaedrus.* Cambridge, Mass.: Harvard University Press, 1966.
Phd. = *Phaedo.*
R. = *Republic.* Edited and translated by Jeffrey Henderson. Cambridge, Mass.: Harvard University Press, 2013.
Tht. = *Theaetetus.* Edited and translated by Harold North Fowler. *Theaetetus. Sophist.* Cambridge, Mass.: Harvard University Press, 1977.
Translated by John McDowell. *Plato. Theaetetus.* Oxford: Clarendon Press, 1973.
Plin. = Pliny the Elder (C. Plinius Secundus). Edited and translated by Jehan Desanges. *Narturalis Historia* (*Nat.*). Book V, 1–46. 1ere partie (L'Afrique du Nord). Paris: Société d'édition "Les belles lettres," 1980.

Plin. = Pliny the Younger (C. Plinius Caecilius Secundus).
Ep. = *Epistulae*
Plu. = Plutarch
Defect. = *De defectu oraculorum.* Edited by W. Sieveking, *Plutarchus, Pythici Dialogi.* Stutgart and Leipzig: B. G. Teubner 1997.
Edited and translated by Frank Cole Babbit. *Moralia, vol. V.* Cambridge, Mass.: Harvard University Press, 1936.
Porph. = Porphyry (Porpyrius Tyrius) *de Abstinentia* (*Abst.*). Edited and translated by Jean Bouffartigue and Michel Patillon. Vol. 1 (book I) and vol. 2 (books II–III). Paris: Société d'édition "Les belles lettres," 1977–1979.
PMG = *Poetae Melici Graeci.* Edited by D. L. Page. Oxford: Clarendon Press, 1962.
RV = Rigveda (R̥gveda). Edited by Barend A. van Nooten and Gary B. Holland. *Rig Veda: A Metrically Restored Text with an Introduction and Notes.* Cambridge, Mass.: Harvard University Press, 1994.
Translated by Stephanie W. Jamison and Joel P. Brereton. *The Rigveda: The Earliest Religious Poetry of India.* Vol. I–III. Oxford: Oxford University Press, 2014.
Translated by Karl Friedrich Geldner. *Der Rig-Veda. Aus dem Sanskrit ins Deutsche übersettzt.* Vol. I–III. Cambridge, Mass.: Harvard University Press, 1941.
S = Sophocles
Ant. = *Antigone*
Snorri Sturluson
Edda. Gylfaginning og prosafortellingene av Skáldskaparmál. Edited by Ann Holtsmark and Jón Helgason. Köpenhamn: Ejnar Munksgaard, 1950.
Soc. = Socrates Scholasticus
HE = *Historia Ecclesiastica.* Edited by Günter Christian Hansen. *Sokrates: Kirchengeschichte.* Berlin: Akademie Verlag, 1995.
Soz. = Sozomen
HE = *Historia Ecclesiastica.* Edited and translated by J. Bidez, Guy Sabbah, and André-Jean Festugière. *Sozomène: Histoire Ecclésiastique. Livres III–IV.* Paris: Les éditions du Cerf.
Tac. = Cornelius Tacitus.
Ann. = *Annales*
Tert. = Tertullian.
Adv. Prax. = *Adversus Praxeam*
Apol. = *Apologeticus.* Edited and translated by T. R. Glover. *Apology. De spectaculis.* London: William Heinemann Ltd., 1931.
Spect. = *De specaculis.* V.s.
Nat. = *Ad nationes.*
Pall. = *De pallio.* Edited and translated by Marie Turcan. Sources Chrétiennes 513. Paris: Les edition du Cerf, 2007.
Translated by Vincent Hunink. *Tertullian, De Pallio. A Commentary.* Amsterdam: J. C. Gieben, 2005.
Praes. Haer. = *De praescriptione haereticorum*
Y = Yasna. Edited and translated by Helmut Humbach, Josef Elfenbein, and Prods O Skjærvø. The Gāthās of Zarathushtra and the Other Old Avestan Texts (I: Introduction – Text and Translation; II: Commentary). Heidelberg: Carl Winter, 1991.
Edited and translated by Jean Kellens and Eric Pirart. *Les textes vieil-avestiques* (I: Introduction, texte et traduction; II: Répertoire, grammatiqaux et lexique; III: Commentaire). Wiesbaden: Dr.

Ludwig Reichert Verlag, 1988 – 1991.
Edited and translated by Stanley Insler. *The Gāthās of Zarathustra.* Téhéran-Liège: Édition Bibliotèque Pahlavi, 1975.
Z. = Zand Avesta. Translated by James Darmesteter. Le Zend-Avesta: Traduction nouvelle avec commentaire historique et philologique. Vol. I–III. Paris: Adrien-Maisonneuve, 1892 – 1893 (reprint 1960).

Secondary sources

Agamben, Giorgio. 2009. *What is an Apparatus? And other essays.* Translated by David Kishik and Stefan Pedatella. Stanford, Calif.: Stanford University Press.
Ando, Clifford. 2008. *The Matter of the Gods: Religion and the Roman Empire.* Berkley/Los Angeles/London: University of California Press.
Anthony, David W. and Don Ringe. 2015. "The Indo-European Homeland from Linguistic and Archaeological Perspectives." *The Annual Review of Linguistics* 1:199 – 219.
AS = *The Arden Shakespeare Complete Works.* Edited by Richard Proudfoot, Ann Thompson, and David Scott Kastan. 1998. Walton-on-Thames, Surrey: Thomas Nelson and Sons Ltd.
Assmann, Jan. 2003. *Die Mosaische Unterscheidung: Oder der Preis des Monotheismus.* Munich: Carl Hanser Verlag.
Assman, Jan. 2010. *Religio duplex: Ägyptische Mysterien und europäische Aufklärung.* Frankfurt am Main: Suhrkamp.
Atkinson, Quentin D., and Russell D. Gray. 2003. "Language-tree Divergence Times Support the Anatolian Theory of Indo-European Origin." *Nature* 426: 435 – 439.
Aubenque, Pierre. 1979. "Les Philosophie hellénistiques." In *Philosophie, t. I, De Platon à saint Thomas.* Edited by François Châtelet. Paris: Marbout Université.
Bachvarova, Mary R. 2012. "The Transmission of Liver Divination from East to West." *Studi Micenei ed Egeo-Anatolici* 54: 1 – 22.
Bartholomae, Christian. 1904. *Altiranisches Wörterbuch.* Strassburg: Verlag von Karl J. Trübner.
Benavides, Gustavo. 2010. "On the Production of Religious Configurations." *Method and Theory in the Study of Religion* 22: 239 – 253.
Benveniste, Émile. 1969. *Le vocabulaire des institutions indo-européennes.* I: *économie, paranté, société;* II: *pouvoir, droit, religion.* Paris: Les Éditions de Minuit.
Blumenberg, Hans. 1987. *Das Lachen der Thrakerin: Eine Urgeschichte der Theorie.* Frankfurt am Main: Suhrkamp.
Blumenberg, Hans. 1989. *Höhlenausgänge.* Frankfurt am Main: Suhrkamp.
Blumenthal, H. J. 1993. "Alexandria as a Centre of Greek Philosophy in Latter Classical Antiquity." *Illinois Classical Studies* 18: 307 – 325.
BNP = *Brill's New Pauly.* Edited by Hubert Cancik, Helmut Schneider, and Manfred Landfester. English translation edited by Christine F. Salazar and Francis G. Gentry. 2002–. Leiden and Boston: Brill.
Boitard, M. [Pierre]. 1861. *Paris avant les homes.* Paris: Passard.
Bottéro, Jean. 1987. *Mésopotamie: L'ecriture, la raison et les dieux.* Paris: Gallimard.
Bredekamp, Horst. 2004. *Die Fenster der Monade: Gottfried Wilhelm Leibniz' Theater der Natur und Kunst.* Berlin: Akademie Verlag.

Bredekamp, Horst. 2005. "Kunstkammer, Play-Palace, Shadow Theatre: Three Thought Loci by Gottfired Wilhelm Leibniz. In *Collection – Laboratory – Theater.* Edited by Helmar Schramm, Ludger Schwarze, and Jan Lazarzig. Berlin and New York: Walter de Gruyter.

Bremmer, Jan N. 1999. "Rationalization and Disenchantment in Ancient Greece: Max Weber among the Pythagoreans and Orphics?" In *From Myth to Reason? Studies in the Development of Greek Thought.* Edited by R. Buxton, 71–83. Oxford: Oxford University Press.

Bremmer, Jan N. and Marco Formisano, eds. 2012. *Perpetua's Passions: Multidisciplinary Approaches to the Passio Perpetuae et Felicitas.* Oxford and New York: Oxford University Press.

Bremmer Jan N. and Birgit van der Lans. 2017. "Tacitus and the Persecution of the Christians: An Invention of Tradition?" *Eirene* 53, 299–331.

Bremmer, Jan N. "Ioudaismos, Christianismos and the Parting of the Ways." In *Jews and Christians. Parting Ways in the First Two Centuries C.E.?* Edited by J. Schröter, Benjamin A. Edsall, and Joseph Verheyden. 57–87. Berlin and Boston: Walter de Gruyter, 2021.

Brenk, Frederick E. 1977. *In Mist Apparelled: Religious Themes in Plutarch's Moralia and Lives.* Leiden: E. J. Brill.

Brereton, Joel P. 1981. *The R̥gvedic Ādityas.* New Haven, Connecticut: American Oriental Society.

Burke, Peter. 1994. *Popular Culture in Early Modern Europe.* Aldershot: Scholar Press.

Burkert, Walter. 1972. *Lore and Science in Ancient Pythagoreanism.* English translation by Edwin L. Minar, Jr. Cambridge, Mass.: Harvard University Press.

Burkert, Walter. 1994. *Antike Mysterien: Funktionen und Gehalt.* Munich: C. H. Beck.

Cage, John. 1961. *Silence: Lectures and Writings.* Middletown, Conn.: Wesleyan University Press.

Cardini, Franco. 2001. *The Chapel of the Magi in Palazzo Medici.* Florence: Mandragora.

Chandler, David. 1996. "Coleridge's 'suspension of disbelief' and Jacob Bruckner's 'assensus suspensioe'." *Notes and Queries* 43, 1: 39–40.

Chastel, André. 1939. "La légende de la Reine de Saba: III: Regina Sibilla (Fin)." *Revue de l'histoire des religions* 120, 160–174.

Chomsky, Noam and Morris Halle. 1968. *The Sound Pattern of English.* New York: Harper & Row.

Chuvin, Pierre. *A Chronicle of the Last Pagans.* Translated by B. A. Archer. Cambridge, Mass.: Harvard University Press.

Coleridge, Samuel Taylor. [1817] 1983. *Biographia Literaria.* Edited by James Engell and W. Jackson Bate. Bollingen Series LXXV. Princeton: Princeton University Press.

Connor, W. R. 1987. "Tribes, Festivals, and Processions: Civic Ceremonial and Political Manipulation in Archaic Greece." *Journal of Hellenic Studies* 107: 40–50.

Cusack, Carole M. and Pavol Kosnáč, eds. 2018. *Fiction, Invention and Hyper-reality: From popular culture to religion.* New York and London: Routledge.

Detienne, Marcel. *Dionysos at Large.* Translated by Arthur Goldhammer. Cambridge, Mass.: Harvard University Press.

DNP = *Der Neue Pauly,* Hubert Cancik, Helmut Schneider, and Manfred Landefester, 1996–. Leiden and Boston: Brill.

Dronke, Peter. 1974. *Fabula: Explorations into the Issue of Myth in Medieval Platonism.* Leiden/Cologne: E. J. Brill.

Eckhardt, Benedikt. 2014. "'Bloodless Sacrifice': A Note on Greek Cultic Language in the Imperial Era." *Greek, Roman, and Byzantine Studies* 54: 255–273.

Edelheit, Amos. 2008. *Ficino, Pico and Savonarola: The Evolution of Humanist Theology.* Leiden: Brill.

Eichner, Heiner. 2002. "Lateinisch *hostia, hostus, hostīre* und die stellvertrende Tiertötung der Hethiter." In *Novalis Indogermanica: Festschrift für Günter Neumann zum 80. Geburtstag.* Edited by Matthias Fritz and Susanne Zeilfelder, 101–156, 715–725. Graz: Leykam.

d'Errico, Francesco. 2003. "The Invisible Frontier. A Multiple Species Model for the Origin of Behavioral Modernity." *Evolutionary Anthropology* 12: 188–202.

d'Errico, Francesco and Jean-Marie Hombert, eds. 2009. *Becoming Eloquent: Advances in the Emergence of Language, Human Cognition, and Modern Cultures.* Amsterdam and Philadelphia: John Benjamins Publishing Company.

EWAia = Manfred Mayrhofer. *Etymologisches Wörterbuch des Altindoarischen*, 1986–2001. Heidelberg: Winter.

Falk, H. S., and Alf Torp. 1907–1911. *Norwegish-dänisches etymologisches Wörterbuch.* Heidelberg: Winter.

Ferguson, Arthur B. 1993. *Utter Antiquity: Perceptions of Prehistory in Renaissance England.* Durham and London: Duke University Press.

Fernie, Ewan, ed. 2005. *Spiritual Shakespeares.* London and New York: Routledge.

Festugière, André-Jean. 1971. *Études de philosophie grecque.* Paris: Libraire Philosophique J. Vrin.

Festugière, André-Jean. 1950. *Contemplation et vie contemplative selon Platon.* Paris: Libraire Philosophique J. Vrin.

Fick, August. 1909. *Vergleichendes Wörterbuch der indogermanischen Sprachen.* 4th ed. revised by Adalb. Bezzenberger, Aug. Fick, and Whitley Stokes. Part 3, *Wortschatz der germanischen Spracheinheit*, revised by Alf Torp. Göttingen: Vanderhoeck & Ruprecht.

Fink, Eugen. [1967] 2010. *Oase des Glücks.* In *Spiel als Weltsymbol.* Edited by Cathrin Nielsen and Hans Rainer Sepp. Freiburg and Munich: Verlag Karl Alber.

Fortson IV, Benjamin W. 2005. *Indo-European Language and Culture: An Introduction.* Oxford: Blackwell Publishing.

Forssman, Berhard. 1998. "Vedisch *átithipati*, lateinisch *hospes*." In *Mír Curad: Studies in Honor of Calvert Watkins.* Edited by Jay H. Jasanoff, H. Craig Melchert, and Lisi Oliver, 715–725. Innsbruck: Institut für Sprachwissenschaft der Universität Innsbruck.

Foucault, Michel. 2001. *L'herméneutique du sujet.* Paris: Seuil/Gallimard.

Freiert, William K. 1991. "Orpheus: A Fugue on the Polis." In *Myth and the Polis.* Edited by Dora Carlisky Pozzi and John M. Wickersham, 32–48. Ithaca: Cornell University Press.

Gadamer, Hans-Georg. 1996. *Der Anfang der Philosophie.* Stuttgart: Philipp Reclam jun.

Geldner, Karl Friedrich. 1951. See above under Abbreviations, RV.

Gemelli Marciano, Laura. 2006. "Indovini, *magoi* e *meteorologoi:* Interazioni e definizioni nell'ultimo terzo del V secolo a.C." In *La costruzione del discorso filosofico nell'età dei presocratici.* Edited by Maria Michela Sassi, 203–235. Pisa: Edizioni della Normale.

Ginzburg, Carlo. 1990. *Clues: Roots of an Evidential Paradigm.* Translated by John and Anne C. Tedeschi. London: Hutchinson Radius.

Gocer, Asli. 1999–2000. "The Puppet Theater in Plato's Parable of the Cave." *The Classical Journal* 95, 2: 119–129.

Goldenbaum, Ursula. 1998. "Leibniz as a Lutheran." In *Leibniz, Mysticism and Religion.* Edited by Alison P. Coudert, Richard H. Popkin, and Gordon M. Weiner, 169–192. Dordrecht: Kluwer Academic Publishers.

Grabar, André. 1967. *Die Kunst des frühen Christentums: Von der ersten Zeugnissen christlicher Kunst bis zur Zeit Theodosius I.* Munich: C. H. Beck Verlag.

Graf, Fritz and Sarah Iles Johnston. 2013. *Ritual Texts for the Afterlife: Orpheus and the Bacchic Gold Tablets* (2nd edition). London and New York: Routledge.
Green, Tamara M. 1992. *The City of the Moon God: Religious Traditions of Harran.* Leiden//New York/ Cologne: E. J. Brill.
Gregory, Timothy E. 1983. "Julian and the Last Oracle at Delphi." *Greek, Roman, and Byzantine Studies* 24: 355–366.
Griggs, Earl Leslie, ed. 1959. *Collected Letters of Samuel Taylor Coleridge.* Volume IV 1815–1819. Oxford: Clarendon Press.
Gunning, Tom. 1989. "An Aesthetic of Astonishment: Early Film and the (In)Credulous Spectator." *Art and Text* 34 (Spring): 31–45.
Guillaumont, François. 2006. *Le* De diuinatione *de Cicéron et les theories antiques de la divination.* Collection Latomus, vol. 298. Brussels: Éditions Latomus.
Hadot, Ilsetraut, ed. 1987. *Simplicius: sa vie, son oeuvre, sa survie. Actes du Colloque International de Paris (28 Sept–1 Oct. 1985).* Berlin and New York: Walter de Gruyter.
Hadot, Ilsetraut, ed. 2014. *Le néoplatonicien Simplicius à la lumière des recherches contemporaines. Un bilan critique.* Sankt Augustin: Academia Verlag.
Hadot, Pierre. 2004. *Le voile d'Isis: Essai sur l'histoire de l'idée de Nature.* Paris: Gallimard.
Hall, Dale. 1980. "Interpreting Plato's Cave as an Allegory of the Human Condition." *Apeiron* 14, 2: 74–86.
Hanegraaff, Wouter. 2012. *Esotericism and the Academy: Rejected Knowledge in Western Culture.* Cambridge: Cambridge University Press.
Hankins, James. 1990. "Cosimo de' Medici and the 'Platonic Academy'." *Journal of the Warburg and Courtauld Institutes* 53: 144–162.
Harrison, Peter. 2007. *The Fall of Man and the Foundations of Science.* Cambridge: Cambridge University Press.
Harrison, Peter. 2015. *The Territories of Science and Religion.* Chicago and London: The University of Chicago Press.
Helbig, Wolfgang. 1868. *Wandgemälde der vom Vesuv verschutteten Städte Campaniens*, Leipzig: Breitkopf und Härtel.
Henrichs, Albert. 1968. "Philosophy, the Handmaiden of Theology." *Greek, Roman, and Byzantine Studies* 9, 4: 437–450.
Henshilwood, Christopher S., Francesco d'Errico, and Ian Watts. 2009. "Engraved Ochres from the Middle Paleolithic Stone Age Levels at Blombos Cave, South Africa." *Journal of Human Evolution* 57: 27–47.
Herder, Johann Gottfried. 1772. *Abhandlung über den Ursprung der Sprache.* Berlin: Christian Friedrich Voß.
Hintze, Almut. 2000. ",Lohn' im Indoiranischen: Eine semantische Studie des Rigveda und Avesta. Wiesbaden: Dr. Ludvig Reichert Verlag.
Hintze, Almut. 2004. "'Do ut des': Patterns of Exchange in Zoroastrianism." *Journal of the Royal Asiatic Society* 14, 1: 27–45.
Hintze, Almut. 2007. *A Zoroastrian Liturgy. The Worship in Seven Chapters (Yasna* 35–41*).* Iranica 12. Edited by Maria Macuch. Wiesbaden: Harrasovitz Verlag
Hoffmann, D. L. et al. 2018. "U-Th dating of carbonate crusts reveals Neanderthal origin of Iberian cave art." *Science* 23: 359, Issue 6378, 912–915.
Hoffmann, Karl and Johanna Narten. 1989. *Der Sasanidischen Archetypus: Untersuchungen zu Schreibung und Lautgestalt des Avestischen.* Wiesbaden: Reichert Verlag.

Hovers, Erella, Shimon Ilani, Ofer Bar-Yosef, and Bernard Vandermeersch. 2003. "An Early Case of Color Symbolism: Ochre Use by Modern Humans in Qufzeh Cave." *Current Anthropology* 44: 491 – 522.

Hunter, Richard and Ian Rutherford. 2009. "Introduction." In *Wandering Poets in Ancient Greek Culture: Travel, Locality and Pan-Hellenism.* Edited by Richard Hunter and Ian Rutherford. Cambridge: Cambridge University Press, 1 – 22

HWPh = *Historisches Wörterbuch der Philosophie.* Edited by Joachim Ritter. Basel and Stuttgart: Schwab & Co Verlag. 1971 – 2007.

Jaccottet, Anne-Françoise. 1990. "Le lierre de la liberté." *Zeitschrift für Papyroilogie und Epigraphik* 80: 150 – 156.

Jackson, Peter. 2012. "Apparitions and Apparatuses: On the Staging and Framing of Religious Events." *Method and Theory in the Study of Religion* 24: 291 – 300.

Jackson, Peter. 2012. "Det urnordiska namnelementet *-gastiz.* Några språk- och religionshistoriska sonderingar." *Studia Anthroponymica Scandinavica* 30: 5 – 18.

Jackson, Peter. 2014. "Themes of Commensality in Indo-European Lore: A propos Greek ξένος and Proto-Germanic **etuna.*" In *Munus amicitiae. Norbert Oettinger a collegis et amicis dicatum.* Edited by H. Craig Melchert, Elisabeth Rieken, and Thomas Steer, 92 – 100. Ann Arbor and New York: Beech Stave Press.

Jackson, Peter. 2016. "The Arrival of the Clients: Technologies of Fame and the Prehistory of Orphic Eschatology." *Historia Religionum* 8: 169 – 194.

Jackson Rova, Peter. 2019a. "Cosmetic Alterations: Religion and the Emergence of Behavioral Modernity." In *Evolution, Cognition, and the History of Religions: a New Synthesis.* Edited by Anders Klostergaard Petersen, Ingvild Saelid Gilhus, Luther H. Martin, Jeppe Sinding Jensen, and Jesper Sørensen, 600 – 608. Leiden and Boston: Brill.

Jackson Rova, Peter. 2019b. "Blood Signals: On the Symbolism and Ritual Pertinence of Blood." *DIN: Tidskrift for religion og kultur* 1: 93 – 102.

Jackson Rova, Peter. 2021a. "The Secret of the Untrembling Heart: A Cryptological Reading of Parmenides' Proem (EGP D4.29/DK B1.29")." *Mnemosyne* 74: 737 – 756.

Jackson Rova, Peter. 2021b. "Itinerancy and the Afterlife." In *Songs of the Road: Wandering Religious Poets in India, Tibet, and Japan.* Edited by Stefan Larsson and Kristoffer af Edholm, 15 – 34. Stockholm: Stockholm University Press.

Jaeger, Werner. 1928. *Über Ursprung und Kreislauf des philosophischen Lebensideals.* Berlin: Walter de Gruyter.

Jamison, Stephanie. 1991. *The Ravenous Hyenas and the Wounded Sun: Myth and Ritual in Ancient India.* Ithaca, N.Y.: Cornell University Press.

Jakobson, Roman. 1971. *Selected Writings II: Word and Language.* Berlin and New York: Mouton de Gruyter.

Jaspers, Karl. 1949. *Vom Ursprung und Ziel der Geschichte.* Munich: R. Piper & Co. Verlag.

Jenkins, Richard. 2000. "Disenchantment, Enchantment and Re-Enchantment: Max Weber at the Millennium." *Max Weber Studies* 1: 11 – 32.

Jakobson, Roman. 1971. *Selected Writings II: Word and Language.* Berlin and New York: Mouton de Gruyter.

Jeyes, U. 1991 – 1992. "Divination as a Science in Ancient Mesopotamia." *Jaarbericht Ex Oriente Lux* 32: 23 – 41.

Jolivet J., and R. Rashed. 2022. "al-Kindī." In *Encyclopedia of Islam, Second Edition.* Edited by P. Bearman, Th. Bianquis, E. van Donzel, W. P. Heinrichs. Consulted online 08 March <http://dx.doi.org.ezp.sub.su.se/10.1163/1573–3912_islam_SIM_4380>

Kahlos, Maiastina. 2016. "Meddling in the Middle? Urban Celebrations, Ecclesiastical Leaders and the Roman Emperor in Late Antiquity." In *Space in Late Antiquity. Cultural, Theological and Archaeological Perspectives.* Edited by Juliette Day, Raimo Hakola, Maijastina Kahlos, and Ulla Tervahauta. London: Routledge, 11–31.

Kahlos, Maiastina. 2019. *Religious Dissent in Late Antiquity, 300–450.* Oxford: Oxford University Press.

Kammenhuber, Annelies. 1968. *Die Arier im Vorderen Orient.* Heidelberg: Carl Winter.

Karanika, Andromache. 2010. "Inside Orpheus' Songs: Orpheus as an Argonaut in Apollonius Rhodius' *Argonautica.*" *Greek, Roman, and Byzantine Studies* 50: 391–410.

Kellens, Jean. 1987. "Characters of Ancient Mazdaism." *History and Anthropology* 3: 239–262.

Kippenberg, Hans G. 1991. *Die vorderasiatischen Erlösungsreligionen.* Frankfurt am Main: Suhrkamp.

Kissel, M. and A. Fuentes. 2018. "'Behavioral Modernity' as a Process, not an Event, in the Human Niche." *Time and Mind* 11, 2: 163–183.

Kindt, Julia. 2012. *Rethinking Greek Religion.* Cambridge: Cambridge University Press.

Klein, Richard G. 2000. "Archaeology and the Evolution of Human Behavior." *Evolutionary Anthropology* 9: 17–36.

Klemming, G. E., ed. 1886. *Sumlen. Där vthi ähro åtskillige collectaneer, som vthi een och annan måtta tiäna till antiquiteternes escolerande af Johannes Thomæ Bureus.* Nyare bidrag till kännedom om de svenska landsmålen ock svenskt folklife. Bih. I.2. Stockholm: P. A. Norstedt & söner

Koch, Ulla Susanne. 2005. *Secrets of Extispicy: The Chapter* Multābiltu *of the Babylonian Extispicy Series and* Niṣirti bārûti *Texts mainly from Aššurbanipal's Library.* Münster: Ugarit-Verlag.

Koch-Westenholz, Ulla. 1995. *Mesopotamian Astrology: An Introduction to Babylonian and Assyrian Celestial Divination.* Copenhagen: Museum Tusculanum Press.

Kurke, Leslie. 2013. *The Traffic in Praise: Pindar and the Poetics of Social Economy.* Berkeley, Calif.: California Classical Studies. Reprint, with minor corrections, of the edition first published 1991 by Cornell University Press.

Kuhlwilm, Martin et al. 2016. "Ancient Gene Flow from Early Modern Humans into Eastern Nenderthals." *Nature* 530: 429–33.

Lambert, W. G. 1967. "Enmeduranki and Related Matters." *Journal of Cuneiform Studies* 21: 126–138.

Lanciani, Rodolfo. 1891. *Ancient Rome in the Light of Recent Discoveries.* London: Macmillan and Company.

Lemke, Harald. 2004. "Feuerbachs Stammtischthese oder zum Ursprung des Satzes: 'Der Mensch ist, was er isst'." *Aufklärung und Kritik* 11, 1: 117–140.

Leuba, James H. 1912. *A Psychological Study of Religion: Its Origin, Function, and Future.* New York: The Macmillan Company.

Lévi-Strauss, Claude. 1955. "The Structural Study of Myth." *Journal of American Folklore* LXVII: 428–444.

Lewis-Williams, David. 2002. *The Mind in the Cave: Consciousness and the Origins of Art.* London: Thames & Hudson.

Lewis-Williams, David. 2009. "Of People and Pictures: The Nexus of Upper Palaeolithic Religion, Social Discrimination, and Art." In *Becoming Human. Innovation in Prehistoric Material and Spiritual Culture.* Edited by Colin Renfrew and Iain Morely, 135–158. Cambridge: Cambridge University Press.

Lieu, Judith. 2016. *Neither Greek or Jew? Constructing Early Christianity.* London: Bloomsbury.

Lincoln, Bruce. 1999. *Theorizing Myth: Narrative, Ideology, and Scholarship.* Chicago: The University of Chicago Press.

Lincoln, Bruce. 2012. *Gods and Demons, Priests and Scholars: Critical Explorations in the History of Religions.* Chicago: The University of Chicago Press.

Lincoln, Bruce. 2018. *Apples and Oranges: Explorations In, On, and With Comparison.* Chicago: The University of Chicago Press.

Lionarons, Joyce Tally. 1996. "Beowulf: Myth and Monsters." *English Studies* 77: 1–14.

LIV[2] = Helmut Rix et al. *Lexikon der indogermanischen Verben.* Wiesbaden: Dr. Ludwig Reichert Verlag. 2001.

Lommel, Herman. 1930. *Die Religion Zarathustras nach dem Awesta dargestellt.* Tübingen: Verlag von J. C. B.
Mohr (Paul Siebeck).

Lubotsky, Alexander. 1997. *A R̥gvedic Word Concordance.* 2 vols. New Haven, Conn.: American Oriental Society.

LSCG = Fraciszek Sokolowski, *Lois sacrées des Cités grecques.* Paris: Éditions E. de Boccard. 1969.

Lürmann, Dieter. 1992. "Faith." In *The Anchor Bible Dictionary* (Vol. 2, D-G). Edited by David Noel Freedman. New York: Doubleday. 744–758.

Mallory, James P., and Douglas Q. Adams. 2006. *The Oxford Introduction to Proto-Indo-European and the Proto-Indo-European World.* Oxford: Oxford University Press.

Mannoni, Laurent. 2000. *The Great Art of Light and Shadow: Archaeology of the Cinema.* Translated by Richard Crangle. Exeter: University of Exeter Press.

Mannoni, Octave. 1969. *Clefs pour l'Imaginaire ou l'Autre Scène.* Paris: Éditions du Seuil.

Marcotte, Roxanne. 2019. "Suhrawardi." In *The Stanford Encyclopedia of Philosophy.* Edited by Edward N. Zalta. https://plato.stanford.edu/archives/sum2019/entries/suhrawardi/. Last accessed on February 28, 2023.

Mariev, Sergei. 2019. "Scholarios' Account of Plethon's Jewish Teacher Elissaios as a Historical Fact and Literary Fiction." In *Verflechtungen zwischen Byzanz und dem Orient.* Edited by Michael Grünbart, 75–92. Berlin: LIT Verlag.

Martin, Luther H., Ruck Gutman, and Patrick H. Hutton, eds. *Technologies of the Self: A Seminar with Michel Foucault.* Amherst: University of Massachusetts Press.

Mayrhofer, Manfred. 1960. "Indo-Iranisches Sprachgut aus Alalaḫ," *Indo-Iranian Journal.* 136–149.

Melchert, H. Craig. 2010. "Indo-European *ḫarp(p)-* and Derivatives." In *Investigationes Anatolicae: Gedenkschrift für Erich Neu.* Edited by Jörg Klinger, Elisabeth Rieken, and Christel Rüster, 179–188. Wiesbaden: Harrassowitz Verlag.

McBrearty, Sally and Alison S. Brooks. 2000. "The Revolution That Wasn't: A New Interpretation of the Origin of Modern Human Behavior." *Journal of Human Evolution* 39: 453–563.

Mithen, Steven. 2009. "Out of the Mind: Material Culture and the Supernatural." In *Becoming Human. Innovation in Prehistoric Material and Spiritual Culture.* Edited by Colin Renfrew and Iain Morely, 123–134. Cambridge: Cambridge University Press.

Montiglio, Silvia. 2005. *Wandering in Ancient Greek Culture.* Chicago and London: The University of Chicago Press.

Neri, Sergio. 2012. "Zum urindogermanischen Wort für 'Hand'." In *Multi Nomini Grammaticus: Studies in Classical and Indo-European Linguistics in Honor of Alan J. Nussbaum on the Occasion of His Sixty-Fifth Birthday.* Edited by Adam I. Cooper, Jeremy Rau, and Michael Weiss, 185–205. Ann Arbor and New York: Beech Stave Press.

Nightingale, Andrea Wilson. 2004. *Spectacles of Truth in Classical Greek Philosophy: Theoria in its Cultural Context.* Cambridge: Cambridge University Press.

Noethlichs, Karl Leo. 2017. "Der rechtliche Status der Juden im römischen Reich: Tradition und Wandel in der römischen Judengesetzgebung vom 2. Jarhundert v.u.Z. bis zm 6. Jahrhundert u.Z. Mit einem Exkurs zur These von Doron Mendels und Arye Edrei über 'Zweierlei Diaspora'." In *Religio licita? Rom und die Juden.* Edited by Görge K. Hasselhof and Meret Strothman, 55–84. Berlin/Boston: Walter de Gruyter.

Norman, K. R. 1972. "Notes on the Greek Version of Aśoka's Twelfth and Thirteenth Rock Edicts." *The Journal of the Royal Asiatic Society of Great Britain and Ireland* 2: 111–118.

Norris, Matthew. 2016. A Pilgrimage to the Past: Johannes Bureus and the Rise of Swedish Antiquarian Scholarship, 1600–1650. Lund: Department for the History of Ideas and Sciences.

Nikolaev, Alexander. 2010. "Indo-European **dem(h$_2$)-* 'to build' and its derivatives." *Historische Sprachforschung* 123: 56–96.

Nyberg, Henrik Samuel. 1938. *Die Religionen des alten Irans.* Reprint 1966. Osnabrück: Otto Zeller.

Ogden, Daniel. 2001. *Greek and Roman Necromancy.* Princeton and Oxford: Princeton University Press.

Owen, W. J. B., ed. 1957. *Wordsworth's Preface to Lyrical Ballads.* Anglistica IX. Copenhagen: Rosenkilde and Bagger.

Parker, Robert. 1996. *Athenian Religion: A History.* Oxford: Clarendon Press.

Parker, Robert. 2011. *On Greek Religion.* Ithaca and London: Cornell University Press.

Perlman, M. 2022. "Ibn Kammūna." In *Encyclopedia of Islam, Second Edition.* Edited by P. Bearman, Th. Bianquis, E. van Donzel, W. P. Heinrichs. Consulted online 08 March http://dx.doi.org.ezp.sub.su.se/10.1163/1573-3912_islam_SIM_3231

Petzold, Leander 2003. "Riesen." In *Reallexikon der germanischen Altertumskunde.* Edited by Rosemarie Müller, 601–607. Berlin: Walter de Gruyter.

Pinault, George J. 1998. "Le nom indo-iranien de l'hôte." In *Sprache und Kultur der Indogermanen: Akten der X. Fachtagung der Indogermanischen Gesellschaft, Innsbruck, 22–28. September 1996.* Edited by Wolfgang Meid, 451–477. Innsbruck: Institut für Sprachwissenschaft der Universität Innsbruck.

Pingree, David. 2002. "The Sābians of Harrān and the Classical Tradition." *International Journal of the Classical Tradition* 9, 1: 8–35.

Poggi, Gianfranco. 2014. Varieties of Political Experience: Power Phenomena in Modern Society. Colchester: ECPR Press.

Possamai, Adam, ed. 2012. *Handbook of Hyper-religions.* Leiden and Boston: Brill.

Renfrew, Colin. 1987. *Archaeology and Language: The Puzzle of Indo-European Origins.* London: Jonathan Cape.

RGA = *Reallexikon der germanischen Altertumskunde.* Edited by Heinrich Beck, Dieter Guenich, and Heiko Steuer. Berlin and New York: De Gruyter. 1973–2008.

Rochberg, Francesca. 2005. *The Heavenly Writing: Divination, Horoscopy, and Astronomy in Mesopotamian Culture.* Cambridge: Cambridge University Press.

Rollinger, Robert. 2017. "Haruspicy from the Ancient Near East to Etruria." In *Etruscology.* Edited by A. Naso, 341–355. Berlin and Boston: Walter de Gruyter.

Ruin, Hans. 2019. *Being with the Dead: Burial, Ancestral Politics, and the Roots of Historical Consciousness.* Stanford: Stanford University Press.

Sachot, Maurice. 2011. *L'Invention du Christ: Genèse d'une religion.* Paris: Odile Jacob.

Sahlins, Marshall. 2013. *What Kinship Is – And Is Not.* Chicago and London: The University of Chicago Press.

Scerri, E. M., M. G. Thomas et al. 2018. “Did our Species Evolve in Subdivided Populations across Africa, and Why Does it Matter? *Trends in Ecology & Evolution* 33, 8: 582 – 594.

Schaafhausen, Hermann. 1888. *Der Neanderthaler-Fund.* Bonn: Adolph Marcus.

Schleiter, Jens. 2022. “Absent Dead, and Abstract Signs for Absence: on the Semiotic Affordance of Religion.” *Religion* 52, 3: 409 – 428.

Schlumberger, Daniel. 1964. “Une nouvelle inscription grecque d’Açoka.” *Comptes rendus des séances de l’Adadémie des Inscriptions et Belle-Lettres* 108, 1: 126 – 140.

Schmitt, Rüdiger, ed. 1967. *Indogermanische Dichtersprache.* Darmstadt: Wissenschaftliche Buchgesellschaft.

Seitter, Walter. 2007. “Was für Bilder gibt es von Plethon?” *Accademia* 9: 7 – 36.

Sierksma-Agteres, Suzan J. M. 2016. “Imitation in Faith: Enacting Paul’s Ambiguous *Pistis Christou* Formulation on a Graeco-Roman Stage.” *International Journal of Philosophy and Theology* 77, 3: 119 – 153.

Smith, Jonathan Z. 1987. “The Domestication of Sacrifice.” In *Violent Origins: Walter Burkert, René Girard, and Jonathan Z. Smith on Ritual Killing and Cultural Formation.* Edited by Robert G. Hammerton-Kelly, 191 – 205. Stanford, Calif.: Stanford University Press.

Smith, Jonathan Z. 1998. “Religion, Religions, Religious.” In *Critical Terms for Religious Studies.* Edited by Mark C. Taylor, 269 – 284. Chicago: The University of Chicago Press.

Smith, Jonathan Z. 2004. *Relating Religion: Essays in the Study of Religion.* Chicago: The University of Chicago Press.

Spreng, Nathan R., Raymond A. Mar, and Alice S. N. King. 2009. “The Common Neural Basis of Autobiographical Memory, Prospection, Navigation, Theory of Mind, and the Default Mode: A Quantitative Meta-Analysis.” *Journal of Cognitive Neuroscience* 20: 489 – 510.

Stausberg, Michael. 1998. *Faszination Zarathushtra: Zoroaster und die Europäische Religionsgeschichte der Frühen Neuzeit.* Berlin: Walter de Gruyter.

Stevens, Wallace. 1997. *Collected Poetry and Prose.* Edited by Frank Kermode and John Richardson. The Library of America.

Stroumsa, Guy. 2009. *The End of Sacrifice: Religious Transformations in Late Antiquity.* Translated by Susan Emanuel. Chicago: The University of Chicago Press.

Suddendorf, Thomas and Michael C. Corballis. 2007. “The Evolution of Foresight: What is Mental Time Travel, and is it Unique to Humans?” *Behavioral and Brain Sciences* 30: 299 – 313.

Stern, S. M. 2022. “ʿAbd al-Laṭīf al-Baghdādī.” In *Encyclopedia of Islam, Second Edition.* Edited by P. Bearman, Th. Bianquis, E. van Donzel, W. P. Heinrichs. Consulted online 08 March <http://dx.doi.org.ezp.sub.su.se/10.1163/1573 – 3912_islam_SIM_0102>

Szpunar, Karl K. 2011. “On Subjective Time.” *Cortex* 47: 409 – 411.

Tardieu, Michel. 1986. “Ṣābiens coraniques et ‘Ṣābiens’ de Ḥarrān.” *Journal Asiatique* 274: 1 – 44.

Tardieu, Michel. 1987a. “Pléthon lecteur des oracles.” *Métis. Anthropologie des mondes grecs anciens* 2.1: 141 – 164.

Tardieu, Michel. 1987b. “Simplicius et les calendriers à Ḥarrān.” In *Simplicius: sa vie, son oeuvre, sa survie. Actes du Colloque International de Paris (28 Sept-1 Oct. 1985)*, edited by Ilsetraut Hadot. Berlin and New York: Walter de Gruyter.

ThesCRA = *Thessaurus Cultus Et Rituum Antiquorum.* Los Angeles: J. Paul Getty Museum. 2004–.

Tomko, Michael. 2015. *Beyond the Willing Suspension of Disbelief: Poetic Faith from Coleridge to Tolkien.* London: Bloomsbury.

Torrance, Thomas F. 1956. "One Aspect of the Biblical Conception of Faith." *The Expository Times* 68: 111–114.
Trivers, Robert. 2000. "The Elements of a Scientific Theory of Self-Deception." *Annals of the New York Academy of Sciences* 907: 113–131.
Tulving, Endel. 1985. "Memory and Consciousness." *Canadian Psychology* 26: 1–12.
Uggla, Arvid Hj., ed. 1933. *Carl von Linné, Fyra Skrifter*, Stockholm: Esselte AB.
Urbano, Arthur. 2017. "Fashion for the Wise: Philosophy, Clothing, and Competition in Late Antiquity." *Ancient Jew Review* (September 12) (ancientjewreview.com).
Vaihinger, Hans. 1922. *Die Philosophie des Als Ob: System der theoretischen, praktischen und religiösen Fiktionen der Menschheit auf Grund eines idealistischen Positivismus.* 7th and 8th edition. Leipzig: Verlag von Felix Meiner.
Van Bladel, Kevin. 2009. *The Arabic Hermes: From Pagan Sage to Prophet of Science.* Oxford: Oxford University Press.
Van der Leeuw, Gerardus. 1961. *Einfürung in die Phänomenologie der Religion.* Darmstadt: Wissenschaftliche Buchgesellschaft.
Vanhaeren, Marian. 2010. *Les fonctions de la parure au Paléolithique supérieur: de l'individu à l'unité culturelle.* Saarbrücken: Éditions universitaires européennes.
Van Straten, F. T. 1995. *Hiera Kala: Images of Animal Sacrifice in Archaic and Classical Greece.* Leiden, New York and Cologne: E. J. Brill.
Waldenfels, Bernhard. 2012. *Hyperpänomene. Modi hyperbolischer Erfahrung.* Berlin: Suhrkamp.
Watkins, Calvert. 1995. How to Kill a Dragon: Aspects of Indo-European Poetics. Oxford: Oxford University Press.
West, Martin L. 2007. Indo-European Poetry and Myth. Oxford: Oxford University Press.
Weber, Max. 1951. Gesammelte Aufsätze zur Wissenschaftslehre. Edited by Johannes Winckelmann. Tübingen: Verlag J. C. B. Mohr (Paul Siebeck).
Weiss, Michael. 2006. "Latin Orbis and its Cognates." *Historische Sprachforschung* 119. 250–272.

Whaley, Diana, ed. 2009. "Þjóðólfr Arnórsson, Lausavísur 5." In *Poetry from the King's Sagas 2: From c. 1035 to c. 1300. Skaldic Poetry of the Scandinavian Middle Ages* 2. Edited by Kari Ellen Gade, 169–171. Turnhout: Brepols.
Wheeler, John Archibald. 1983. "On recognizing 'law without law,' Oersted Medal Response at the joint APS-AAPT Meeting, New York, 25 January 1982." *American Journal of Physics* 51 (5): 398–404.
Wheeler, John Archibald. 1990. "Information, Physics, Quantum: The Search for Links." In *Complexity, Entropy, and the Physics of Information.* Edited by W. H. Zurek. Redwood City: Addison-Wesley, 354–368.
Willamowitz-Moellendorff, Ulrich von. 1922. *Pindaros.* Berlin: Weidmannsche Buchhandlung.
Willcock, Malcolm., ed. 1995. *Pindar Victory Odes: Olympians 2,7 and 1; Nemean 4; Isthmians 3, 4 and 7.* Cambridge: Cambridge University Press.
Wilson, Peter. 2009. "Thamyris the Thracian: The Archetypal Wandering Poet?" In *Wandering Poets in Ancient Greek Culture: Travel, Locality and Pan-Hellenism.* Edited by Richard Hunter and Ian Rutherford. Cambridge: Cambridge University Press, 46–79.
Woodhouse, C. M. 1986. *George Gemistos Plethon: The Last of the Hellenes.* Oxford: Oxford University Press.
Yelle, Robert. 2012. The Language of Disenchantment. Protestant Literalism and Colonial Discourse in British India. Oxford: Oxford University Press.

Zanker, Paul. 1996. *The Mask of Socrates: The Image of the Intellectual in Antiquity.* Berkeley: University of California Press.

Ziai, Hossein. 2004. “Illuminationism.” In *Encyclopedia Iranica* XII/6, 670 – 672 and XIII/1, 1 – 2. An updated version is also available online at https://www.iranicaonline.org/articles/illuminationism. Last accessed on February 28, 2023.

Ziegler, Konrat 1964. *Plutarchos von Chaironeia.* Stuttgart: Alfred Drückenmüller Verlag.

Zilhão, João et al. 2010. “Symbolic Use of Marine Shells and Mineral Pigments by Iberian Neanderthals.” Proceedings of the National Academy of Sciences. January 19, vol. 107, no. 3: 1023 – 1028.

Index

Abaris 79
Abbasid caliphate 147
academy
– *Accademia Romana* 152
– Florentine Academy 85, 91, 139, 145, 153, 159, 163, 175
Adad (god) 80
Adam (first man) 36, 48
ad hominem reasoning 5
Aesop 82 f., 119
affirmative participation 9, 101, 133, 174
afterlife 27, 51, 53 f., 57, 67, 69 f., 77, 132
Agamben, Giorgio 98 f.
Agni (god) 41, 62, 65
Agohya (god) 62–64
agýrtai (Gr.) 54, 88, 90
akoúsmata (Gr. pl.) 87 f.
alazṓn (Gr.) 81, 83
alḗtheia (Gr.) 114, 118
Alexander of Alexandria 127–130
Alexander the Great 72
Alexandria 127 f., 130 f., 133, 147, 157
alien abductions 22
al-Kindī 157
allegory of the cave, see also parable of the cave 169
All's Well That Ends Well 140
al-Ma'mūn (caliph) 148, 157
al-Mas'ūdī 149 f.
al-Mu'taṣim (caliph) 157
al-Nadīm 147, 157
al-Šahrastānī 147
al-Suhrawardī 155
Amphion and Zethys 85
Anatolian 37, 59
anatomical modernity 5, 23–25, 28–29
Anaxagoras 85
Ancient Egypt 79, 85, 128, 147
Ancient Mesopotamia 79, 81, 147
Anebo 162
animal sacrifice, see also sacrifice 34–36
anthroponomastics 37
anti-guest 44, 46 f.
anti-host 46
antinomy 11, 58, 72, 79, 82, 86, 130, 178
Apollo 35, 101, 144
Apologeticus 109 f., 118, 123
Apology 10, 102, 118, 129
aporía (Gr.) 97, 100
apparatus 8, 11, 93 f., 98–100, 105, 107, 134
Aquinas, Thomas 167
archaeology 34, 36
Argippeans 19–21
Aristophanes 81, 84 f., 129
Aristotle 6, 84 f., 87, 90, 92, 97, 103, 108, 114, 148 f., 154 f.
Arius 128–130
Ars Magna Lucis et Umbrae 169
artefact 28, 30 f.
artifice 13, 95, 106, 119, 169
artificiality 4, 8, 10, 26, 29 f., 93
asceticism 52, 71 f., 88, 133
Ásgarðr 45 f.
as if, see also play and pretense 8, 17, 27, 31 f., 40, 68, 102, 106, 132, 150, 166, 179
Aśoka 72
Assmann, Jan 110
Aššurbanipal 80
Assyria, see Ancient Mesopotamia
astrology 79
Aśvins (gods) 61
Athens 10, 54, 59, 82, 84 f., 93 f., 96, 102 f., 106, 123, 129, 139, 142, 146 f., 149 f., 158
átopos (Gr.) 83, 130, 179
Augustine of Hippo 120, 125, 133, 143, 148
Averroes (Ibn Rušd) 155
Avestan 40, 51, 67
Avicenna (Ibn Sīnā) 155
axiality, see Jaspers, Karl

Babylonia, see Ancient Mesopotamia
bacchanalia sacrilege 72
Baghdad 147 f., 158
behavioral modernity 6, 10, 13, 23 f., 27, 33, 77
belief, see faith
Beowulf 45–48, 70

https://doi.org/10.1515/9783110460605-015

Berossus 162
Bible 146, 148
biology 24, 30 f., 33, 127, 175
bíos (Gr.) 66, 84 f., 87, 90, 92, 109, 134
Blumenberg, Hans 25, 82, 84, 95, 120, 142
Boileau, Nicolas 4
Bosch, Hieronymus 163 f.
Buddhism 71
Bureus, Johannes 173–176
burial 13, 23–25, 27, 29–31, 33
Burke, Peter 172
Burkert, Walter 87 f., 106
Byzantine Empire 125, 139, 149, 151, 162

cabinet of curiosities 169
Cacus 49
Cage, John 104
Cain 47 f.
Calabi-Yau manifold 180
Carneades 166
Carthage 118
Catalogue of Women 34
Catholic Church 145, 165
Cavalcade of the Magi, see Gozzoli, Benozzo; and three Magi 162
cenae (Lat. pl.) 42
Chaldean Oracles 156
Chapman brothers 179
Chastel, André 164
Chomsky, Noam 182
Christ 92, 111, 114–117, 121, 123, 128, 143, 146, 152, 161, 163, 171
Christianity 4, 13, 72, 78, 99, 109–135, 139, 144, 151, 154, 162 f., 165, 176
Christians 40, 92, 109, 111 f., 115–118, 120 f., 123, 130–133, 147 f.
Cicero, Marcus Tullius 92, 100–103, 105, 124, 144 f., 166
cinema 9, 171
civic spectacle 13, 120
civic worship 82, 87, 110, 112 f., 151, 177, 181
civilization 21, 44, 112, 142, 175, 177
Claudian 55
Clausewitz, Carl von 49
Clement of Alexandria 119
cliens (Lat.) 57
client, see also *cliens* 36 f., 39, 42, 50–55, 57, 59, 62, 89, 107
cognition 5–8, 24–25, 30, 98, 100, 107, 166,
Coleridge, Samuel Taylor 2–5, 166, 170
commensality 42 f., 45, 48, 60, 77
communion, see also eating 88, 134, 143, 150
Conclusiones CM 159 f.
Connor, W. R. 93 f.
consanguinity 33, 47 f.
consciousness 6, 20, 25 f., 170
Constantine I 72, 112 f., 127–130, 151
Corneille, Pierre 4
Corpus Hermeticum 148
cosmetics 27 f., 30, 77
council of Ferrara-Florence 153
council of Nicea 127, 130
council of Trent 171
counter-reformation 165
creativity 104 f., 107, 168
credo (Lat.) 113, 143
credulity 14, 20, 143, 167, 178
culture 2, 10, 18, 20, 22, 28, 37, 39, 44, 70, 72, 100, 108, 110, 119 f., 123, 125, 127, 133 f., 172 f., 175, 177 f., 181
– cultural difference 19–21, 178
– cultural modernity, see behavioral modernity
– cultural origins 21, 28
curiositas (Lat.) 120
curiosity, see also *curiositas* 2, 14, 119, 123, 145, 168, 170, 172, 174, 181

Damascius 139
Darmesteter, James 61, 67
Darwin, Charles 17, 21, 98
deception 2, 6 f., 14, 64
De defectu oraculorum 102–105, 161
De divinatione 101–103
defamiliarization 9, 23, 28, 141
default mode 6
De hominis dignitatae 157, 159 f., 162
della Mirandola, *Giovanni* Pico 157, 159–162, 165
Delphi 102, 104, 144 f.
delusion 25 f., 94, 96, 98 f., 118
de' Medici, Cosimo 153, 159, 162 f.
demigods 161
dēmioergoí (Gr. pl.) 60 f.

Democritus 72, 85
demystification 169–171
De natura deorum 101
De pallio 122–124
De raptu Proserpinae 55
Derrida, Jacques 100
De spectaculis 120
deus ex machina (Lat.) 23, 93
devotion 12 f., 82, 109, 116, 130, 142, 175
diatribḗ (Gr.) 72
differentiation 20, 32, 88
dikaiosýnē (Gr.) 114
Diogenes Laertius 85, 87, 89
Dionysus (god) 59, 131
disenchantment 89, 140 f., 143, 145
dispositio (Lat.), see also apparatus 2, 8, 77, 98 f., 115, 170
dissimulation 9, 27, 30
distance 9, 20 f., 25, 48, 178
divination 11, 79–81, 100–105, 144, 149
divinity 65, 91, 142 f., 162
Dream of Scipio 124
dreams 20 f., 27, 106
Drôle de Pensée 167–169
Dumézil, Georges 73

eating, see also communion 33 f., 40, 42 f., 49, 51, 55, 87
Edda 45, 173
eikṓn (Gr.) 95 f.
Eirene (goddess) 81
Eleusis 87
Elia del Medigo 159
Eliade, Mircea 21
Elissaeus 155–158, 160
Empedocles 88, 90–92, 156
encryption 165
Enlightenment 99, 145, 175
Enmeduranki of Sippar 80
entertainment 13, 44, 96 f., 113, 130, 167, 180 f.
Epicurus 31, 123
epistḗmē (Gr.) 114
epistemic commitment 115, 117, 180
epistemology 2, 4
epokhḗ (Gr.) 2, 5, 8, 105, 127, 166, 172
epopteía (Gr.) 161
eschatology 54, 67, 81
êthos (Gr.) 41
etiology 27, 35, 98
Eumolpus 53
Euripides 65, 85, 103
Eurydice 55
Eusebius of Cesarea 129
exchange 29, 33, 36, 39, 52, 67, 78, 86, 90
expenditure 34, 36, 86
experiment 3, 91, 127
extispicy 79–81

faith, see also *fides* and *pístis* 3 f., 8, 13, 92, 112–121, 123, 125, 127–129, 132–134, 143, 158, 167, 170, 177 f., 180
fame, see also glory 33–35, 37, 39 f., 42 f., 46, 49–52, 55, 57 f., 62, 67 f., 71, 90
Festugière, André-Jean 79, 86, 96
Feuerbach, Ludwig 33
Ficino, Marsilio 153, 157, 159 f., 162 f., 165
fides (Lat.) 13, 113, 117
Fihrist 147 f., 157
Fink, Eugen 7
First Alcibades 10, 150, 161
Florence 146, 153 f., 158 f., 162
Florentinus 55
food and food-sharing, see eating
Foucault, Michel 10, 98–100
Frazer, James George 98
Friedrich, Caspar David 176

Gāthās 51, 67, 70
Geldner, Karl Friedrich 62, 64
Gemistos Plethon 153–157, 159 f., 162 f.
Gennadios Scholarios 154–156
George of Trebizond 154
Germanic 40, 45, 48 f., 69, 77
Geryon 49
ghost 167, 170, 175
gift 33, 38 f., 43, 51 f., 58, 69, 109, 115
Ginzburg, Carlo 1
glory, see also fame 35, 38–40, 49, 58, 71, 89, 91, 111
Gozzoli, Benozzo 160, 162 f.
Gray aliens 21 f.
Greek religion 11, 59
Grendel 46–48
guest 35, 37, 39–42, 44–47, 51 f., 67–70, 90

guest-friendship, see also *xenía* 41
Gunning, Tom 9

Hades 53, 58
Hadot, Ilsetraut 146
Hadot, Pierre 161
Ḥarrān 146–151, 157, 161 f.
Hávamál 48
Hawking, Stephen 179
Hegel, Georg Wilhelm Friedrich 98 f.
hepatoscopy 79, 101
Heraclitus 58, 89
Hercules 55 f.
Herder, Johann Gottfried 26, 49 f.
Hermes (god) 35, 148, 155
Hermes Trismegistus 148
Hermetic tradition 146, 148, 156, 159
Herodotus 19–21, 93 f., 106
heroism 49 f.
Hesiod 34, 146
heterodoxy 54
Hierocles 81 f., 85
Higgs particle 180
himátion (Gr.) 122
Holy Trinity 128
Homer 87, 146
Homeric Hymn to Hermes 35 f.
homoíōsis theôi (Gr.) 84, 114
Hoogstraten, Samuel van 168 f.
host 8, 33, 37, 40–45, 47 f., 50 f., 60, 63, 67, 82
hostility 33, 43–45
hostis (Lat.) 41 f., 44, 49
House of Deceit 52
House of Laudation 52, 66, 68–70
Hrungnir 45–47
Hume, David 176
hunting rituals 49
hyperbole 17, 27, 29 f., 32, 43, 50, 58
Hyperborea 79
hyperphenomena (pl.) 30
Hyppolite, Jean 98 f.

Iamblichus 87 f., 170
Ibn Kammūna 158
Ibn Taymiyyah 147
identity 9, 17, 22, 24, 27–30, 32 f., 77, 103, 110, 122 f., 148, 155
idolatry 94, 111, 120, 134, 148
Idrīs, see Hermes
Iliad 57
Illuminationism 155, 158
illusion 4 f., 27, 86, 96, 170
imagination 3 f., 6 f., 44, 52, 59, 94 f., 104 f., 119, 121
indeterminacy 8, 44, 99 f., 107
indeterminate dyad 103
Indo-Aryan society 72
Indo-European 34, 36 f., 41 f., 45, 47, 61, 69, 72 f.
Indra (god) 38, 61 f., 65, 68
inhibition 7, 94, 108, 169
in illo tempore (Lat.) 21
initiation 54, 87, 110, 161, 179
Innocent VIII 160
integumentum (Lat.) 124
intellectuals 90, 102, 105, 116, 122 f., 129, 144 f., 150–152, 162, 165
Iranian religion 67, 72, 138
Islam 9, 135, 147, 154, 162
itinerancy, see wandering

Jaeger, Werner 85
Jahweh 110
Jainism 71
Jakobson, Roman 61
Jaspers, Karl 53
Jerusalem 123
Jesus of Nazareth 111, 114, 118, 121, 123, 125 f., 130, 161
Jews 78 f., 82, 85, 91, 109–111, 115, 130, 147 f., 152, 159
– as “race of philosophers” 78,
Judaism 109 f.
Julian (emperor) 144, 155, 170
Julius Pomponius Laetus 152
Justinian (emperor) 112, 139, 149
Justin the Martyr 99

Kabbalah 159
Kamnamaēzā Hāiti 51–54, 63
katábâsis (Gr.) 106
Kellens, Jean 51, 67
Khosrow I 149
kinship 33, 48

Kircher, Athanasius 169 – 171
kléos (Gr.), see fame and glory 35, 58
Knight, Chris 27
kósmēsis (Gr.), see cosmetics 28

language 4, 19 – 21, 25 f., 36, 40, 100, 141, 162, 182
Lascaux cave 182
Latin 2, 9, 11, 40 – 42, 44 f., 49, 99, 102, 110, 113, 153, 155, 157, 159
Latour, Bruno 166
lecanomancy 79 f.
Leibniz, Gottfried Wilhelm 167 – 171
Lévi-Strauss, Claude 31, 181
Leviticus 78
Lewis-Williams, David 24 – 26
Lincoln, Bruce 19, 45, 102
Linnaeus, Carl 173, 175 f.
Lionarons, Joyce Tally 47
liver as "mirror" 80 f.
lógos (Gr.) 114
Lukács, Georg 98
Lutheran confession 170
lyric performance 91

magic 52, 65, 168, 171
mágoi (Gr. pl.), see also three Magi 90, 92
Mālik ibn ʿUqbūn 150, 157
manipulation 7 f., 106, 169 f.
Mannoni, Octave 171, 182
Manuel II Palaeologus 153
Marciano, Laura Gemelli 90
Marx, Karl 98
Master of Animals 49
mathesis divina (Lat.) 171
Mazdayasnian religion 51
McCutcheon, Russel 1
mechanics, see also *mēkhanḗ* 94, 97, 168
Megarian laughter 96
mēkhanḗ (Gr.), see also mechanics 93, 96 f.
Menoecus 31
mental time travel 6
metaphor 61, 120 – 124, 127, 161
metaphysics 99, 103, 163
Metaphysics (work by Aristotle) 97
metempsychosis, see also transmigration 147
metonymy 61, 153,
Middle Platonism 103
mind-wandering 6
misthós (Gr.) 90
Mithen, Steven 24 f.
Mitra/Mithras (god) 37, 39, 110
modernity 9, 12, 26, 139, 141 – 146, 166 f., 176, 178
Molière 12
monster 34, 44, 47 f.
mōría (Gr.) 115
multi-species model 24, 27, 29
Musaeus 53 f., 146
Muslims 148
Muʿtazilites (pl.) 147
mysteries 53 – 55, 109, 131, 140, 153, 161 f., 171
myth 20, 35, 45, 47, 57, 59, 82, 91 f., 97, 108, 124 f., 127, 134, 181
mythology 48, 65

natural theology 171, 181
Neanderthals 17, 24 f., 29
Nebuchadnezzar I 80
Neoplatonism 139, 147, 170
New Age spirituality 180
Nightingale, Andrea Wilson 86
noûs (Gr.) 103, 143
Nyberg, Henrik Samuel 66 f.

oath, see also vow 89, 114, 117, 123
Odin (god) 45, 48
Odysseus 43 f., 60
Odyssey 43, 60
oikonomía (Gr.) 2, 98 f.
oîkos (Gr.) 79
Old English 45 f., 48
Old Norse religion 45, 48, 70
Olympius 131 – 133
omen 79, 173
ontology 33, 182
optics 150
oracle 80, 102, 104, 106, 144 f., 156
oracle of Trophonius 106
Origen 119, 161
Orpheotelests 53, 66
Orpheus 53 – 59, 61, 65 f., 79, 146
Orphic gold tablets 68
Orphism 53, 88, 90

orthodoxy 160
ostracism 47
Otto, Walter 59

paideutics 97
pallium (Lat.) 122 – 125, 132
Pāṇini 182
Paṇis (pl.) 49
parable of the cave, see also allegory of the cave 94, 96 f., 142
Parmenides 54, 90 f., 150, 182
paronomasia 47
patron 36 – 42, 50 – 52, 54 f., 57, 62, 68 – 71, 81, 89 f., 94, 121, 153, 163
patronage 13, 36, 52, 63, 85 f.
patron-clientage 36, 52, 55, 57, 73, 89 f.
Paul of Tarsus 98, 111, 113 – 116, 119 – 122, 128, 152
Pausanias 100, 106 f.
personal ornaments 13, 23, 28 – 30, 33, 77
phantasmagoria 171
phenomenology 7 f.
Philo of Alexandria 109, 146, 162
philosophical dress code, see *pallium*
philosophy 7 f., 10, 54, 71, 82 – 87, 91, 97, 101 f., 105, 109 – 113, 115, 120, 123 – 125, 130, 139, 145 – 147, 151, 153, 155 – 158, 162, 172, 178
– Christian critique of, see Paul of Tarsus and Tertullian
– pagan philosophy 13, 120, 123 f., 146 f., 154, 157 f., 161
Physics (work by Aristotle) 149, 178
PIE (Proto-Indo-European) 34, 36 f., 40 – 42, 44 f., 53, 59 – 61, 66 – 69, 199
Piero ("the Gouty") 162
piety 10, 12, 42, 78, 85, 113, 116 f., 123, 133 f., 166, 177, 180
Pindar 41 f., 57, 70, 89 f.
pisteúō (Gr.) 113, 115
pístis Christoû (Gr.) 114 f., 118
pístis (Gr.) 13, 113 f., 117
Plautus 42
play-palace 168 f.
play, see also pretense and *as if* 7, 12, 42, 67, 77, 82, 94, 98, 125, 129, 140 f., 147, 160, 165
Pliny the elder 20, 52
Pliny the younger 113, 116 – 118
Plotinus 153, 159, 163
Plutarch 92, 100, 102 – 105, 107, 145, 156, 161
poet 34, 38 f., 41 f., 47 f., 51 f., 54 f., 57, 60 – 65, 67 – 71, 86, 88 – 90, 121, 124, 168, 173
poetics 4, 34, 37, 42 f., 51, 161
poetry 3 f., 38, 42, 48, 53, 57, 61 f., 66, 68, 70 f., 86, 96, 124, 145 f.
polis 11, 34, 58, 92, 96
politics 8, 58, 84 f., 97 f., 103
Polyphemus 43 f.
Pontius Pilate 118
popular culture 173
popular science 180
Porphyry 72, 87
prehistoric archaeology 19
pre-Socratic philosophy 87
pretense, see also play and *as if* 12 f., 34, 58, 77, 93, 133, 166 f., 180, 182
preternatural 44, 47, 49
prisca religio (Lat.) 163
Prometheus 35, 88
prophecy 102, 143
Proto-Germanic 40, 45
Proto-Indo-European (PIE) 34, 50
Proto-Indo-Iranian 50
Protrepticus 90
Psellos 156
psógos (Gr.) 53, 89 f.
Purifications, see Empedocles
puritans 172
Pūṣan (god) 62
Pythagoras 71 f., 85 – 87, 89 f., 148, 156
Pythagoreans 10, 86 – 89
Pythia 102, 104 f., 107

Qafzeh cave 27
Queen Sheba 163 f.
Qur'ān 146, 148

Rabbinic Judaism 162
Ṛbhus (pl.) 53, 61 – 65
reality-testing 178
Reformation 73, 165
religio falsa (Lat.) 180
religio (Lat.) 11, 110, 113, 118 f., 122, 134, 180
religion 1 f., 7 f., 10 f., 13, 19, 25, 27, 32, 51, 66 f., 71, 91, 98 f., 108 – 110, 112 f., 121, 125,

129, 131, 133–135, 143 f., 147–149, 154, 163, 166 f., 171 f., 176–178, 180 f.
- concept of 1, 5, 24 f., 37, 47, 57 f., 66 f., 99 f., 103, 115, 119, 141, 145, 177
religious residuals 13, 177 f., 180 f.
Renaissance 124, 139, 141 f., 146, 151, 157–165
representation 4, 7, 17–19, 26 f., 31, 66, 84, 93, 113, 127, 130 f., 177
Republic 53, 88, 94
residual religion 177, 180 f.
Ṛgveda/Rigveda (RV) 38 f., 42, 59, 61 f., 65, 67–69, 199
rhetoric 2, 17, 37, 43, 45, 77, 120, 122, 125, 130, 170 f., 173, 175
Ricœur, Paul 98
ritual 9, 27, 33, 35 f., 38–42, 49, 52 f., 55, 57–59, 61 f., 64–67, 71 f., 77, 79, 81 f., 86–91, 94, 106–108, 110, 117 f., 141, 147, 170, 182
Robertson, Etienne-Gaspard 171
Roman Empire 92, 116, 134 f., 139
Roman religion 118

Sabellius 128
Ṣābians of Ḥarrān 147–149, 157, 162
sacrality 11, 19, 21, 35, 43 f., 47, 54, 65, 67, 69, 78, 86, 88, 109 f., 115, 117, 128, 131, 134, 148, 151, 172, 176, 180
sacrifice 9, 11, 34–38, 41, 44, 49, 62, 67, 72, 78–82, 86–88, 91 f., 110 f., 123, 131, 143, 147, 149
- bloodless sacrifice 87, 91 f.
- sacrificial economy 11, 34, 115
- sacrificial exegesis 52
Saenredam, Jan 169
sage 52, 71, 78 f., 85 f., 90, 92, 115, 121, 130, 146, 149 f., 154–156, 160 f., 164, 178 f.
Sahlins, Marshall 33
Salem witch trials 172
salvation 50, 53, 59, 88, 109, 127
Šamaš (god) 80
Santa Maria della Concezione dei Cappuccini 31
Savitar (god) 62–64
Savonarola 165
scapegoating 47
scepticism 2, 5
Schaffhausen, Hermann 18
scholasticism 158
science 1, 5, 7, 81, 98, 101, 140, 142, 148, 167 f., 171, 175, 178, 180–182
Scythians 19
Second Temple 109 f.
secular 139
self-care 10 f.
self-deception 7, 167
self-projection 6, 30
self-sacrifice 179
Serapeum 127, 131 f.
Serapis (god) 133
Shakespeare, William 140, 165 f.
shaman 59
Siddhārtha Gautama 71
Simonides 57 f., 65
Simplicius 139, 146, 149–151
single-species scenario 24, 28
skaldic poetry 45
Skáldskaparmál 45, 173
Slava feast 40
Slavic 40
Smith, Jonathan Z. 18–20, 22, 49 f.
Snorri Sturluson 45, 47, 173
Socrates 10 f., 53 f., 58, 82–85, 94, 122, 129, 133
Socrates Scholasticus 128
sodālis (Lat.) 41 f.
Solomon 163 f.
Soma (god) 41, 59, 61
sophía (Gr.) 115
soteriology 91, 181 f.
Sozomen 131–133
spectacle 32, 86, 90, 96, 108, 111 f., 120–122, 130, 133, 167 f., 171 f.
speculation 27, 80, 85
spirituality 110 f., 145, 167
stargazer 58, 78 f., 82 f., 90, 92, 119
stargazer's plummet 82, 91, 119, 122
Stevens, Wallace 71
stocisim 5, 92, 101, 146
stranger 33, 40 f., 43–45, 47, 49, 58, 60, 69, 84
Stroumsa, Guy 110, 112, 127
structural anthropology 181 f.
Suda 133

supernatural 3, 24, 28, 49, 140 f., 165
suspension 2–11, 13, 27, 31, 50, 92, 95, 101, 105, 107, 118, 127, 166, 177
- of disbelief 2–4, 10 f., 13, 20, 27, 31, 50, 101, 166
- of judgement 2, 5 f., 11, 13, 95, 101, 105, 121, 127, 166, 177
symbol 23, 28, 132, 156
sýmbola (Gr. pl.) 87
symbolic behavior 23 f., 26 f.

Ṯābit ibn Qurra 157
Taborin, Yvette 29
Tacitus, Publius Conrelius 81, 116
Talayesva, Don Chuka 182
Tardieu, Michel 146, 149 f., 155–157
Tartuffe 12
technology 9, 21, 168
Tertullian 109 f., 113, 118–125, 130, 133, 143
Thales 58, 82–85, 119 f., 122, 133
Thamyris the Thracian 57
thaûma (Gr.) 93, 96 f.
thaumatopoiía (Gr.) 96 f.
thaumaturgy 65, 170
Theaetetus 82, 97
theatre 112, 121, 128 f., 168
Theodosius I 113, 131
theology 2, 31, 82, 98 f., 109, 130, 133 f., 146, 154 f., 158, 161, 167
Theophrastus 78 f., 82, 85, 91 f., 109
theōría (Gr.) 78, 86, 91, 112, 120
theory of mind 6
Thor (god) 45, 173 f.
Thrace 55, 59, 79
Thracian maid 84, 120
Thrasybulos 41
three Magi, the; see also *mágoi* 162 f.
Þjóðólfr Arnórsson 45
Tocharian 37
Trajan (emperor) 113, 116–118
transformation 11, 35, 86, 112, 127, 134, 150, 179
transmigration, see also metempsychosis 88
tribal society 37, 49 f., 52, 66, 73
Triptych of the Adoration of the Magi, see Bosch, Hieronymus 163 f.
troglodyte 17 f., 20 f., 44, 95
trolls 173–176
truth 3, 10, 13, 54, 58, 68, 70 f., 77, 86, 90, 100, 109, 112–114, 118–121, 133, 142 f., 145 f., 150, 176 f., 180 f.
Tulving, Endel 6
Tvaṣṭar (god) 61

unconscious mind 7
Universal Declaration of Human Rights 160
Útgarðr 48
utopia 26, 168 f.

Vala 49
Van Bladel, Kevin 146, 148 f.
Vardhamāna 71
Vedic religion 37–40, 42, 45, 51, 53, 59–62, 65 f., 68, 72 f., 77
Vera religio (Lat.) 13, 113, 121
virtuality 27, 30 f., 60, 77
Vištāspa 52, 63
volition 7, 95
vow, see also oath 118

Waldenfels, Bernhard 30, 77
wandering 6, 51 f., 60, 66, 72, 81, 88, 91
Watkins, Calvert 34, 38, 44, 47
wealth 10–12, 37–39, 46, 49 f., 57, 91
Weber, Max 11, 89, 141–143
Wheeler, John Archibald 104, 182
Whitehouse, Harvey 1
wisdom, see also *sophía* 10, 58, 79, 85, 91, 115, 120, 123, 133, 149, 154, 157, 163, 168, 179
wonder, see also *thaûma* 25, 93 f., 96 f., 105, 125, 140, 142, 165, 167, 180
Wordsworth, William 3 f.

xeînos (Gr.) 41, 43, 59
xenía (Gr.) 41 f.
Xenophanes 58, 91
xénos (Gr.) 40, 42

Zanker, Paul 122
Zarathushtra, see also Zoroaster 51, 68
Zeus 35, 37, 40, 43 f., 78
Zilhão, João 29
Zoroaster, see also Zarathushtra 52, 154–156

www.ingramcontent.com/pod-product-compliance
Lightning Source LLC
Chambersburg PA
CBHW050525170426
43201CB00013B/2087